Women and the Media in Asia

Youna Kim is Associate Professor of Global Communications at the American University of Paris, France. She was formerly at the London School of Economics and Political Science, UK, where she taught after completing her PhD at Goldsmiths College, University of London, UK. Her books are *Women, Television and Everyday Life in Korea: Journeys of Hope* (2005, Routledge), *Media Consumption and Everyday Life in Asia* (2008, Routledge) and *Transnational Migration, Media and Identity of Asian Women: Diasporic Daughters* (2011, Routledge).

At a time of significant change, when women's lives are entering a much larger but precarious world of female individualization, this book explores such phenomena by critically incorporating the parameters of popular media culture into the overarching paradigm of gender relations, economics and the politics of everyday life. Drawing on a wide range of perspectives from media and communications, sociology, cultural studies and anthropology, the book provides an insightful investigation into the evolving phenomena.

Also by Youna Kim

WOMEN, TELEVISION AND EVERYDAY LIFE
IN KOREA: Journeys of Hope (2005)

MEDIA CONSUMPTION AND EVERYDAY LIFE
IN ASIA (2008)

TRANSNATIONAL MIGRATION, MEDIA AND IDENTITY
OF ASIAN WOMEN: Diasporic Daughters (2011)

Women and the Media in Asia

in Asia

The Precarious Self

Edited by

Youna Kim
American University of Paris, France

palgrave
macmillan

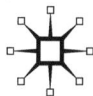

First published 2012 by
PALGRAVE MACMILLAN

Palgrave Macmillan in the UK is an imprint of Macmillan Publishers Limited,
registered in England, company number 785998, of Houndmills, Basingstoke,
Hampshire RG21 6XS.

Palgrave Macmillan in the US is a division of St Martin's Press LLC,
175 Fifth Avenue, New York, NY 10010.

Palgrave Macmillan is the global academic imprint of the above companies
and has companies and representatives throughout the world.

Palgrave® and Macmillan® are registered trademarks in the United States,
the United Kingdom, Europe and other countries.

ISBN 978–0–230–29272–7

This book is printed on paper suitable for recycling and made from fully
managed and sustained forest sources. Logging, pulping and manufacturing
processes are expected to conform to the environmental regulations of the
country of origin.

A catalogue record for this book is available from the British Library.

A catalog record for this book is available from the Library of Congress.

10   9   8   7   6   5   4   3   2   1
21   20   19   18   17   16   15   14   13   12

Printed and bound in the United States of America
by Edwards Brothers Malloy, Inc.

To OH, SOOAN and OH, JEILL

Contents

viii *Contents*

**Part III   New Consumption Practices of Female
Individualization**

Illustrations and Table

Illustrations

Table

Acknowledgements

This book has been developed along with my research monograph *Transnational Migration, Media and Identity of Asian Women: Diasporic Daughters* (2011, Routledge). I am especially grateful to Anthony Giddens for his valuable advice and friendship, as always. Thanks also to Chris Berry for his continual support and suggestions in reaching participants for this book. I have also appreciated encouraging words from Rosalind Gill, Stevi Jackson, Maria Jaschok, Lily Kong, Tara McPherson, Rachel Moran, Alondra Nelson, Susan Pharr, Anna Reading, Liesbet Van-Zoonen and Jing Wang, among many scholars around the world.

In Paris, I want to express my personal gratitude to the lovely expatriate families in Champ de Mars Tour Eiffel, who continued to offer much-needed care and hospitality by looking after the precious small details of everyday life, especially when I had to travel abroad for research and meetings – Stephanie Xatart and her daughter Albane; Isabelle Tadmoury and her daughter Zena; Becca and Thomas Valente and their children Kate and Thomas have shared enjoyable times during their sabbatical leave here.

Special thanks go to the publisher, Palgrave Macmillan, and particularly to Felicity Plester and Rebecca Barden, for showing interest in this book project, and to my dedicated PA and friend, Diane Willian, for helping me wherever I am.

I am deeply appreciative of the contributors to this book for collaborating so willingly and delightfully. Thank you all.

Youna Kim
Paris, July 2011

Notes on Contributors

Susan Dewey is a cultural anthropologist teaching gender and women's studies at the University of Wyoming, USA. She is the author of *Neon Wasteland: On Love, Motherhood and Sex Work in a Rust Belt Town* (2011); *Making Miss India Miss Universe: Constructing Gender, Power and the Nation in Postliberalization India* (2008); and *Hollow Bodies: Institutional Responses to Sex Trafficking in Armenia, Bosnia and India* (2008).

Radhika Gajjala is Professor of Communication and Cultural Studies and Director of American Culture Studies at Bowling Green State University, USA. She is the author of *Cyber Selves: Feminist Ethnographies of South Asian Women* (2004) and *Techno-Cultural Agency: Identity at the Interface* (forthcoming). She teaches and researches on topics related to digital media, feminism and globalization.

Alexandra Hambleton is a doctoral candidate at the Graduate School of Interdisciplinary Information Studies, University of Tokyo, Japan. Her research interests include Japanese popular culture, nationalism and gender. She is currently researching the connection between mainstream and online media representations of sex and the sexual identities of women in contemporary Japanese society.

Bliss Cua Lim is Associate Professor of Film and Media Studies at the University of California, Irvine, USA. She is the author of *Translating Time: Cinema, the Fantastic, and Temporal Critique* (2009). Her research and teaching centre on Philippine cinema, temporality, postcolonial feminist film theory, transnational horror and the fantastic, and taste cultures. Her next book project is entitled *Troubled Archive: Race, Sex, and Language in Filipino Film Stardom*.

Fran Martin has published widely on gender, sexuality and media cultures in Taiwan, China and Hong Kong. Recent publications include *Backward Glances: Contemporary Chinese Cultures and the Female*

Homoerotic Imaginary (2008) and the co-edited collection *AsiaPacifiQueer: Rethinking Genders and Sexualities* (2008). Her current collaborative research project focuses on life-advice TV in Asia. She is Senior Lecturer in Cultural Studies at the University of Melbourne, Australia. Her co-author in this collection, Tania Lewis, is a Vice Chancellor's Senior Research Fellow in the School of Media & Communications at RMIT University, Melbourne, Australia. She is the author of *Smart Living: Lifestyle Media and Popular Expertise* (2008), editor of *TV Transformations: Revealing the Makeover Show* (2009) and co-editor of *Ethical Consumption: A Critical Introduction* (2011).

Pam Nilan is Associate Professor of Sociology at the University of Newcastle, UK. She has conducted research on youth in Indonesia, Vietnam, Fiji and Australia. She has been a chief investigator on two externally funded research projects in Indonesia, and has published widely on youth, gender relations, education and popular culture. She is the author of two books on youth and youth culture, and is currently co-writing a book entitled *The New World of Adolescents in Indonesia* (2012) and another book entitled *Spaces and Times of Youth Cultures in the Global City* (2012).

Fatimah Tobing Rony is a film-maker and a scholar, and is Associate Professor in Film and Media Studies as well as Visual Studies at the University of California, Irvine, USA. She was one of the directors of the narrative feature film *Chants of Lotus [Perempuan Punya Cerita]* (2008). Her book *The Third Eye: Race, Cinema, and Ethnographic Spectacle* (1996) won the 1998 Katherine Kovacs Book Prize from the Society of Cinema and Media Studies. Her current book project is *Annah la Javanaise*.

Ping Shaw is Professor of Communications Management at National Sun Yat-sen University, Taiwan. She specializes in feminist criticism, media content analysis, advertising and culture research. She has published numerous articles in *Journal of Communication*, *Sex Roles*, *Asian Journal of Communication*, and in many other scholarly journals in Chinese. Her co-author in this collection, Chin-yi Lin, works as a research assistant at the same University.

Sue Thornham is Professor of Media and Film at the University of Sussex, UK. She is the author of *Passionate Detachments* (1997), *Feminist Theory and Cultural Studies* (2001), *Approaches to TV Drama* (2004, with Tony Purvis) and *Women, Feminism and Media* (2007). She is also the editor of two key collections: *Feminist Film Theory: A Reader* (1999) and, with Paul Marris and Caroline Bassett, *Media Studies: A Reader* (2009, third edition).

Jing Wu is Associate Professor at the School of Journalism and Communication at Peking University, China. Her research areas are media and cultural studies, social theories of mass communication, media and the public sphere, identity and ideology, and media and modernity. She has published numerous articles in Chinese and English on topics concerning various aspects of media and society.

Audrey Yue is Senior Lecturer in Cinema and Cultural Studies at the University of Melbourne, Australia. She is the author of *Ann Hui's Song of the Exile* (2010) and co-editor of *AsiaPacifiQueer: Rethinking Genders and Sexualities* (2008) and *Mobile Cultures: New Media in Queer Asia* (2003).

Introduction: Female Individualization and Popular Media Culture in Asia

Youna Kim

To what extent do women have control over their lives? How do the media intersect with imagining different lives for women? This book is concerned with the changing lives of women; the troubling signs of female individualization as intersected by everyday media culture – a new arena of anxiety for women in contemporary Asia.

Since the 1980s, women in Asia have gained higher levels of education, and the commensurate expectations have become a driving motor in their aspirations for work, economic power, independence, freedom and self-fulfilment. However, women often experience gendered labour market inequity setting limits on patterns of participation, women's socio-economic position on the margins of work systems and thus the illusion of the language of choice that the new capacities of education appear to promise. The enlargement of choice can be particularly illusory for women in contemporary Asia where gendered socio-economic and cultural conditions persist and continue to structure labour market outcomes and lifestyles.

Yet signs of female individualization have been proliferating as a defining feature of contemporary modes of identity, albeit untenable and ambivalent, within the discursive regime of self – embodied in regulatory practices in society where individualism is not placed at the heart of its culture. Arguably, the media are central to the signs of emergent cultures of female individualization producing the alternative social, cultural and symbolic relations women wish to live within and define the kind of self they wish to become. Seeming suggestions of individualization are encountered, mediated through popular media imaginaries that are present and often intentionally used as resources for reflexivity and self-imagining. This also provides a condition for an increased awareness of cultural differences and of women's own positions in

1

relation to global Others, new symbolic objects of identification and contestation.

At a time of significant changes in women's lives entering a much larger but precarious world of female individualization, this book explores such phenomena by critically incorporating the parameters of popular media culture into the overarching paradigm of gender relations, economics and politics of everyday life. The chapters in this book examine everyday media culture and the issues of women as 'consumers', women as 'representations' and women as 'creators', to offer an understanding of changing lives and frustrated desires, contradictions and dispersed sites of female individualization that are refracted into various degrees and forms.

Gendered socio-economic change

While there is significant variation in the extent and depth of social change between Asian societies, the changing socio-economic status and desires of women today indicate some noticeable transformations in the ongoing processes of modernization. Education is widely perceived as an indicator of the status of women and, more importantly, as an agent for the empowerment of women, although there is 'no positive linear relationship' between the role of education and the socio-economic and political empowerment of women in Asia, as a consequence of the continuing interface of traditional gender ideologies and structural constraints (Jayaweera, 1997). Nevertheless, improvements in the living conditions of women and their subjectivities constructed within unequal relations of power are generally assumed to depend on their access to education, and growing numbers of urban middle-class women across Asia participate in higher education.

In contemporary Korea, 95.3 per cent of women go to high school and 63 per cent go on to higher education. High school education in Japan has also reached equal levels for men (96.0 per cent) and women (96.7 per cent), and 45.3 per cent of these women advance to higher education (Kim, Chapter 1 in this volume). Taiwan, too, notes the high rate (86 per cent) of women's tertiary education (Martin and Lewis, Chapter 2 in this volume), and Taiwanese women receive higher returns on investments in their own human capital than their counterparts in Japan and Korea (Brinton, 2001). Women in Singapore currently equal men in educational achievements and literacy rates (Yue, Chapter 12 in this volume). Young women in urban China who were born in the era of the single-child policy, with the emphasis on individual success, become the focus of parental expectations and the product of a fiercely competitive education system, in which gender difference is not recognized (Thornham and Feng, Chapter 4 in this volume). Lower fertility in transitional societies leads to increased human capital investment per child. Muslim women in Malaysia and Indonesia have experienced significant improvements in educational attainment, although the nature of education is influenced by the 'Asian way' model of political development, and its reinforcement of patriarchal values and institutional impact on women (Rahim, 1998).

There is greater gender equality in education and the expansion of educational opportunities for urban middle-class women. Therefore gender inequality is often thought to be diminished or non-existent at the educational level of the urban middle class. On the other hand, there is also evidence regarding the implications of poorly educated and low-status women in parts of Asia. Decisions about education depend on competing forces at both the family and the macro-economic levels; parental enthusiasm for education is largely motivated by its private economic returns, which are determined in labour markets (Montgomery et al., 2000). Women face poorer economic incentives to invest in education than men because they generate lower labour market returns to education than men. Labour market discrimination against women and parental discrimination against daughters are two of the most common factors of the gender gap in education, and this is the case in many countries, including India (Kingdon, 1998).

Women's desire to participate in the labour market is certainly on the rise, and educated women's choices in life appear to have become more varied, available yet unviable. The entrance of women into the paid workforce is driven by the role of education in mediating job aspirations, the seeming promise of liberation from traditional feminine identities through the achievement of economic independence and empowerment. However, the gendered division of the labour market continues to promote inequality, and it is still organized by markedly regressive forms of stratification, new risks and contradictions. Employment represents a measure of women's empowerment, acquiring the ability to make strategic life choices and to exercise choice by incorporating 'material and human resources, agency, and achievements of well-being outcomes' within the structural parameters of individual choice (Kabeer, 1999). The operation of choice is regulated and constrained by social structures and persisting patriarchal cultures that continue to influence women's education–work transition and create new inequality, insecurity and a precarious self.

Young women's work participation in Singapore seems remarkable (85.5 per cent of 25–29-year-olds in 2009). However, women are over-represented in the services (79.1 per cent) and clerical industries (76.1 per cent), with only 26 per cent working as legislators, senior officials and managers. Furthermore, once Singaporean women leave the workforce to get married and have children, they tend not to return (Martin and Lewis, Chapter 2 in this volume). Gender gaps in employment are strongly related to family status; married women and mothers in urban China face significant disadvantages as a result of family–work conflict and lack of childcare policies, an issue which looms large in most Asian countries (Zhang et al., 2008). Working women in Hong Kong, too, are under-represented in higher status occupations, and their role in the workplace is substantially constrained by their familial caring role (Lee, 2000). Labour markets are gendered regimes operating at the intersection of the productive and reproductive economies, where work experiences of women often demonstrate the profound limitations on choice and flexibility in their struggle to combine paid work and familial care labour. In almost all the countries of Asia, decision-making management positions are dominated by men (Omar and Davidson, 2001). Organizational performance constructed by gender discrimination and the culturally assumed, private/public, gendered division of labour accounts for the under-representation of women (Benson and Yukongdi, 2005).

While advances in new information and communication technologies are said to have the potential to dissolve old bases of discrimination, such potential has yet to be realized in the patriarchal and unreflexive organization of work in Asia (Kelkar and Nathan, 2002). Despite the impressive level of higher education in Korea, only 46.7 per cent of women graduates are employed, mostly in traditional female tracks, non-managerial and secretarial positions in small firms. These educated women can be seen as 'reflexivity losers' (Lash, 1994) as they are excluded from the new labour spaces of reflexive production in large corporations with knowledge- and information-intensive forms of work. A wage differential of 76 per cent compared with male wages gives Korean women little economic security (Kim, Chapter 1 in this volume). Yet the problematic wage differential remains unexplained (Kim and Voos, 2007) and similar conditions are widespread in Asia. Japanese women in full-time employment earn only 65 per cent of male wages, far from being economically rewarding or emotionally fulfilling. Japan's male-dominated labour system divides recruits into 'career track position' and 'general clerical work', with 80 per cent of women being hired in the second category. The perception of education has become 'consumption' – a thing to be consumed by Japanese women without any expectations as to the consequences (Kim, Chapter 1 in this volume). Middle-class women in urban China have to compete for jobs in a post-socialist context in which gender difference – officially denied in their school years – seems 'suddenly very pronounced' (Thornham and Feng, Chapter 4 in this volume).

The idea of empowerment in South Asian women's development considers not only gender inequalities of labour but also class differences among women (Rozario, 1997). Through rural–urban labour migration, poor rural women strive to negotiate the conflict between their new individual desires and their family household's well-being (Luo, 2005). Young women in rural Thailand who migrate to Bangkok for employment and aspirations for new identities face significant exploitation as low-wage, low-status migrant labour (Mills, 1997). A large proportion of women in Asia toil in vulnerable, low-paid, informal jobs with long hours of work, which implies that poor-quality jobs are a greater labour market challenge for women than is unemployment (ADB, 2011). Labour migration has become increasingly feminized since the 1990s, with growing numbers of young Asian women having to migrate transnationally in search of better work, while suffering from the feminization of poverty and violence. Although the level of poverty remains high in Indonesia, significant numbers of women are receiving a college education and working for national and transnational corporations. However, not all academic degrees have the same value on the labour market; while an Indonesian woman educated abroad in Australia, the US or Europe may have much more success in the corporate labour market, someone from a less prestigious Indonesian university may have to seek work abroad in the care-related service sector as a nanny (Rony, Chapter 8 in this volume).

Socio-economic opportunities motivate women to postpone marriage and childcare in order to actualize rising aspirations for material well-being, higher education and occupational mobility (Chowdhury and Trovato, 1994). Increasingly, educated women are choosing to invest their resources into their career, rather than into marriage and family. The effects of the choices they are making can be seen in the growth of singles, delayed marriage, low fertility and high divorce rates. The average age of marriage for Japanese women increased from 24.5 in 1975 to 28.5 in 2008, making Japan one of the latest-marrying populations in the world (Retherford et al., 2001; Hambleton, Chapter 5 in this volume). Similarly in Taiwan, the figure rose from 22.3 in 1975 to 29.2 in 2009, and more than 30 per cent of Taiwanese women aged 30–40 remain unmarried (Shaw and Lin, Chapter 6 in this volume). Non-marriage for women has become common in many urban areas of East and Southeast Asia (Jones, 2005). Women's choices against marriage are affected by the conflicting burden of caring roles, and the seeming implausibility of combining paid work and domestic labour.

Women with higher educational attainment and stronger career commitment tend to marry later but not necessarily abandon marriage, as pronounced in many countries, including Hong Kong (Wong, 2005) and Japan (Raymo and Iwasawa, 2005). The latter, paradoxically, exhibits educated women's continued dependence on men's economic resources, rather than increasing economic independence, and a decline in the relative supply of highly educated men as potential spouses. There is increasing concern over the difficulty of finding the right husband among better-educated career women in urban China, which in part explains why TV dating shows have become a significant and popular form of entertainment (Wu, Chapter 11 in this volume). The majority of marriages in India are arranged with careful regard to social class as well as educational and ethno-religious background. Nonetheless, urban professional women are increasingly opting for individual control over partner selection, as evidenced by the later age at which women choose to marry, albeit in a deficit of eligible men (Banerjee, 1999; Dewey, Chapter 10 in this volume). While early marriage in Indonesia is still common in rural areas and marriage remains almost universal, these trends are moving into reverse for urban, tertiary-educated middle-class young women (Nilan, 2008). More and more young women in urban Singapore are opting out of married life, marking a significant generational shift from a more family-based mode of modernity to an increasingly individualized form of social organization (Martin and Lewis, Chapter 2 in this volume).

A trend towards delayed marriage and non-marriage has brought fertility rates to unprecedented low levels in many countries of East and Southeast Asia (Jones, 2007), whereas changes in marriage patterns have played a small role in reducing fertility in South Asia (Caldwell, 2005), with the exception of India, where female education and urbanization in some areas, and the modern media and consumer culture, have contributed to fertility decline since the 1980s (Murthi, 2002). Son preference, however, tends to persist in the face of sweeping economic and social change in modernizing Asia (Gupta et al., 2003). The total fertility rate for Asia as a whole dropped from approximately six children per woman in the period 1950–1955 to approximately 2.7 children per woman by 1995–2000 (Chan and Yeoh, 2002). Although there are regional variations, the current average level of fertility in Asia is slightly less than the world average of 2.8. Korea, Japan, Taiwan and Singapore are among the lowest fertility rates that are below replacement levels.

Low fertility countries are characterized by low gender equity, robust marriage institution and strong familism (Suzuki, 2008). The robustness of traditional gender role division impedes any improvement in compatibility between work and family, generating a high opportunity cost of childbearing. Korea, a typical case, shows one of the world's lowest birth rates – 1.15 (KWDI, 2009) – as a growing number of women delay marriage/family life in pursuit of employment and self-actualization, which further pushes the state and individuals towards transnational marriage (Shim and Han, 2010). Migrant women from the Philippines may look for modern husbands and modern marriages because of local constraints on their marriage opportunities. Philippine transnational marriage migration blurs the dominant division between marriage migrants and labour migrants, since women not only marry in order to migrate but also migrate in order to marry (Lauser, 2008). Japan, too, is at risk owing to its low birth rate of around 1.3, undergoing a major demographic transition and prompting the state to consider childcare policies and work–life balance (Coleman, 2005).

Amid these transformations, divorce rates have increased, although in some countries more radically and more quickly than in others. The Korean divorce rate has rapidly increased from 5.8 per cent in 1980, to 11.1 per cent in 1990, 16.8 per cent in 1995, 33 per cent in 2000 and today, almost 50 per cent (KWDI, 2009). Since the 1990s the divorce rate in China has increased quickly in urban cities, with Beijing at 39 per cent and Shanghai at 38 per cent today (*Sina*, 2010). In Singapore the overall rate has risen from 10 per cent in 1985 to 31 per cent in 2008 (Martin and Lewis, Chapter 2 in this volume). About 39.5 per cent of marriages in Taiwan today are ending in divorce (Taiwan Ministry of the Interior, 2010). As more women enter the workforce, they are increasingly making choices of independence from unfaithful or uncaring husbands. The predominantly Muslim societies of Malaysia and Indonesia historically had low divorce rates due to traditional systems of arranged marriage and polygamy. Recently, however, divorce rates have been rising in both countries, driven in part by the relative economic independence of women and their changing expectations of a social life (Nilan, Chapter 3 in this volume).

Social life in many countries of Asia, including Japan, has been historically orientated towards hierarchical networks of social integration, starting in the family and extending to the neighbourhood, company and nation (Ronald and Hirayama, 2009). Many of Japan's company workers, called 'salary-men', are devoted to their jobs apart from their families, whereas today's well-educated and worldly Japanese women watch *Sex and the City* and wonder why their husbands are not more intimate and dynamic (*Telegraph*, 2011). The pressures of the modern workplace, and concentration more on careers and less on personal lives, are increasing divorce rates in India among the urban middle class, whose aspirations are radically different and more complex from those of their parents: 'Today the Indian male, as opposed to earlier, is a very complex entity. We want our wives to be really progressive, modern, so to say, which is why we married them in the first place. But at the same time we still want our wives to cook food for us. We want our wives to be there when we get back home' (BBC News, 2011). While women in Singapore are encouraged to become educated and pursue a modern career, they are also expected to maintain traditional family roles as wives and mothers (Martin and Lewis, Chapter 2 in this volume). Nation-building strategies of gendered state policies encourage women to identify as members of families and to structure life decisions around the family, rather than gender-based individualized identity, which ultimately works to reinforce state/male power as the only agent able to deal with difficult modernizing conditions not of its own making (Yue, Chapter 12 in this volume).

The rise of female individualization and its limits

The rise of female individualization, albeit complex and often contradictory, has been reflected in, and enabled by, the gendered socio-economic changes discussed above – higher levels of educational attainment than ever before, labour market participation, feminization of migration, delayed marriage and non-marriage, declining fertility, increasing divorce rates and family breakdown. These indicators of the family at risk represent visible and provisional, if not permanent, cases of individualization. The social transformations in many parts of contemporary urban Asia appear to engender similar trends and consequences of individualization, which is notably linked to Western/European social theory in the processes of second modernity (Beck, 1992) or liquid modernity (Bauman, 2001) of post-traditional society (Giddens, 1991).

The notion of individualization in Western theory of reflexive modernization is seen as an ongoing shift from a traditional gender role-oriented, collective, normal biography to a labour market-steered, elective, do-it-yourself biography, or an extended, Others-related, reflexive project of self (Giddens, 1991; Beck, 1992; Bauman, 2001; Beck and Beck-Gernsheim, 2002). Individualization is characterized by a growing emphasis on individual autonomy and independence from traditions and social institutions. Women are now released from traditional gender roles and find themselves forced to build up a 'life of their own' by way of the labour market, training and mobility (Beck and Beck-Gernsheim, 2002). Confronted with a plurality of choices, individuals' life politics is organized around an increasingly reflexive and calculable mode of thinking to colonize the future with some degree of success (Giddens, 1991). At the heart of life politics lie enterprising agents who strategically plan, avidly self-monitor and manage a life of their own. Crucially, this do-it-yourself biography is planned around labour market freedom in a neo-liberal economy emphasizing the importance of a flexible labour market and competition (Beck, 1992). The entrance of women into paid work liberates them from inherited gender fates and traditional roles of compulsory housework and dependency on men, as the structural constraints of gender as well as class, ethnicity and other social markers become less significant in structuring the opportunities and identities available to individuals (Beck and Beck-Gernsheim, 2002). This tends to intensify the fluidity of human relationships not only at work but also at home, including intimate relationships, with the melting of previously solid bonds of collective identity into the less determined forms of individually conducted life policies (Bauman, 2001). Marriage has become a chosen construct as well as a risk. Rather than a way to pool resources for risk coping, family is a source of economic and social risks, wherein familial relationships must be constantly negotiated and patterns of intimacy are contested, uncertain or chaotic (Beck and Beck-Gernsheim, 1995). With the rise of post-familial families in a variety of organizational forms, such as cohabitation, with or without children, the individual is becoming the basic unit of social reproduction. Family members form an elective relationship or a permanent do-it-yourself project, shifting from traditional expectations of 'being there for others' to contemporary notions of 'living one's own life' as a free and independent individual (Beck and Beck-Gernsheim, 2002).

What does it mean to be a free and independent individual in Asian societies today? Individualization is not an all-encompassing trend or a radically sweeping process that shares different developments in social structures and cultural domains, as well as the levels of agency and reflexivity operating within. It is necessary to recognize the partial nature of agency and reflexivity in relation to the relative openness of the social world and the different restraints on agency in contemporary Asian societies (Kim, 2008). Despite high levels of reflexivity and possibilities potentially available for change, agency is not 'becoming freed, unleashed or released from structure and its constraints' (Beck and Beck-Gernsheim, 1995), but agency is regulated by structure, operating within broader systems of constraint. The social and cultural fields are not totally restrictive but dialectically positioned; the complexity neither closes the avenue for change for women nor holds it wide open for any kind of empowerment.

There is no doubt that with higher educational attainment and assumed empowerment, women in Asia are seeking to plan a life of their own with a greater capacity for the reflexive project of self. It is the educational achievement that engenders a fundamental shift towards the choice of individualization departing from a normative female biography. Indeed, higher education has become a new normative expectation for middle-class women, or a compulsion towards individualization, albeit a paradoxical one. The promise of higher education and the assumed enlargement of choice can be particularly illusory for highly educated women in Asia, where gendered socio-economic and cultural conditions persist and continue to structure labour market outcomes and lifestyles (Kim, 2011; Kim, Chapter 1 in this volume). The language of choice obscures the ongoing existence of gender inequalities, the highly exclusionary and regulatory function of the labour market in structuring the opportunities and identities available to women. Employment experiences of women are far from being directed by individualization but by inequalities – unequal access to work, gendered wage differential, low pay, chronic economic insecurity and the possible fragmentation of the female life course (Lee, 2000; Brinton, 2001; Benson and Yukongdi, 2005). Educated and skilled women are not necessarily mobile or upward in the labour market, which is still profoundly gendered, nor are they likely to achieve full economic individualization as a free female subject.

Enduring inequalities in the labour market intimately linked to family and care work further impede the logics and possibilities of female individualization. As in other parts of Asia, in Indonesia, women are encouraged to become educated in order to pursue a career, while also maintaining familial roles of being head of the domestic household as wife and mother (Rony, Chapter 8 in this volume). The mutually imbricated structures of family and work in Taiwan are distinct from Euro-American models, where the separation of the family from the economic sphere has been a key feature in the formation of modernity (Martin and Lewis, Chapter 2 in this volume). Families have been an engine of compressed modernity in East Asia, and such familial burdens and dilemmas are particularly onerous to women due to the fundamentally gender-based structure of family relations and duties influenced by Confucianism (Chang and Song, 2010). The possibility of female individualization in Muslim Asia involves a confluence of political, religious and cultural factors, entailing ruptures and contradictions. Women are brought up with ideals of individual autonomy but are expected to put them aside at the moment they raise a family, as motherhood is not merely valued but acknowledged as an important performance equal to labour (Nieuwkerk, 2006).

The neo-liberal idea of the individualized subject is ultimately an economically viable and single individual unfettered by family and care work. It is premised on the assumption that everyone must be free and independent, available for the demands of the market and harsh market competition in order to guarantee one's economic existence and individual performance. Surely women in contemporary Asia still take much more responsibility for the unpaid work of family care than men (Lee, 2000; Brinton, 2001; Zhang et al., 2008), not necessarily being released from gender fates or moving towards more equal, flexible and democratic relationships between women and men and within families. Rather, working women are burdened as a professional family coordinator, which requires a great deal of strategic life-planning and skilful juggling to gain some control over their otherwise risky lives. The constant balancing of work and home renders processes of female individualization much more complex and conflictual, not easily resulting in a shift from 'being there for others' to 'living one's own life'. This means that the movement of women into the labour market has not necessarily undermined the traditional model of male breadwinner/female carer, with women unlikely to become free and fully autonomous citizen workers.

The limitations and contradictions of female individualization within the key parameters are continually salient yet unresolved, giving rise to transnational mobility as a temporary resolution and a form of defection from an expected normative biography (Kim, 2011; Kim, Chapter 1 in this volume). The disjuncture between higher educational attainment and labour market inequity prevents individualization, yet simultaneously generates the individualized, choice-based narratives that women tend to construct in talking about an imagined future of individualization, while finding their ambivalent transition from education to work and independent adulthood unattainable. Female individualization has emerged as a major mode of identity formation that is now operating in a transnational flow of desire, giving rise to the experience of increased freedom as well as growing insecurity and personal responsibility in every move. A defining characteristic of migration patterns today has been initiated by the particular circumstances of the sending countries, which put an extremely high value on education yet offer an extremely low level of certainty in the labour market, and so this has increased the likelihood of migration. In a sense, the new generations of women in Asia are perhaps moved by a 'myth of education', a human capital-focused view that may not necessarily work for particular social categories (Kim, 2011). This global mobility often stems from an individualist faith that the 'human capital of education' can take one where one wants to go, and make it work anywhere, regardless of social structure or social reproduction (Smith and Favell, 2006). Nevertheless, this mode of migration embraced by educated women is predicated on the untenable assumption of secure, or better, employment, and in that sense an occupational and experiential trajectory that is increasingly shaping transnational ways of being. Identity itself is predicated on mobility, involving an openness to risk and a discursive space that is uncertain, highly contingent and unguaranteed (Kim, 2011).

The current growth of singles, and delayed marriage in pursuit of higher education and work, can be seen as an indicator of precarious individualization, which may challenge the stability of family but not necessarily hold a privileging logic of self-invention and freedom. What does individualization mean in the context of the family? Changes in family structure and size in China, for example, have led to the rising importance of the individual in family life, and to a process of the 'individualization of the family' that is mostly reflected in the weakening of the bonds between the family and the larger kinship/community organization (Yan, 2009). Despite the lack of a culturally embedded democracy and a welfare system, a growing individualization has been registered in the rising expectations of individual freedom, choice and individuality (Hansen and Svarverud, 2010). Nevertheless, traditional external constraints on marriage and family – the hetero-normative expectation of marriage by 30 in East Asia or much earlier in South Asia – have not progressively disappeared. The family, not the individual, is still the basic unit of social reproduction in Asia. Mainstream discourse is heavily slanted towards seeing unmarried women, rather than unmarried men, as socially problematic and pathological (Wu, Chapter 11 in this volume). The popular expression 'Defeated Dog' in Japan is seen as a personal responsibility that must be dealt with individually by women who fail to live up to the society's exacting standards and expectations, especially in terms of an age-specific hetero-normative biography: getting married by 30 and establishing a normal family (Kim, Chapter 1 in this volume). Individualization, or family-oriented individualization, encompasses a much more complex and delicate, culture-bound balance between individual and family (Shim and Han, 2010), whose values and practices differ significantly from the individualizing trend of the West. Often, an imagined future of individualization is simultaneously organized around the modalities of marriage and family. This is evident in the varying degrees to which transnational Asian women remain both autonomous from, and dependent upon, concrete familial relations in their diasporic existence and do not necessarily desire individual autonomy or freedom from the notions of marriage and family, even while continually transgressing national borders and producing new narratives of individual freedom (Kim, 2011).

Delayed marriage, childless marriage and declining fertility may readily be regarded as a symptom of social risk, not just a sign of precarious individualization. Although reproduction is regarded as an individual choice, and although low fertility is attributed to cultural patterns going beyond family policies in Korea (Suzuki, 2008), policymakers in Japan justify policies to boost the declining birth rate within a 'risk management' frame, suggesting that personal lifestyle choices are, and should be, politically regulated (Coleman, 2005). State policies aimed at boosting marriage and fertility in Singapore operate as new forms of social control over the choices that women make over various aspects of their lives, while reinforcing the state's non-liberal position towards the family (Yue, Chapter 12 in this volume). On the one hand, today's women appear to be liberated through their educational attainment and labour market participation, but on the other hand, their emancipation is also constrained by the state's bio-political control of their bodies and reproductive choices.

The personal choice of divorce is also a sign of the present uncertainty within the precarious process of female individualization – excruciatingly painful, and not automatically a liberating transition to self-improvement and independent life. What is striking in Asian societies is the extent to which women lack control over their lives, and when women do exercise control they are subjected to violence (Manderson and Bennett, 2003). While divorce may be viewed as an opportunity to construct one's life radically in a non-traditional way, it is usually experienced as a failed life history, a result of wrong choice. Most female divorcees have to face chronic economic insecurity as well as cultural discrimination – people in more conservative parts of Asia will segregate and never speak to them again (*Time Asia*, 2004). Any possibility of creating a biography of one's own is far from reflecting freedom of choice and individualization, but rather represents very limited possibilities and new forms of risk and injury embodied in the regulatory regime of the self.

The notion of the self that is 'free to choose' is not simply a cultural fact but becomes an autonomous self when a woman is able to make a life for herself in her everyday existence, to make herself the centre of her biography. Gender is not losing its decisive influence but is still operating as a powerful category of social stratification, and women are more conscious about it (Kim, Chapter 1 in this volume). Women are not actually living through individualization that has not yet become lived experiences and viable aspects of identity formation in the social landscape of contemporary Asia. As its precarious processes and limitations indicate, female individualization is unlikely to be implemented in a full sense, yet is endlessly played out at the level of imagination, within women's imaginative self-reflexivity, compounded by feelings of uncertainty and anxiety about everyday life.

Popular media culture in everyday life

Individualization in transnational flows

The unresolved identity of individualization, as addressed above, serves as a necessary context within which this book explores the role of the media, the troubling signs of female individualization as intersected with popular media culture in everyday life. Significant changes in media globalization and the rise of Asian economies are affecting the scale and manner in which individuals consume the media today (Kim, 2008). The emerging socio-cultural consequences deserve to be analysed and explored fully in an increasingly global media environment. This book explores the dynamic and complex implications of the everyday media for an understanding of socio-cultural change, female individualization, in the lives and diverse experiences of women across and within Asia, not a singular and unitary region. Asia is a conceptual category of vast differences – economically, politically, culturally and historically. What is meant by Asia does not always garner consensus or generate one Asia but many Asias (Berry et al., 2003; Erni and Chua, 2005; Holden and Scrase, 2006). Each contextual analysis in this book acknowledges unique social spaces and contexts, conveying the diversity of Asia's spaces today at a time of globalization in an increasingly mediated, precarious everyday life.

As Part I demonstrates, transnational flows of the media have emerged in globalizing Asia with a seeming emphasis on individualization and new heterogeneous choices within a neo-liberal capitalist culture of freedom. Although the regulation of the transnational media remains a serious domestic affair and there are worrying signs of the influences of commercialization over local cultural formations (Servaes and Wang, 1997), new media developments have nonetheless stimulated individualization. One of the most important resources for individualization is the availability of a variety of media cultural materials, from which one can choose in order to create a life of one's own, or a do-it-yourself biography as an enterprising agent, although this does not necessarily lead to an unfettered self-creation in the world. Proliferating media images, expressive symbols and globalized narratives reflect the emerging yet precarious trend of individualization of Asian societies, and at the same time they profoundly frame the place of individualization, articulating the multiplication of consumer choices, lifestyle differentiation and imagined empowerment. The transnational media appear to resist patriarchal institutional structures in order to encourage the intertwined trends of individualization and capitalist consumerism, particularly on the part of women who are increasingly tied to global cultural Others, while enabling the imagination of the fluid connections of consumerist agents between the local, the national and the transnational. As a new cultural phenomenon, imagined individualization propelled by everyday media culture opens up new spaces for the pluralization of lifestyles, freedom and the imagined democratization of work opportunities, with the emphasis on self-realization as opposed to traditional values of self-sacrifice.

In Korea, Japan and China, the attainment of higher education does not necessarily increase women's work opportunities and the subsequent role of work in developing individualization. Despite the paradoxical outcomes and anxieties of where women actually stand regarding a move towards individualization, multiple ways of imagining such a possibility are widely available in mediated cultural domains with proliferating resources for the mobilization of self (Kim, Chapter 1 in this volume). Currently proliferating in various forms across the Asian media landscape, lifestyle TV in Singapore and Taiwan is promoting models of individualized femininity and enterprising modes of selfhood, but within structural constraints and gendered social and economic inequities (Martin and Lewis, Chapter 2 in this volume). Lifestyle-themed self-improvement TV programmes, from beauty and career planning to travel and child-rearing, borrow heavily from Western makeover formats but combined with regional East Asian television conventions. Women are exposed to a range of transnationally inflected engagements with neo-liberal economic and consumerist models of female individualization and self-monitoring practices. The engagement with online and cell phone technologies, especially the Internet, involves young Muslim women of Malaysia and Indonesia in a creative enterprise and self-representation that is also a form of control over their lives in the transition to adulthood (Nilan, Chapter 3 in this volume). While young women in Muslim Southeast Asia are able to choose, consume and connect instantly with local, regional and global media resources for self-imagining, the discursive regime of the female self-embodied in the regulatory practices of Islam emphasizes the strict moral behaviour of young women, producing anxieties at the intersection with ideals of individualized modernity.

Often the neo-liberal social changes surrounding individual rights to choice that centre upon beauty, consumption and sexuality are embedded in gendered social morality that polices women's sexuality in India (Dewey, Chapter 10 in this volume). Young women's choices about what to wear, revealing forms of fashion and bodily practices hold a deeply ambivalent social status and tension in a moral economy that places a high value on pre-marital female chastity and absolute post-marital fidelity. A huge influx of Western fashion magazines into the urban centres of Asia has offered shifting conceptions of female identity, as reflected in the Chinese versions of Western magazines: *Cosmopolitan*, *Elle* and *Marie Claire* (Thornham and Feng, Chapter 4 in this volume). It is this continual intersection of local cultural space with the transnational flows of media culture in which re-fashioned modern women reflect on a future different from their mothers' lives of self-sacrifice. They develop a half-imagined future ('maybe one day') characterized by self-actualization, career success and a consumer lifestyle, while negotiating both the identities and choices on offer in such global media culture, and the contradictions between these choice-based identity positions and those experienced elsewhere, self-reflexively, in their gendered lives.

Increased choices in light of mediated non-local knowledge can create the conditions for the operation of reflexivity, heightened self-consciousness, self-monitoring and the possible re-defining of self, as a response to growing knowledge about one's own life circumstances in relation to global cultural Others, other lifestyles and other gender relations (Kim, 2005, 2008, 2011). Global media culture is clearly one of the new, mundane and prime sites in which self-reflexivity is operating continuously, and some knowing self-monitoring subjects are more likely than others to be reflexive about gender relations, inequalities and oppression within the larger context of the mediated world. Reflexivity, as an everyday practice, allows women to reflect upon their social conditions and sometimes criticize existing structures and given dimensions of social order in a new light. The often intended consequences of everyday media consumption on the part of women – not only deriving pleasure and gratification but also gaining routine access to alternative forms of knowledge – contribute to the increasing likelihood of a habitual reflexivity and moreover, a transnational reflexivity through which the self can be regularly examined, re-thought and re-defined, even if not always discursively accomplished. Everyday reflexivity facilitates women in realizing the capacities of socially and culturally situated agents, albeit partial and precarious, leading to new possibilities of identity transformation, or mediated experiences of individualization, with unpredictable consequences within the competing regime of signifiers.

Competing regime of signifiers: Representation and production

As Part II demonstrates, the media, not only the global cultural force but also the national and local mediation, can be understood as a key cultural mechanism creating the emergence of precarious individualized identities in the region. On the one hand, the media's growing emphasis on individualization and lifestyle choices, as well as a process of reflexivity at work, apparently signifies de-traditionalization, individual autonomy and emancipation from oppressive traditional social forms, including the conventional family and gendered self. New ways of conducting life and constructing the self with changing expectations and relations between men and women are playfully signified in the various images, symbols and narratives of popular media culture, which appear to weaken the determining influence of gender and represent imagined empowerment through the de-traditionalization of the private and public spheres. The often de-contextualized representation and playful engagement invite individuals to compare experiences, to become free from fixed gender identities and unequal power, and to orientate themselves towards free choices in the consumerist market or further relate to a cosmopolitan outlook transcending national cultural boundaries.

On the other hand, there are also emerging forms of re-traditionalization, new models of cultural continuity and re-integration replacing ongoing rupture, and the symbolic production of regulative forms of social control over the lives of individuals, and women in particular. The pulls of regulative traditions still operate in the competing regime of signifiers, of dialectical relations between gender, work, sexuality and family that are being reconstituted in ambiguous and sometimes contradictory ways that simultaneously de-traditionalize and re-traditionalize contemporary female subject formation. Pre-existing social structures, regulative traditions and families, if not overly deterministic, continue to play an integral role in structuring the parameters and workings of contemporary media culture, while prompting a relational reflexivity, a relationally constructed emotionality and sociality to function as a moral ideal in a wider, complex and uncertain cultural narrative and vision about social change in Asia (Kim, 2008).

Women's social roles in some parts of Asia have undergone a rapid transformation from the traditional image of the 'good wife and wise mother' to the career women working and playing for pleasure. The Japanese popular media have historically pushed the boundaries of social acceptability with increasingly unconventional content, from women's magazines with a 'sex special' to TV programmes advising women about pornographic videos and even love hotels they might enjoy (Hambleton, Chapter 5 in this volume). Men's bodies are now commoditized and consumed with the same passion as women's bodies have been for many centuries. However, women's shifting relationships with the media and the contradictory images of their bodies are often represented as both the protectors of traditions and consumers for pleasure. Women are invited to feel empowered and modernized through the liberalized consumption, while at the same time dutifully maintaining their traditional role as mothers in the family. Contemporary TV advertising animates the multiple points of divergence and tension between the discourses of neo-liberal individual subjectivity and neo-familism. Although rapid economic growth has benefited Taiwanese women with regard to educational opportunities and employment, and although single-person households are the fastest-growing group in Taiwan, the media produce a symbolic resolution reconstituting the traditional family and articulating the emergence of individualization (Shaw and Lin, Chapter 6 in this volume).

With growing purchasing power as consumers, single working women are increasingly portrayed as gaining more mobility and freedom through the possession of commodities, which is nevertheless framed in the continuity of tradition. Fashion, beauty and luxuries become signifiers of independence and hard work, the markers of a life of one's own, and an identity successfully achieved; but at the same time they need to portray a traditional, 'soft and gentle' femininity seen as a specifically Chinese quality quite unlike the nature of Western women (Thornham and Feng, Chapter 4 in this volume). The premise of lifestyle TV in Singapore and Taiwan underlines young female workers' labours of individual self-management, self-branding and success that are, nonetheless, strongly gender-inflected, advising them how to look professional at work while avoiding appearing 'too powerful' (Martin and Lewis, Chapter 2 in this volume). Popular media discourses seemingly produce new models for the empowerment and freedom of women, yet simulateneously continue to deepen gender inequality and existing social oppression by re-stabilizing and regulating the gendered self.

Empowerment, independence and much of what women aspire to rests upon the premise of their equality with men. Young urban Indian women working in media-related professions act upon their desire for social mobility and individual autonomy under multiple levels of restrictions, rendering them both objects of desire and at risk of sexual harassment from employers and others in positions of power (Dewey, Chapter 10 in this volume). Ironically, the ways in which seemingly de-traditionalizing women seek to gain that equality often end up reproducing the processes that enable male privilege and gender re-traditionalization. Such contradictions, tensions and conflicts abound. The media in contemporary Asia have introduced quite new images and aspirations for women, suffused with values about individual choice, gender equality and freedom of action as independent consumers, whose femininity nonetheless remains intact, whose femaleness is always the core issue (Gallagher, 2002). Television dramas, created by women and for women, present the central conflicts of career vs. family, divorce vs. social norms, asserting new female independence 'without overtly rebelling against men' (Chen, 1998). The new representation of women in globalized advertising is seen to be a sign of female empowerment, as well as subjugation by the continuing influence of Confucianism in China, Korea, Taiwan and Singapore; the traditional Hindu beliefs in India; and the role of Islam in construct-ing social norms for women in Islamic countries like Pakistan (Frith and Karan, 2008).

Empowerment, as a bottom-up approach, is seen to enable subaltern women to become an equal part in social processes and to represent their interests in the public and private spheres. The capacity of popular media culture, albeit limited, can raise subaltern voices that articu-late different interests, express social and political discontent, mediate between the subordinate and the dominant, or transcend hierarchical boundaries of gender and power. Women's voices are not being heard enough, although women's visibility in media content appears to have increased dramatically in otherwise male-dominated fields of media pro-duction (IPS, 2011). In a multi-ethnic society like Malaysia, the gender dimension is closely linked to ethnicity, religion and class, and repre-senting their voices on mainstream TV becomes much more complex given the diversities of identity politics (Balraj-Ambigapathy, 2000).

Voicings, or producing/staging voice from the margins in a global economy, are heard only when the speaker/agent voices her issues and concerns within the frameworks that are recognizable within existing discursive logics shaped by current power hierarchies. Therefore rather than celebrating the emergence of voices from thus far marginalized groups on the Internet and social online networks, it is important to interrogate the implications of these voicings for the existing and emerging structures of power (Gajjala, Chapter 7 in this volume). The Internet today appears to create a space for enacting the empowerment of women while simultaneously highlighting the desirability of female individualization, which can only occur in specific circumstances of access and literacy, and the complex gendered, raced, classed and embodied nature of technological production and representation. Mod-ern documentary film, produced by self-reflexive younger generations of female directors, provides radical voices and views of controversial mate-rial about women, sexuality and power, as well as the basic human right of women's sovereignty over their own lives and health. In Indonesian contexts, this genre of do-it-yourself filmmaking has given voices to female subjects who have been silenced or marginalized by mainstream public culture due to differences in gender, race, class and sexuality (Rony, Chapter 8 in this volume). Such changes in imagery, represen-tation and production of the contemporary media have become both new arenas for signifying women's desires and identities, and new strug-gles over the construction of individualizing subjectivity through new consumption practices.

New consumption practices of female individualization

Consumption, a site of leisure and pleasure, is also a key site for the production of the self that becomes integrated into everyday life with new openings and possibilities, tensions and contradictions of transition in the interplay between lived relations and mediated processes (Kim, 2005, 2008). The precarious nature of female individualization intersected with media consumption is explored in Part III of this book, which addresses the media's profound significance in and for individualization. The increasingly diverse and intrusive media today are intentionally used as resources for the organization of social life and for the awareness of new lifestyles, individual choice and differentiation that are somehow universally shared by global consumers. This increased awareness is not only the outcome of education but also significantly the consequence of the proliferation of sites of mediated experience offering wider contexts of knowledge and images concerning different discourses outside local networks of experience (Kim, Chapter 1 in this volume). Subordinate women, unsatisfied with gendered inequalities and constraints, may find fulfilment through media cultural consumption practices, the often trivialized yet becoming-significant developments for the culturally specific ways in which individualization and de-traditionalization are imagined and searched for, albeit not always accomplished. Modernity is inescapably gendered and reflexively embodied – often performed by female bodies in transit as a particular site of struggle over identities, unequal power and some degree of control to resist, yet sometimes complicit with, the gendered norms of the modernizing and globalizing neo-liberal economies of Asia.

Modern women's high levels of education and participation in the labour market have increasingly focused attention on their individualizing lifestyles and consumption culture in Hong Kong (Leo et al., 2001). For many educated Chinese women, the belief that they will succeed in consuming luxuries as long as they work hard is bound up with a belief in the power to become self-made (Thornham and Feng, Chapter 4 in this volume). Consumption as success is seen to be an outcome of individual ability and, above all, self-determination. The dream of self-transformation is similarly a dream of independence and success, albeit acknowledged to be fragile. New cultural consumption practices may enable women, regardless of their class positions, to imagine self-transformation and empowerment and to become agents hidden behind social transformations. Gendered yearning for empowerment is expressed in the historical phenomenon of the Philippine New Cinema, the cult fandom surrounding the nation's first media-convergent female superstar (Lim, Chapter 9 in this volume). Its overwhelmingly female and working-class fandom can be read as allegories for gendered collective desires for social and political transformation, which contests patriarchal authority in the family and the religious power structure of the everyday.

The Miss India Pageant and Bollywood stardom – key sites of popular media consumption in a South Asian context – are envisioned by many middle-class young women as self-transforming opportunities (Dewey, Chapter 10 in this volume). As the Indian media landscape becomes increasingly integrated into the global economy, it is significant that such rapid upward and global mobility is tied to women's capacity to impress others through their beauty, grace and body. This presents an apparent paradox that reinforces gendered stereotypes while simultaneously situating female performances within the discourse of female achievement and the burden of self-development. Mediated experience often leads to an unresolved precarious identity – an ambivalence of close identification and distancing, contestation and resistance (Kim, 2005, 2008). Middle-class young women's experience of popular reality TV and new media convergence culture surrounding TV dating shows in China generates multiple discourses of love, gender, class, sexuality and the unsayable, as well as the widening gap between men and women in their self-understandings and expectations of each other (Wu, Chapter 11 in this volume). The seemingly self-choosing subjects negotiate real-life tensions between traditional values and modern consumerism while manifesting a dialectic of freedom and constraint in a rapidly globalizing Asia.

Since the late 1980s, trends towards individualization and identification with such lifestyles have been produced by the media industry in all of Southeast Asia, particularly Indonesia, Malaysia and Vietnam, with the emergence of the new urban middle classes and their capitalist consumption practices that have been used in the construction of modernity (Evers and Gerke, 1997). The modern media, consumerism and porous socio-religious boundaries have significantly influenced the current realities of Muslim women's lives in South Asia (Mehta, 2010). Religious practices are highly gendered and implicated in the formation of the modern in Indonesia, as women's Islamic practices have been part of the creation of a particular kind of urban middle-class subjectivity, enacting class and gender difference and simultaneously producing modern selves (Rinaldo, 2008).

Media access of rural women is particularly low, and their mediated experiences are of an entirely different nature from those of urban women in highly dense media environments (Gallagher, 2002). Rural women in Thailand, who move to Bangkok for employment, confront significant social and economic constraints as low-wage, low-status migrant labour; yet experiences of exploitation in the workplace are widely mediated by aspirations for and participation in new patterns of consumption (Mills, 1997). These consumption practices are important sites of cultural struggle in which young women seek to construct new identities and contest their marginalization within the wider society. Constructions of new identities through pop culture, such as music TV in India, are strategically appropriated by marginalized young Indian women to imagine alternatives to both national and transnational institutions of political and patriarchal power (Curtin and Kumar, 2002). While the increasingly globalized and more liberal media culture prevails in India, the private world of the family nevertheless retains many aspects of traditional moral and hierarchical principles (Scrase, 2002).

There is a much more peculiar trend in Asia, given its collectivistic cultural traditions (Qiu, 2010), in which the consumption of mobile media technologies becomes a conspicuous means to achieve social differentiation and highly differentiated sociality among urban youths (Wei, 2006). New media technologies – the Internet in particular – are often uncritically celebrated as a democratic revolution in everyday life, and a seemingly free-floating move towards individualization, a do-it-yourself lifestyle culture that is continually produced and consumed in neo-liberal consumer societies of Asia. Women, as producers and consumers of social media, have increasingly appropriated female blogging to fashion new self-narratives of female individualization. Recent developments in Singapore's transition to the new knowledge and creative economy have witnessed the rise of a highly educated, media-savvy and entrepreneurial population. While women in Singapore have been at the forefront of these changes, their mediated discourses and new life politics are both complicit with, and resist, illiberal pragmatism that is governed and regulated by the interventions of government (Yue, Chapter 12 in this volume). New consumption practices of female individualization are constituted by a paradoxical modality that not only creates new modes of self-choosing, self-fashioning female life politics but also possibly reproduces gendered subjects and the nature of gendered identity that is resonant with gendered state policies.

This indicates the complex and often contradictory status of female individualization, regulated and confined but also challenging and contesting at the intersection with popular media culture in everyday life, its imagined modes of self-actualization but also new forms of social control operating in an expanded world of mediation. Mediated experience heightens reflexive awareness of the deeply embedded aspects of identities given by social structural locations, and also provokes confusion or anxiety over the construction of new individualized identity projects and intended effects on life politics. Amid the proliferation of the media, the seeming pluralization of choices in life and the deepening of the self, ongoing identity work is struggled for by women, who create the expressive possibilities for identity transformation but may also face considerable difficulties, may still not know which way they are going, or may potentially suffer from unintended consequences. The achievement of a reflexive self-identity – female individualization in this social context – can be understood as a precarious process, not simply flexible but much more complex, constantly being reconstituted through, and simultaneously competing with, normatively directed constraints and available discursive resources as well as capacities to reduce inequalities in the life trajectories of women of rapidly changing Asia.

References

ADB (Asian Development Bank) (2011) 'Women and Labour Markets in Asia: Rebalancing for Gender Equality', report by the ADB and the International Labour Organization.

Balraj-Ambigapathy, S. (2000) 'Dis-Empowering Women on Malaysian TV', *Asia Pacific Media Educator*, 9: 148–163.

Banerjee, K. (1999) 'Gender Stratification and the Contemporary Marriage Market in India', *Journal of Family Issues*, 20(5): 648–676.

Bauman, Z. (2001) *The Individualized Society*, Cambridge: Polity.

BBC News (2011) 'Not So Happily Ever After as Indian Divorce Rate Doubles', 1 January.

Beck, U. (1992) *Risk Society: Towards a New Modernity*, London: Sage.

Beck, U. and Beck-Gernsheim, E. (1995) *The Normal Chaos of Love*, Cambridge: Polity.

Beck, U. and Beck-Gernsheim, E. (2002) *Individualization*, London: Sage.

Benson, J. and Yukongdi, V. (2005) 'Asian Women Managers: Participation, Barriers and Future Prospects', *Asia Pacific Business Review*, 11(2): 283–291.

Berry, C., Martin, F. and Yue, A. (2003) *Mobile Cultures: New Media in Queer Asia*, Durham: Duke University Press.

Brinton, M. (2001) *Women's Working Lives in East Asia*, Palo Alto: Stanford University Press.

Caldwell, B. (2005) 'Factors Affecting Female Age at Marriage in South Asia', *Asian Population Studies*, 1(3): 283–301.

Chan, A. and Yeoh, B. (2002) 'Gender, Family and Fertility in Asia', *Asia-Pacific Population Journal*, 17(2): 5–10.

Chang, K. and Song, M. (2010) 'The Stranded Individualizer under Compressed Modernity: South Korean Women in Individualization without Individualism', *The British Journal of Sociology*, 61(3): 539–564.

Chen, Y. (1998) 'In Search of the Essential Woman in National Development: China's First TV Drama Series on Women, by Women, for Women', *The Journal of Development Communication*, 9(2): 1–17.

Chowdhury, F. and Trovato, F. (1994) 'The Role and Status of Women and the Timing of Marriage in Five Asian Countries', *Journal of Comparative Family Studies*, 25, http://soci.ucalgary.ca/jcfs/.

Coleman, L. (2005) 'Social Risk, Value Change and the Life Course', *Social Science Japan*, September, 19–21.

Curtin, M. and Kumar, S. (2002) 'Made in India: In between Music Television and Patriarchy', *Television & New Media*, 3(4): 345–366.

Erni, J. and Chua, S. (2005) *Asian Media Studies*, Malden: Blackwell.

Evers, H. and Gerke, S. (1997) 'Global Market Cultures and the Construction of Modernity in Southeast Asia', *Thesis Eleven*, 50(1): 1–14.

Frith, K. and Karan, K. (2008) *Commercializing Women: Images of Asian Women in the Media*, New York: Hampton Press.

Gallagher, M. (2002) 'Women, Media and Democratic Society: In Pursuit of Rights and Freedoms', paper of the United Nations EGM/Media, November.

Giddens, A. (1991) *Modernity and Self-Identity: Self and Society in the Late Modern Age*, Stanford, CA: Stanford University Press.

Gupta, M., Zhenghua, J., Bohua, L., Zhenming, X., Chung, W. and Bae, H. (2003) 'Why Is Son Preference So Persistent in East and South Asia?', paper in the World Bank e-Library.

Holden, T. and Scrase, T. (2006) *Medi@sia*, London: Routledge.

IPS (Inter Press Service News Agency) (2011) 'Forget Gender', 25 May.

Jayaweera, S. (1997) 'Women, Education and Empowerment in Asia', *Gender and Education*, 9(4): 411–424.

Jones, G. (2005) 'The Flight from Marriage in South-East and East Asia', *Journal of Comparative Family Studies*, 36, http://soci.ucalgary.ca/jcfs/.

Jones, G. (2007) 'Delayed Marriage and Very Low Fertility in Pacific Asia', *Population and Development Review*, 33(3): 453–478.

Kabeer, N. (1999) 'Resources, Agency, Achievements: Reflections on the Measurement of Women's Empowerment', *Development and Change*, 30(3): 435–464.

Kelkar, G. and Nathan, D. (2002) 'Gender Relations and Technological Change in Asia', *Current Sociology*, 50(3): 427–441.

Kim, H. and Voos, P. (2007) 'The Korean Economic Crisis and Working Women', *Journal of Contemporary Asia*, 37(2): 190–208.

Kim, Y. (2005) *Women, Television and Everyday Life in Korea: Journeys of Hope*, London: Routledge.

Kim, Y. (2008) *Media Consumption and Everyday Life in Asia*, London: Routledge.

Kim, Y. (2011) *Transnational Migration, Media and Identity of Asian Women: Diasporic Daughters*, London: Routledge.

Kingdon, G. (1998) 'Does the Labour Market Explain Lower Female Schooling in India?', *Journal of Development Studies*, 35(1): 39–65.

KWDI (Seoul: Korean Women's Development Institute) (2009) http://www2.kwdi.re.kr.

Lash, S. (1994) 'Reflexivity and Its Doubles', in Ulrich Beck et al. (eds) *Reflexive Modernization*, pp. 110—173, Cambridge: Polity.

Lauser, A. (2008) 'Philippine Women on the Move: Marriage across Borders', *International Migration*, 46(4): 85–110.

Lee, W. (2000) 'Women Employment in Colonial Hong Kong', *Journal of Contemporary Asia*, 30(2): 246–264.

Leo, Y., Sin, S., So, O. and Yau, K. (2001) 'Chinese Women at the Crossroads: An Empirical Study on Their Role Orientations and Consumption Values in Chinese Society', *Journal of Consumer Marketing*, 18(4): 348–367.

Luo, G. (2005) 'Effects of Rural-Urban Migration on Rural Female Workers', paper for NACS conference, June.

Manderson, L. and Bennett, L. (2003) *Violence against Women in Asian Societies*, London: Routledge.

Mehta, S. (2010) 'Commodity Culture and Porous Socio-Religious Boundaries: Muslim Women in Delhi', *South Asia Research*, 30(1): 1–24.

Mills, M. (1997) 'Contesting the Margins of Modernity: Women, Migration and Consumption in Thailand', *American Ethnologist*, 24(1): 37–61.

Montgomery, M., Arends-Kuenning, M. and Mete, C. (2000) 'The Quantity-Quality Transition in Asia', *Population and Development Review*, 26: 223–256.

Murthi, M. (2002) 'Fertility Change in Asia and Africa', *World Development*, 30(10): 1769–1778.

Nieuwkerk, K. (2006) *Women Embracing Islam: Gender and Conversion in the West*, Austin: University of Texas Press.

Nilan, P. (2008) 'Youth Transitions to Urban, Middle-class Marriage in Indonesia', *Journal of Youth Studies*, 11(1): 65–82.

Omar, A. and Davidson, M. (2001) 'Women in Management: A Comparative Cross-cultural Overview', *Cross Cultural Management: An International Journal*, 8(3): 35–67.

Qiu, J. (2010) 'Mobile Communication Research in Asia: Changing Technological and Intellectual Geopolitics?', *Asian Journal of Communication*, 20(2): 213–229.

Rahim, L. (1998) 'In Search of the Asian Way: Cultural Nationalism in Singapore and Malaysia', *Commonwealth & Comparative Politics*, 36(3): 54–73.

Raymo, J. and Iwasawa, M. (2005) 'Marriage Market Mismatches in Japan: An Alternative View of the Relationship between Women's Education and Marriage', *American Sociological Review*, 70(5): 801–822.

Retherford, R., Ogawa, N. and Matsukura, R. (2001) 'Late Marriage and Less Marriage in Japan', *Population and Development Review*, 27(1): 65–102.

Rinaldo, R. (2008) 'Muslim Women, Middle Class Habitus and Modernity in Indonesia', *Contemporary Islam*, 2(1): 23–39.

Ronald, R. and Hirayama, Y. (2009) 'Home Alone: The Individualization of Young, Urban Japanese Singles', *Environment and Planning*, 41(12): 2836–2854.

Rozario, S. (1997) 'Development and Rural Women in South Asia: The Limits of Empowerment and Conscientization', *Bulletin of Concerned Asian Scholars*, 29, http://criticalasianstudies.org/bcas/back-issues.html.

Scrase, T. (2002) 'Television, the Middle Classes and the Transformation of Cultural Identities in West Bengal, India', *International Communication Gazette*, 64(4): 323–342.

Servaes, J. and Wang, G. (1997) 'Privatization and Commercialization of the Western-European and South-East Asian Broadcasting Media', *Asian Journal of Communication*, 7(2): 1–11.

Shim, Y. and Han, S. (2010) 'Family-Oriented Individualization and Second Modernity: An Analysis of Transnational Marriages in Korea', *Soziale Welt*, 61(3–4): 237–255.

Sina (2010) 'Beijing Divorce Rate Skyrockets', Sina.com, 8 February.

Smith, M. and Favell, A. (2006) *The Human Face of Global Mobility*, New Brunswick: Transaction Press.

Suzuki, T. (2008) 'Korea's Strong Familism and Lowest-Low Fertility', *International Journal of Japanese Sociology*, 17(1): 30–41.

Taiwan Ministry of the Interior (2010) *Statistical Yearbook*, Taipei: Department of Statistics.

Telegraph (2011) 'Tokyo Sees Rise in Divorce Ceremonies', 17 June.

Time Asia (2004) 'Asia's Divorce Boom', 29 March.

Wei, R. (2006) 'Lifestyles and New Media: Adoption and Use of Wireless Communication Technologies in China', *New Media & Society*, 8(6): 991–1008.

Wong, O. (2005) 'The Socioeconomic Determinants of the Age at First Marriage among Women in Hong Kong', *Journal of Family and Economic Issues*, 26(4): 529–550.

Yan, Y. (2009) *The Individualization of Chinese Society*, Oxford: Berg.

Zhang, Y., Hannum, E. and Wang, M. (2008) 'Gender-Based Employment and Income Differences in Urban China', *Social Forces*, 86(4): 1529–1560.

Part I
Individualization in Transnational Flows

1
Female Individualization? Transnational Mobility and Media Consumption of Asian Women

Youna Kim

Women are travelling out of South Korea (hereafter, Korea), Japan and China for very different reasons than those that sent them into diaspora only 20 years ago. From the mid-1980s onwards there has been a rising trend in women leaving their country to experience life overseas either as tourists or as students, which has eventually surpassed the number of men engaging in foreign travel. Now, 80 per cent of Japanese people studying abroad are women (Kelsky, 2001; Ono and Piper, 2004); an estimated 60 per cent of Koreans studying abroad are women; and more than half of the Chinese entering higher education overseas are women (HESA, 2006; IIE, 2006). This phenomenon is part of a larger trend described as the 'feminization of migration', yet there remains a striking lack of analysis on the gender dimension (World Bank, 2006). Today women are significant and active participants in the increased scale, diversity and transition in the nature of international migration. Studying abroad has become a major vehicle for entry into Western countries (Lucas, 2005) and East Asia continues to be the largest sending region every year. In 2005, 53,000 Koreans, 42,000 Japanese and 62,000 Chinese students moved to US institutions of higher education; and 4000 Koreans, 6000 Japanese and 53,000 Chinese students moved to UK institutions of higher education. Studying abroad has become a common career move for relatively affluent women in their twenties. This new generation of women, who depart from the usual track of marriage, are markers of contemporary transnational mobility, constituting a new kind of diaspora – a 'knowledge diaspora'.

Why do women move? What are the social conditions, the push-and-pull factors that compel women to move away from Korea, Japan

31

and China? How do the media play a role in this process? The purpose of this study is to analyse the highly visible, fastest-growing, yet little-studied phenomenon of women's transnational mobility and its relationship to the impact of media consumption on everyday life. While this transnational mobility has been recognized as important from an economic perspective in Western higher education (Nania and Green, 2004), there has been very little research from a socio-cultural angle. In particular, scant attention has been paid to the gender composition of transnational mobility and what it actually means to the women on the move. Questions of identity are reconfigured by flows of desire that now operate transnationally, aided by Asia's economic growth and integration into a globalized world that has enabled new generations of women to experience and then create a different life trajectory using Western educational institutions as a contact zone. This study explores the nature of women's transnational mobility and the role of the media, providing detailed empirical data from young Korean, Japanese and Chinese women living and studying in the West.

Specifically, this study begins by analysing the gendered socio-economic and cultural conditions of each society, with a particular focus on systems of education and employment. It will argue that higher education does not necessarily increase women's work opportunities and the subsequent role of work in developing a new mode of identity formation – individualization.

In Korea, there is an inverse relationship between a woman's higher education and her subsequent job opportunities; female individualization as an alternative, emancipatory life politics remains frustratingly limited for reasons that are structural to the labour market (Kim, 2005: 169–177). With the rapid expansion of education throughout the 1980s and 1990s, the value of a university education in Korea declined, guaranteeing neither employment nor middle-class life (Abelmann, 2003). The unmet promises of education, the increasing awareness of inequalities and the lack of job opportunities have propelled a new surge of movement to the West.

Similarly, in Japan, it is increasingly common for women to quit their 'office lady' (OL) jobs and move to a Western destination (Kelsky, 2001). Half of the employed women in Japan are temporary part-time workers; highly educated women are often under-employed; and the rapid rise of youth unemployment since the 1990s has led to the ambivalent lengthening of the transition from school to work (ILO, 2006). Ironically, some Japanese women feel that education could actually damage their chances of getting a job (Ono and Piper, 2004). A new desire has emerged among young women, who are making a westward journey to redefine their work identity and to have a degree of control over their individual lives (Ichimoto, 2004).

In contemporary China, increasing international openness and the country's economic development since the 1980s appear to encourage the right conditions for job opportunities, yet traditional gender dynamics within Chinese work environments limit women's employment. In the urban labour market, young women graduating from university find it particularly difficult to get their first job (Jiang et al., 2004). Urban women tend to postpone marriage for the sake of a career, independence and personal freedom, seeking opportunities in Western higher-education institutions that will allow them to access international jobs outside of the Chinese labour system. Exposure to international education and a progression towards working in foreign-invested companies – effectively moving out of the domestic work environment altogether – may be one of the few legitimate avenues open to Chinese women to live in a non-traditional, personally emancipatory and individualized fashion (Turner, 2006).

Arguably, female individualization has emerged as a major mode of identity formation that is now operating in a transnational flow of desire, giving rise to the experience of increased freedom, as well as increased insecurity and personal responsibility for every move. A generalization about women's decisions to move can be grounded in an understanding of the transnationally dispersed sites, instances and cultures of female individualization that are refracted into various degrees, forms and interests. Educated women have a strong interest in the idea of individualization, autonomous choice and the aspiration for self-actualization; however, interest in individualization is a growing response not to the successful actualization of that aspiration but to the frustrated desire for subjective autonomy that is increasingly felt in the 'no choice' situation. This study intends to draw attention to the rise and the problematic nature of female individualization among young Korean, Japanese and Chinese women in the context of transnational mobility, while making a case for a more interrogatory approach towards gender and social change in the male-stream debate about individualization.

The individualization of life experiences has become one of the central claims of contemporary social theory (Giddens, 1991; Beck, 1992; Bauman, 2001; Beck and Beck-Gernsheim, 2002). Education and career opportunities are generally regarded as the driving forces behind the individualization of people's lives and social mobility. It is suggested that a person's position in the labour market is now constituted less by determinants such as gender, class, age and place, but more by self-design, self-creation and individual performance: 'The educated person becomes the producer of his or her own labour situation, and in this way, of his or her social biography' (Beck, 1992: 93). The emergence of privatized work, the devaluation of social order by globalization processes and the uncertainty of changing societies have become powerful individualizing forces as the borders between social institutions disappear and fluidity becomes more characteristic than structure (Bauman, 2001). There is a tendency to emphasize the increased fluidity of contemporary social life, as well as the mobile reflexive individual and his or her freedom of movement, along with a consequence of personal choice. This individualization process is characterized by growing reflexivity, self-monitoring and awareness, and an expansion of disembedding mechanisms (Giddens, 1991), including global media flows that lift social interaction out of the individuals' local context and allow them to relocate themselves in a transnationally dispersed culture. The result of these social conditions is seen to be an individualized individual. It is up to each individual to decide if she wants to or must be economically active (Beck and Beck-Gernsheim, 2002), and to choose for herself and plan what she will do with her choices and capacities. Significantly, work is regarded as a 'motor of individualization' (Beck, 1992: 92).

A shared ground and the possibility of individualization are predicated by the labour market – finding work and achieving equality as well as success in education. This study will argue that the claim that education encourages work freedom, economic power and the enlargement of choice can be illusory for educated women in Korea, Japan and China, where gendered socio-economic and cultural conditions persist and continue to structure labour-market outcomes and lifestyles. Whose individualization? A contradiction lies at the heart of female individualization. The individualization of life experiences may reflect a discursive shift in the ways that women today 'imagine' and 'talk' about their lives, rather than a substantive change in actual life conditions. Regulative dimensions of gender and social structure continue to shape available opportunities and constrain personal choice and freedom. The resulting contradiction of female individualization and women's stories that do 'not reach beyond the narrow and painstakingly fenced off enclosure of the private and subjective self' (Bauman, 2001: 12) now become apparent in the growing phenomenon of transnational mobility. Free mobility is itself a deception, since the seemingly voluntary movement – or a woman's self-determined choice to move – is a forced, gendered process mediated by larger forces that push women into different routes across the world.

Against these social contexts, this study will also consider the pull-effect of the media, which means that women's mediated symbolic encounter with the West generates 'imaginations of alternative lifestyles and work' (Kim, 2005: 184–192). The media play a significant role in the symbolic and cultural forms that people live by, constituting a 'residual culture' (Williams, 1977) that has been accumulated throughout a life history and that is still active as an effective element in the present. People seem to imagine routinely the possibility that they will live and work in places other than where they were born, and their plans are affected by a mass-mediated imaginary that frequently transcends national space (Appadurai, 1996). Since the 1990s, the media landscape of Asia has been rapidly globalizing; the growth in satellites, transnational TV channels and online networks in Asia is said to be the most rapid worldwide (Thomas, 2005). Such profusion of the media, with new imaginations, choices and contradictions, generates a critical condition for reflexivity, providing everyday people with the resources to learn about self, culture and society in Asia (Kim, 2008). This plausibly powerful capacity of the media, deeply ingrained in what people take for granted, should be recognized in any attempt to understand the present phenomenon of transnational mobility.

TV in particular has become a key site for the emergence of a new contemporary subject, 'migratory youth', and for the construction of a 'migratory project' (Mai, 2004). This mobility is seen as an extension of the previous immersion of young people in consuming images transmitted from a Western destination, while dreaming of escape from their social constraints. In Asian society, where women's social roles and public voices are otherwise highly constrained, women are either allowed to be, or coerced into being, the primary agents of cultural media consumption (Skov and Moeran, 1995). Under social controls that deny women the ability to act on their own, the chances for individualization become smaller, and so individualization can be sought in an ever-greater participation in media cultural consumption – the complex symbolic project that women engage with. Media consumption can be understood as a key cultural mechanism in creating the emergence of individualized identities, both imagined and enacted. This study will therefore show how the West is represented in the imagination of young Korean, Japanese and Chinese women through engagement with the media in their homeland by which female individualization operates as a self-reflexive and imaginative social practice. It will argue for the potential role of the media in triggering enactment of transnational mobility; the interplay between media consumption and physical displacement towards a deliberately encouraging yet precarious movement of freedom.

Why do women move? Tackling this question requires that transnational mobility should be understood with multi-faceted insights; considering some of the key macro factors affecting women's decision to move and the micro processes of the ways in which women experience the mediated world of everyday culture, while reflecting the interconnection of these seemingly opposite and contradictory levels of push-and-pull elements within the particular socio-economic and cultural contexts in which women live their everyday lives.

Method

In what follows, this study will offer an insight into the causes and implications of women's movement, using data drawn from personal in-depth interviews and diaries from the period 2006–2008. As part of a larger project exploring women's diasporic lives and identities and their intersections with the media, interviews were conducted with 60 Asian women (20 Koreans, 20 Japanese and 20 Chinese) who had been living and studying in the UK/London for three to seven years. The women's ages were between 26 and 33 years. They were recruited by the snowball method of sampling, which is based on the friendship networks of participants, and several snowballs were used to ensure that interviews were conducted with women from different universities. Interviews were open-ended and unstructured; at least three follow-up interviews were conducted for a consistent flow of data. Also, a panel of 30 diarists (10 Koreans, 10 Japanese and 10 Chinese) were recruited from the women interviewed and asked to write/email diaries about their experiences and to express in detail the key issues raised during the interviews. This method was designed to generate biographical material accounts from the women and incorporate a reflexive biographical analysis.

Female individualization in transnational flows

Korean women: 'It's the only exit'

> Education guarantees nothing. In Korea, the more women are educated, the more we would find it difficult to get a job. Not just any kind of job that doesn't need a university degree or

just a low-paid secretary.... There was no job future, no hope to make my own life. It's the only exit.

I am doing another MA degree (in the UK), moving from this country to another country, until I find a solution. Don't know if another degree will give me a better job in Korea, or the same job, or a jobless life.

'Education without a guarantee' is illustrated in Korea, where 95.3 per cent of women go to high school and 63 per cent of the women go on to higher education, yet only 46.7 per cent of university graduates are employed – mostly in traditional female roles; non-managerial and secretarial positions unrelated to their educational qualifications (KWDI, 2006). A wage differential of 76 per cent compared with male wages gives women little economic security, and the gendered division of the labour market is a site of continuing inequality. A contradiction of female individualization lies in the gap between the growing expectations of education and the reality of work inequality. The culture of uncertainty is so pervasive that women's work identity is fraught with feelings of hopelessness and ambivalence.

Feeling I was getting smaller and smaller every day, exhausting myself, I quit the job and moved to study. Job satisfaction was very low, even erosive to the self. Working from morning until 9pm, 10pm with everybody as a team, there was no self.

Is this work for me? What do I work for? Work was self-destructing, not self-building. I was constantly searching for my self.

What actually happens in the workplace and to the role of work in defining women's identities is often revealed as 'self-destructive' or 'self-erosive'. Koreans work the longest hours in the world (OECD, 2007), working overtime until late in the evening is the norm and the work–life balance is a serious concern. This enormous work stress can produce a paradox; people work intensely under great pressure, but their relations to others remain curiously superficial (Sennett, 2006), leading to a diminution of collective consciousness and to a self-oriented individualism (Park and Kim, 2005). Work identity is a central feature of women's modern life. The workplace can be a distinctive site for the construction of identity, and work satisfaction can build a renewed sense of self, but none of this seems necessarily available to Korean women. Nevertheless, the ambivalent sense of work identity is primarily and most intimately connected with their conceptions of self-identity. The self is sought in work biography, the 'working self'.

> If work life is not fulfilling, mothers' generation would choose marriage. We try to find an alternative, such as studying abroad, hoping to find better work. Work comes first, marriage later.... When will I be able to marry? Finding the right man is equally difficult as my expectations are much higher than my mother's.

> I want happiness. I want both work and marriage, not to self-sacrifice like old mothers, however illusory having it all is.

> I am highly educated and believe I can have it all. But nothing is certain about work or marriage.

With the rising expectations of education, the younger generation of women seek to find their individuality through work and somehow feel obliged to construct their own identities in opposition to their mothers' lives ('self-sacrifice'), yet they are simultaneously expecting their own feelings ('happiness') to be fulfilled also by marriage and family life. There emerges an ambivalent sense that they have to take on a self-fulfilling but less predictable life course and the burden of the choices; the illusion of 'having it all' or the belief that women 'can have it all' becomes an imperative rather than a choice for educated women. This highly ambivalent desire to 'have it all' is commonly expressed and shared, marking a generational difference. While marriage is not repudiated but postponed, the women's socio-economic status has not been improved enough to operate individualization through work.

> I was looking for an escape from that hopeless job. It's the only exit, however uncertain. Finding a new job was difficult and other jobs would be the same.

> If you can't get a good job and don't want to marry yet, but while approaching the age 30, you become not desirable in the marriage market either, then what can you do? There was no choice. I am willing to move until there is change in my life.

'It's the only exit'. This indicates a deep dissatisfaction with the systematic contradictions that make women feel that there is little they can do to change the 'no choice' situation. Women are frustrated in varying degrees by the way that they find themselves disempowered in social conditions that limit work possibilities and choices. The lack of fit between the role of education in opening up the possibility of mobility and female individualization, and women's unemployment and under-employment propel them to move away from Korea. This may be an expression not only of their own hopes but also of their rage against the unproductive consequences of education and the determinacy of structure. They are becoming a 'nomadic subject' (Braidotti, 1994), expressing a desire for an identity made up of transitions and changes and a discursive freedom from dominant fixity, while moving with the indeterminacy of risk or a gamble.

Japanese women: 'It's like a gamble'

> Education is consumption. We pay for it without expecting economic returns, because there is no guarantee for a job or a better salary. It's not easy to get a good job, even with a top university degree. Job recruitment works favourably for men ... I disliked the ordinary office job. The salary was low, though I had a materially good life living with my parents.

> I am not sure if a MA or a PhD overseas will help me find a fulfilling job in Japan. It's like a gamble. Without knowing the chance of success, I try it.

The perception of education has become 'consumption', a thing to be consumed by women without any expectations as to the consequences. Japanese women are among the world's best educated but most under-utilized (Social Science Japan, 2005). High-school education has reached equal levels for men (96.0 per cent) and women (96.7 per cent), and 45.3 per cent of women advance to higher education. However, Japan's male-dominated labour system divides recruits into 'career track position' and 'general clerical work', with 80 per cent of women being hired in the second category. Shorter-term work and clerical tasks are reserved for women, who are widely known as 'office ladies'. Women in full-time employment earn only 65 per cent of male wages. Unlike their parents' generation, many younger workers are getting part-time or temporary employment – a situation that is neither efficient nor equitable (*Japan Times*, 2007). This inequity, along with the rise of youth unemployment since the early 1990s, has caused the phenomenon of 'Parasite Singles', which refers to those Japanese who continue to live with their parents for a longer period of time than in previous generation – 60 per cent of single men and 80 per cent of single women between the ages of 20 and 34 live with their parents. They are the first new generation of women to stay single beyond their twenties, while recognizing the social pressure to get married.

> A woman who is not married, does not have children and is over 30, is called a 'Defeated Dog' (title of a Japanese bestseller book), a loser in life. We laugh about it, but are serious too.... No matter how successful I am in my profession, society will see me as a personal failure if I stay single.

> Work is important in my life, travelling with women friends, having fun too...I am not excluding marriage. But it seems so difficult for women to have work, freedom, marriage and children.

The popular expression of 'Defeated Dog' is seen as a personal responsibility that must be dealt with individually by women who fail to live up to the society's exacting standards and expectations, especially in terms of an age-specific hetero-normative biography – getting married by 30 and establishing a normal family. This institutionalized normalization, along with society's fears regarding the declining birth rate of 1.29, excludes the wishes of young women who aim to establish a career first and hesitate to prioritize marriage. Single women fear it is unlikely that they will be able to continue in full-time work after marriage and when dealing with childcare, and they will eventually become part-time workers with no career future. Being unmarried and approaching the age of 30 is precisely the time when women's longings to move abroad generally peak, in conjunction with the social pressure to marry, which also peaks at 30 (Kelsky, 2001).

> It's like a gamble. I think we women are more willing to take a gamble, willing to move around to find a better life, because there is no better life in Japan anyway.

> I wanted to get away and find something new...I think about my self, my work, my independent life, marriage someday when I can find the right man, regardless of whether he is a Japanese or Western man, understanding of my self-fulfilment, not just his own.... We women want happy family life, don't we?

'It's like a gamble'. Women are willing to be risk-takers in a denormalization of gendered roles through transnational relocation in order to find an individual and independent self. However, the search for self is a kind of gamble in a limited sense since Japanese women are 'not always willing to forsake their traditional selves in order to take on the new' (Rosenberger, 2001). Hetero-normative marriage and family life is temporarily delayed, not discarded, within the new transnational framework of self in which Japan is seen as failing in its attitude towards women as individuals. Rather than a desire to live in a particular Western country, what seems to be the case is that women often feel trapped within, and have an 'urge to leave Japan' (Fujita, 2008) or seek to escape it for a time. Contemporary Japanese society has become something to escape from rather than to find one's place within.

Chinese women: 'We call it a golden certificate'

> We all know it is difficult to get a job for women, and extremely difficult to get a satisfying job in China. After graduating from university, luckily I got a job but a very ordinary one where I could not expect self-development, so I quit.

> It is hard to find a job when you have just graduated from university, though you are so ready to work! Just a BA degree is not sufficient to get a good job in the competitive market. An overseas MA degree with English and work experience is preferred. We call it a golden certificate.

Although modern women have learned to seek and embrace 'self-development' through pursuing education, the Chinese labour market impedes such possibilities. Education in China has witnessed a rapid development since the 1990s. The enrolment rate for women in higher educational institutions reached 44 per cent in 2003 (China Ministry of Education, 2004), and in Shanghai and Beijing more than half of those of school age can go on to higher education. However, the rise of unemployment in the urban labour market has put great pressure on China, where a million people join the workforce every year, and women are removed from the workforce to control surplus labour problems (Jiang et al., 2004). Educated women are discriminated against during hiring and are euphemistically called 'waiting for work' (Wallis, 2006). Although 'so ready to work', new women graduates in Chinese cities have a hard time locating their first job.

> Chinese companies think women are not profitable as we will leave on maternity. They follow their own rules.... We call ourselves a 'Super Girl'. Most of us are from a one-child family, growing up as

'Super' encouraged by parents. At work, we seem surprising ordinary, nothing.

Young women like me prefer to work in foreign-invested companies. They have a modern culture appealing to women.... An overseas degree is called a golden certificate. I want to have a global career and a life of a global woman, not like old mothers staying inside China for life.

Young women self-proclaim themselves as 'Super Girls' (referring to the Chinese version of popular TV *American Idol*), since China's one-child policy has enabled them to grow up with significant parental investment in education and domestic empowerment. Yet the perceived discrepancy between women's empowerment in the private sphere and their disempowerment in the work sphere presents a puzzling paradox to these women. Traditional gender identity and the ghettoizing of women in the workforce are governed by unwritten rules and the market logic of productivity, which treat women as less efficient and an economic liability. There emerges a desire for what they call a 'golden certificate' to access a 'global career' and a life of a 'global woman', effectively moving out of the constraints of the domestic work environment. It is against this context that Chinese women manifest an emerging attitude towards individualization and the construction of 'self-responsible' life politics.

We can't rely on men! I want to be self-reliant, not dependent on a husband for my happiness. My parents expect me to marry before 30.... Actually, we can't find a man. A highly educated woman is not approved of by a man's family. A woman with a MA degree should find a man with the same level of education or higher. Marriage becomes more difficult for a highly educated woman aged over 30.

Do it myself! I will find a suitable job, a suitable husband, a suitable place to live in.... Don't know how. I am not eager to go back to China.

'We can't rely on men!' What comes across forcefully is a self-determined attitude towards individualization, highlighting the degree to which women desire to become the actors in their own biography and for the happiness of their own existence. A 'do-it-myself' identity is embraced as a positive yet anxious expression, as well as a marriage relationship without the sacrifice of independence. Women feel pressure to get married before the age of 30, recognizing hidden costs and stringent criteria within a gendered discourse of power relationship: 'A highly educated woman is not approved of by a man's family.' In a society that places a primary value on family life, men also feel the burden of family pressure to marry younger and less well-educated women (Higgins and Sun, 2007). Highly educated professional women are emerging as a 'new social class' (Turner, 2006), or a new minority that may not fit into the mainstream of society but is potentially marginalized from dominant aspects of family social life.

Consuming the West: Imagining an individual

Despite the paradoxical outcomes and anxieties of where women actually stand regarding a move towards individualization, multiple ways of imagining such a possibility are widely available in mediated cultural domains with proliferating resources for the mobilization of self. Women's desire to move is constituted by contradictory socio-economic relations, as well as the cultural-symbolic forms by which everyday life is lived out, re-thought and re-articulated in its intersection with the emergence of precarious individualized identities. This frequently figures in their imagination of the West through everyday media.

Korean women: 'The more I see it on the media, the more I think'

> I don't like marriage pressure from the whole family, 'When will you get married?' Everybody interferes in my life.... One time, I wore a shoulder-revealing top and took a bus. Everybody stared at me! Nobody would make such interference in men.

> I was once smoking on the street and nearly hit by an old man, 'How can a woman dare to smoke on the street?' Life is under the eyes of society.... In Western society, people choose any kind of life they want. The more I see it on the media, the more I think. If I go there, wouldn't life be free?

'The more I see it on the media, the more I think.' The media are implicated in the imaginative pull towards mobility and the emergence of fledgling individualized identities within Korean women's socio-cultural landscape, public and private sites, where the multitude of quotidian constraints and expressions for a not-yet-realized-self take place in their lack of choice and control. Gender inequality and modes of 'neo-Confucian governmentality to control the female body and self'

(Kim, 2003) remain active through the surveillance of society. While society does not encourage women to pursue different ways of being without external intervention, notions of a new self – an individualized individual – are effectively discovered and articulated within their mediated experience in a culture-specific manner. For instance:

> She (in *Sex and the City*) works only briefly at night sitting alone and writing, and during the day, she meets friends, chats and laughs. It's totally unrealistic. But Western people work much less, they would not work like us from morning until late evening. They would have their own life.

> I don't envy free sex, sleeping with any man you like, but envy the individual life (in *Sex and the City*). There is no self-sacrifice or social pressure. They get what they want. They get a career, their own life, and are happy.... We are highly educated, but why can't we live like that?

This reflects how a US cultural text intersects distinctively with a sociological moment in Korean culture that continues to be a site of contestation. The programme's appeal is associated not primarily with sexuality and sexual identities, but with issues of work, economic freedom, women's individuality and choice (although the world of work ironically disappears from their TV viewing). This irony might be the emotional resolution of a continuing contradiction in Korean women's lives, or a wishful projection of opportunities for educated women in the labour market and the balance they wish to seek between work and life. The careerists on TV, in their 'totally unrealistic' representation, are seen to be 'happy'.

> My job might be OK, my life might be OK compared to my mother's. But I didn't feel happy, couldn't be satisfied with just that! I have bigger desires.... The more I got to know bigger things through the media, the more I thought about them.

> This (Korean drama) showed beautiful scenery of Cambridge and London where they met while studying. It's a typical romance, an illusion made by TV. But I wanted to believe that could happen. Life would feel different there... I imagined myself and anticipated to go.

Young women today appear to have more choices and capacities in life, higher education and better material provisions compared with past generations, yet this does not necessarily translate into greater happiness. Expectations of satisfaction have risen, affected by what other people have or an insatiable endless desire to have, which occurs due to the intrusion of cultural Others via the media and has the consequence of causing both rising expectations and rising frustrations. The construction of an autonomous illusion – 'I wanted to believe that could happen', the ability to create an illusion that is known to be false but felt to be true – suggests that the knowing individual creates an existence for herself in her imagination, as both actor and audience in her own drama, thereby obtaining pleasure as she 'constructs a more realistic anticipation of those events yet to come' (Campbell, 1987). Considerable meaning is gained, not merely from the illusion, but from 'imagining that illusion as actuality', mobilizing the self towards a hoped-for future.

Japanese women: 'Something you like always affects you somehow'

> I always liked watching European films, beautiful images of cities, buildings, diverse cultures. They look better. Although real things might not be beautiful as the images, I anticipated in my memory.

> I have gathered bits and pieces of images from TV, magazines, websites. Something you like always affects you somehow.... You wait for that moment and go, at least once, to fulfil an endless desire to go.

'Something you like always affects you somehow.' Bits and pieces of media culture, which create a self-constructed collage of images, have been elaborated in mediated memory in order to contain pleasure, an element of possibility or an 'endless desire to go'. The media play an important role in inducing transnational mobility for many young Japanese (Fujita, 2008). They have grown up much exposed to Western architecture, city landscapes, cultures and lifestyles, while reconfiguring a preferred view of the world and an ideal lifestyle that they desire. The desire for the foreign permeates many Japanese women's lives with a belief that the West is better (Kelsky, 2001). Such a belief resonates in the representation of the West in the imagination of Japanese women:

> There is no one standard for all, the Western is open to diversity. In Japan, one standard dominates. If you don't fit into this, you are

seen as a failure like the Defeated Dog ... I wanted to move away and develop my own self.

Those women (in *Sex and the City*) are old but still enjoy romance! They are over 35 or 40, have lots of wrinkles under make-up. How can women enjoy life at that age? They live like young women in their 20s. That's unimaginable in Japan.

'There is no one standard for all.' 'How can women enjoy life at that age?' The West is idealized in a desire for cultural diversity, an unfixed heterogeneous self and a greater range of possible lives, which marks a contrast to their own living conditions as constrained by gender and age. The significance of media consumption cannot be separated from the particular socio-economic and cultural contexts within which they are embedded and which they are called into. In Japanese society that asserts a fairly homogeneous identity, everyone should conform to the classificatory status and role to which they are assigned (Skov and Moeran, 1995). A desire to move away from such a collectivist self can be seen as one of the possible outcomes of the mediated relationships related to the plurality of individual lifestyles and the process of disembedding from a hierarchically gendered society.

Japanese women's magazines showed photo essays about experiences of travelling and living abroad, which inspired me a lot.... A 30-year-old TV announcer quit her job because old women are not considered suitable for that job in Japan. Her job was replaced by a younger woman. So she moved to Paris to study.... Her photo essay shows, Paris is beautiful! The beautiful illusion arouses such a good feeling that you want to be there.

So sick and tired of office work, one day I decided to do nothing and watched this film *Noting Hill*. Romance, freedom, laughter, London parks are so green! I felt, go there! It makes you feel something good can happen there.... You know that is an illusion but you want to believe that illusion and go.

The aestheticization and romanticization of Western cities is known to be false but felt to be true or suggestive of possibility, 'something good can happen there'. A general awareness of the link between media consumption and physical displacement exists in the women's emotional investment in the media at a level of utopian sensibility. It is intertwined with good feelings that the media embody and evoke – 'utopian feelings of possibility' (Dyer, 1992) acting as temporary answers to the specific inadequacies of society and showing what solutions feel like. The media certainly construct an illusion or an image of something better that these women's day-to-day lives do not provide. But it is the intelligently detectable illusion that is put to work by the knowing individuals with intentionality of knowledge: 'You know that is an illusion but you want to believe that illusion and go.'

Chinese women: 'The decision to believe the media is made by us'

While watching Western movies, I found them open to expressing self, there seemed more space for self-development.... When I see a good image that I really like, I want to believe that is true, although that may not be true in reality. The decision to believe the media is made by us.

The media help me see things that cannot be seen in real life. It's a different kind of knowledge.... While noticing differences, more freedom and choice, I was curious to go and experience. It may sound silly, but I cannot deny the power of the media.

'The decision to believe the media is made by us'. Media culture is a powerful pull factor in stimulating mobility, but this symbolic power is certainly recognized and intentionally allowed by educated women. This intentionality is at centre stage in the way the media are used and this meaning is mobilized by the 'knowledge class'. The significance of media consumption can be understood as a dynamic and transformative process, often involving active and intended engagement (Kim, 2008). The construction of transnational subjectivities by the Chinese is facilitated by the mobility of media images and the media images of mobility (Sun, 2002). The flow of the media is a significant mediator of knowledge and an extension of social imagery from which women can reconstruct their conceptions of self in relation to the lived realities of global Others.

Their life looked so free (on DVD dramas). Is it true? I must see it myself.... Here in London I like walking along the Thames while listening to music and singing along. If I do so in China, people would look at me, 'She is crazy!'

I watched lots of movies.... Western men seem romantic, set the table, pull up a chair for a woman. Chinese men would not do so.... But I was surprised at sexual freedom in *Sex and the City* and *Desperate Housewives*. I wondered about real life.

'Is it true? I must see it myself.' Travel is related to the increasingly mobile patterns of the everyday, taking on a new significance in the construction and narration of women's life stories and their mobility biographies. Travelling is seen as a 'must see' practice, and part of what travelling means is to affirm cultural differences and acquire a wider transnational meaning through the recognition and experience of differences in the realm of individual freedom and gender modality. Although the proliferation of Western media in China has increased the awareness of greater freedom, attitudes to sexuality are much less open than in the West (Higgins and Sun, 2007). The media constantly present the prisms of possible lives upon which women can reflect on their life conditions through a dialectics of imaginary closeness and distance.

> Life in China is so competitive, crowded and stressful. People work so hard, try to survive and win in competitive society.... Bus is so crowded that you have to squeeze in. There is no space for your self. I started the every day with this crowded bus.... A bus ride in the West seemed fun, pleasant (on TV), people easily got on and got off. Wouldn't it be nice to live in that environment? I saw this empty bus on TV a long time ago but still remember.... Here, London, bus is not crowded, most of time I can sit down and think. There is a space for thinking about my self.

This mediated experience can powerfully create and allow a space for the self to emerge within the fluidities of transnational imagination, while engaging with a newly found curiosity and a search for a new self that can be played out and actualized. Different ways to conceive the self are emerging in more individualist terms, marked by an outward-looking reflexivity. Contemporary Chinese female identities are being shaped by cultural consumption within mediated transnational networks, thus complicating an understanding of women's position within, and as belonging to, the nation (Ferry, 2003). Women have been subject to different imaginary social spaces, which enable them to reflect upon their lived experiences within multiple and competing regimes of identification and expand their potential for self-invention that divergent cultural experiences give rise to and mobilize.

Conclusion

With a heightened self-awareness, educated women now hope to grasp what is going on in the world and to understand what is happening in themselves as minute points of the 'intersections of personal biography and larger forces of social structures at work within everyday worlds' (Mills, 1959) that are now operating transnationally, thus entering a much larger but precarious world at this particular historical and cultural juncture. From the 1980s onward, women in Korea, Japan and China have gained a remarkably high level of education, and its commensurate expectations have become a driving force behind women's aspirations for work, economic freedom and imagined futures of individualization. However, they often experience the gendered labour-market inequity that sets limits on their patterns of participation and women's socio-economic position on the margins of work systems, and hence experience the illusion of the language of choice or choice biography that the new capacities of higher education appear to promise. The limitations and contradictions of female individualization within the key parameters are continually salient yet unresolved, giving rise to transnational mobility as a temporary resolution and a form of defection from an expected normative biography.

Signs of female individualization have been proliferating as a defining feature of contemporary modes of identity, albeit they appear untenable and ambivalent within the discursive regime of self embodied in regulatory practices in society which does not put individualism at the heart of its culture. The notion of the self that is 'free to choose' is not simply a cultural fact, but becomes an autonomous self when a woman is able to make a life for herself in her everyday existence – to make herself the centre of her biography. There are troubling signs of female individualization alongside an ambivalent extension of the transition from education to work/independent adulthood; thus the question as to whether and when to achieve such an autonomous subject position, separate from family economic resources, becomes a new arena of anxiety for young women. Gender is not losing its decisive influence; it is still in operation and people are more conscious of it. There is a lack of fit between the cultural shifts manifested in the transformation of women's consciousness and the structural shifts largely unchanged in structural relations and systems, so the perceived gap between the cultural and the structural has become too wide for women to resolve within the nation they were born into. Women may have developed a different relation to the nation, since they are not represented by it and are generally subordinate to men; they may be quick to abandon it when it no longer provides strategies of survival and fulfilment (Kelsky, 2001) and move the strategic locus of self in transnational flows.

The media are central to the signs of emergent, transnationally dispersed cultures of female individualization, producing the alternative social, cultural and symbolic relations that women wish to live within and to define the kind of self they wish to become. Seeming suggestions of individualization are encountered, mediated through the global imaginaries that are present and often intentionally used as resources for reflexivity and self-imagining at a level of utopian sensibility. This intentionality provides a condition for an increased awareness of cultural differences and of women's own positions in relation to global Others, new symbolic objects of identification and contestation. This increased awareness is not only the outcome of education but also significantly the consequence of the proliferation of sites of mediated experience that offer wider contexts of knowledge and images concerning different discourses outside local networks of experience. The mediated experience can have the effect of transforming women's sense of self, of the world beyond and their imagined place in it, while mobilizing the always-already orientation towards displacement. The media are constitutive of transnational mobility, and are the potentially compelling but taken-for-granted force behind physical displacement.

Acknowledgement

This chapter has previously been published in *Media, Culture & Society*, 32(1), 2010, and appears here with the permission of the publisher.

References

Abelmann, N. (2003) *The Melodrama of Mobility: Women, Talk and Class in Contemporary South Korea*, Honolulu: University of Hawaii Press.

Appadurai, A. (1996) *Modernity at Large: Cultural Dimensions of Globalization*, Minneapolis: University of Minnesota Press.

Bauman, Z. (2001) *The Individualized Society*, Cambridge: Polity.

Beck, U. (1992) *Risk Society: Towards a New Modernity*, London: Sage.

Beck, U. and Beck-Gernsheim, E. (2002) *Individualization*, London: Sage.

Braidotti, R. (1994) *Nomadic Subjects: Embodiment and Sexual Difference in Contemporary Feminist Theory*, New York: Columbia University Press.

Campbell, C. (1987) *The Romantic Ethic and the Spirit of Modern Consumerism*, Oxford: Blackwell.

China Ministry of Education (2004) *Survey of the Educational Reform and Development in China*, Beijing: China Ministry of Education.

Dyer, R. (1992) *Only Entertainment*, New York: Routledge.

Ferry, M. (2003) 'Advertising, Consumerism and Nostalgia for the New Woman in Contemporary China', *Continuum*, 17(3): 277–290.

Fujita, Y. (2008) 'Cultural Migrants and the Construction of the Imagined West', in Y. Kim (ed.), *Media Consumption and Everyday Life in Asia*, pp. 217–230, New York: Routledge.

Giddens, A. (1991) *Modernity and Self-identity: Self and Society in the Late Modern Age*, Cambridge: Polity.

HESA (Higher Education Statistics Agency) (2006), data from http://www.hesa.ac.uk.

Higgins, L. and Sun, C. (2007) 'Gender, Social Background, and Sexual Attitudes among Chinese Students', *Culture, Health & Sexuality*, 9(1): 31–42.

Ichimoto, T. (2004) 'Ambivalent Selves in Transition', *Journal of Intercultural Studies*, 25(3): 247–269.

IIE (Institute of International Education) (2006) Open Doors Annual Data, from http://opendoors.iienetwork.org.

ILO (International Labour Organization) (2006) Statistics and Databases, http://www.ilo.org.

Japan Times (2007) 'Sustained Growth Needs More Access', 9 June.

Jiang, L., Gao, E. and Huang, L. (2004) 'Situation of Female Employment in China', Working Paper of the Research Group of Shanghai Urban Women Project, Shanghai: East China University of Science and Technology.

Kelsky, K. (2001) *Women on the Verge: Japanese Women, Western Dreams*, Durham: Duke University Press.

Kim, T. (2003) 'Neo-Confucian Body Techniques', *Body & Society*, 9(2): 97–113.

Kim, Y. (2005) *Women, Television and Everyday Life in Korea: Journeys of Hope*, London: Routledge.

Kim, Y. (2008) *Media Consumption and Everyday Life in Asia*, New York: Routledge.

KWDI (Korean Women's Development Institute) (2006) Documents and Databases, http://www2.kwdi.re.kr.

Lucas, R. (2005) *Diaspora and Development: Highly Skilled Migrants from East Asia*, Washington, DC: World Bank Publications.

Mai, N. (2004) 'Looking for a Modern Life', *Westminster Papers in Communication and Culture*, 1(1): 3–22.

Mills, C. W. (1959) *The Sociological Imagination*, New York: Oxford University Press.

Nania, S. and Green, S. (2004) *Are Mainland Chinese Students Saving Britain's Universities?* London: Royal Institute of International Affairs.

OECD (Organization for Economic Co-operation and Development) (2007) Statistics Portal, http://www.oecd.org/statsportal.

Ono, H. and Piper, N. (2004) 'Japanese Women Studying Abroad', *Women's Studies International Forum*, 27(2): 101–118.

Park, G. and Kim, A. (2005) 'Changes in Attitude toward Work and Workers' Identity in Korea', *Korea Journal*, 45(3): 36–57.

Rosenberger, N. (2001) *Gambling with Virtue: Japanese Women and Sense of Self in a Changing Nation*, Honolulu: University of Hawaii Press.

Sennett, R. (2006) *The Culture of the New Capitalism*, New Haven: Yale University Press.

Skov, L. and Moeran, B. (1995) *Women, Media and Consumption in Japan*, Honolulu: University of Hawaii Press.

Social Science Japan (2005) 'Youth Employment', September.

Sun, W. (2002) *Leaving China: Media, Migration and Transnational Imagination*, Boulder: Rowman & Littlefield.

Thomas, A. (2005) *Imagi-Nations and Borderless Television*, New Delhi: Sage.

Turner, Y. (2006) 'Swinging Open or Slamming Shut?' *Journal of Education and Work*, 19(1): 47–65.

Wallis, C. (2006) 'Chinese Women in the Office Chinese Press', *Westminster Papers in Communication and Culture*, 3(1): 94–108.

Williams, R. (1977) *Marxism and Literature*, Oxford: Oxford University Press.

World Bank (2006) *The International Migration of Women*, Geneva: World Bank Publications.

2
Lifestyling Women: Emergent Femininities on Singapore and Taiwan TV

Fran Martin and Tania Lewis

The recent rise of lifestyle TV in Anglophone markets reflects the increasing dominance of an individualistic, consumer-driven approach to lifestyle issues in which late modern selfhood is seen as endlessly malleable, a project to be worked on and invested in (Wood and Skeggs, 2004). Popular-factual programmes offering advice on life skills for surviving and thriving in late modern capitalist culture are also in evidence across Asia. As this chapter will demonstrate, some of these are similar to their Anglo-American counterparts, while others present life advice in ways clearly shaped by distinct local and regional televisual and cultural codes and conventions. We propose, as others have argued in relation to this genre in Western markets (Palmer, 2004; Redden, 2007; Lewis, 2008), that lifestyle-themed shows in Asia may be playing a significant role in modelling particular lifestyle behaviours and, concomitantly, social identities, offering not just consumer advice but life guidance in a period of rapid cultural and social change. This chapter analyses selected examples of life-advice TV in Taiwan and Singapore, looking in particular at the highly feminized subgenre of 'fashion and beauty advice' TV. With a focus on the question of gendered individualization, our analysis examines the contradictions between the ideals of reflexive, choice-based selfhood that are promoted by such programmes, and the structural constraints on this emergent feminine subject in the context of ongoing gendered social and economic inequities. As we will see, these are contradictions that the programmes themselves reveal and explore.

Numerous social theorists have suggested that what distinguishes identity in late modernity is a heightened sense of individualization and

'reflexivity' (Giddens, 1991; Beck, 1992), with the responsibility for dealing with the complexities of everyday life increasingly lying with the
'enterprising' self and the privatized, 'informed' citizen (Bauman, 1991;
Rose, 1996; Schudson, 1998). For Beck, institutionalized individualization in the sociological sense is a corollary of reflexive modernization
in Europe. The disintegration of the social, cultural and political forms
of the 'first modernity' of the early twentieth century, and the new
demands, controls and constraints placed on individuals as part of 'second modernity' – in particular, incentives to take action rather than
old-style prohibitions – have led to the rise of the reflexive or 'DIY
biography'(Beck, 1994). The shift towards reflexive individualization
means that 'choice' (or at least the rhetoric of choice) becomes central to people's existence as their identities are increasingly formed
through lifestyle-oriented decision-making rather than through older-
style 'ascribed' social collectives such as social class, family, gender or
occupation.

In the discussion that follows, we are interested in examining the
function of popular lifestyle discourses in constructing and regulating
the gendered (feminine) self. This analysis recognizes the critical insight
provided by Beck and others that contemporary selfhood has become a
pre-eminent site for social transformation, in particular, individualization processes. At the same time, however, we strive to examine how
the forms of selfhood modelled on life-advice TV may also involve
re-inscriptions of older forms of ascribed identity, especially gendered
identity.

Women's socio-economic status, female individualization and Singapore modernity

Singapore is a highly developed city state with a per capita income
that matches that of Canada. It has moved from a successful export
economy in the sixties and seventies to a growing focus on positioning itself as a regional and global hub for the new knowledge
economy. As Aihwa Ong notes (2006), in rapidly transforming into
a post-industrial nation, this 'global city' has sought to 're-engineer'
its citizens, orienting them towards a new focus on neo-liberal models of risk-taking and entrepreneurialism. The push to neo-liberalism
means that Singaporean 'citizens are now expected to develop new
mindsets' (Ong, 2006: 194) and to embrace enterprising individualism, albeit an individualism that is manufactured and engineered by
the state.

The statistics on the socio-economic status and role of women in relation to this shift to neo-liberalism present a rather complex picture. The state has sought equity in education, with growing numbers of women participating in higher education – in 1999 just over half the graduates from Singapore's two universities were women, with the percentage of resident women aged 25–29 years with a completed university degree increasing from 3.2 per cent in 1980 to 12.6 per cent in 1995 (Mukhopadhaya, 2001: 551). The combination of education and lower fertility rates has seen work participation rates for women increase significantly in the 1980s and 1990s, to 85.5 per cent of 25–29 year olds in 2009 and 55 per cent of resident women overall (Statistics, 2010b). However, as in Taiwan (see below), women are still over-represented in the services (79.1 per cent) and clerical industries (76.1 per cent) with only 26 per cent working as legislators, senior officials and managers and only 38.9 per cent of professional workers being female (Haspels and Majurin, 2008: 32–33). Further, while young women (25–30 years old) have higher work participation rates than in the US (over 80 per cent in 2006), unlike in other developed nations, once Singaporean women leave the workforce to get married and/or have children they tend not to return. Consequently, labour participation rates drop to just over 60 per cent in women over 40 years, with a steady decline from then on (Haspels and Majurin, 2008: 29). At the same time, more and more young Singaporean women are opting out of married life, despite government attempts to encourage dating. Between 2000 and 2009, the proportion of single women aged 25–29 years rose from 40 per cent in 2000 to 53 per cent in 2009 (Statistics, 2010a: 5). A relatively high proportion of females in their thirties were also never married in 2009, with 24 per cent of females aged 30–34 years being single in 2009 compared with 19 per cent of females in 2000 (Statistics, 2010a: 5). Singapore's divorce rate has also increased notably over the past two decades, up from around 10 per cent in 1985 to about 31 per cent in 2008 (Seah, 2007; Department of Statistics, 2011).[1]

This split between stay-at-home housewives and increasing numbers of young unmarried working women speaks of a significant generational shift in Singapore as it moves from a more family-based mode of modernity to an increasingly individualized form of social organization. At the same time it also reflects some of the contradictions of Singaporean (late) modernity, marked as it is by a combination of economic liberalism and entrepreneurialism on one hand, and authoritarian modes of governance and Chinese-dominated multiracialism on the other. These contradictions are also apparent in the mixed messages that Singaporean women receive from the government, where policy initiatives and workplace culture have not kept pace with state rhetoric around economic liberalization and progressivism, at least in relation to gender equity. On the one hand, women are encouraged to become educated to pursue a career and support the economy (at a time when highly skilled labour is at a premium in Singapore). On the other hand, they are expected to also maintain their traditional domestic roles as wives and mothers, while often not being provided with the options of childcare and flexible part-time work that would usually accompany a high-tech economy (Mukhopadhaya, 2001: 555).

Professional but not too powerful: Lifestyled individualization on Singaporean TV

How are these competing images of women's familial versus wage-earner identity negotiated in the media? What kinds of discourses of feminine selfhood circulate within Singaporean popular media? A recent study of advertising on the English-language Singaporean channel, Channel Five, found that 'female and male characters (were) portrayed in line with traditional gender role stereotypes, both during prime time and daytime TV with representations of women more likely to be associated with body-care, housekeeping and food products' (Lee, 2003). Our interest here is whether representations of femininity are equally conventional on lifestyle TV or whether we are seeing a shifting, more negotiated understanding of identity in these programmes, reflecting both Singapore's complex hybrid modernity and lifestyle TV's nature as a genre where questions of life choice, individualism and self-making are often central.

Lifestyle-advice TV – modes of programming that provide guidance on everything from health, beauty and career planning to travel, child-rearing and relationships – represents a significant proportion of programming on broadcast TV in Singapore, along with newspapers and other media that also devote considerable space and time to lifestyle issues. Women's advice magazines such as *Singapore Women's Weekly* and *Her World* are a booming industry in Singapore, with a range of foreign titles such as *Good Housekeeping* and *Oprah* in the market since the 1990s, meaning that Singaporean women are exposed to a range of local and globally inflected engagements with contemporary femininity. Despite the qualifications noted above, women's roles have changed dramatically in post-socialist and post-independence Singapore, with the emergence of equal employment and education rights and an increasingly liberalized economic agenda. As in Taiwan in a similar time period, such shifts have seen older-style Chinese patriarchal conceptions of family and femininity increasingly challenged by liberalized and individualized consumerist models of women's roles. In examining how such shifting gender roles might be played out on Singaporean TV our focus here is primarily on Chinese-language TV, given its dominance in the market (with three out of four Singaporeans being Chinese) and the necessarily finite scope of this chapter.

While, as in Taiwan, drama dominates evening TV schedules in Singapore, in contrast to Taiwan, lifestyle TV is also a very popular and recognized genre within the Singaporean industry (though lifestyle content is often labelled as 'variety' or 'info-ed') and has increasingly found itself moving from traditional daytime slots to prime time. Over the past couple of years, programming on Channel 8 aired in the 8–9 p.m. slot (traditionally prime time in Europe and the US), for instance, has included a range of lifestyle and variety shows from cooking (*Celeb's a Cook*) and consumer advice (*King of Thrift*), to popular factual/human interest shows (*Life Transformers* 心晴大动员) and pop doc-reality shows (*With You 1000 Miles*, a local variation on *The Amazing Race*). Our focus for both Singapore and Taiwan is on prime-time shows in the fashion-and-beauty lifestyle subgenre. Personal makeover formats are becoming an increasingly familiar feature on prime time TV in Singapore, often borrowing heavily from Western makeover formats though combined with a variety of regional East Asian TV conventions. Singapore has produced a number of beauty and fashion makeover shows, aimed at female audiences, and usually sponsored by make-up or fashion companies. Examples include Channel 8's fashion-and-beauty makeover show *Beautiful People*, first aired in 2002, Channel U's *Closet Affair* (IN女皇, 2005) aimed at making over 'clueless individuals', and Channel 8's *Be Somebody* (魅力新姿采, 2005), which sought to transform 'wallflowers', who had been 'nominated by their thoughtful friends or family', into 'stunning babes'.

Channel 5's locally produced English-language show *Style Doctors* is an interesting example of a show specifically targeted at working women. Aired in 2004, it is hosted by two celebrity consultants (MTV media personality, or VJ, Nadya Hutagalong, and her funky male counterpart, singer/actor RJ Rosales), who aim to transform the lives, homes, wardrobes and personal grooming routines of 'style-deficient' ordinary Singaporeans. Not just focusing on fashion, but also, as the show's website explains (Mediacorp, 2011), offering 'an extreme style makeover in attitude (and) self-confidence', the style gurus' 'patients' we are told, 'are women in their early 20s to late 40s who have neglected themselves because of busy work schedules'. Borrowing heavily in presentation and style from Western reality makeover shows such as *Queer Eye for the Straight Guy*, *Style Doctors* is playful and performative, distancing itself from 'straighter', more didactic versions of the lifestyle-advice genre, though, like *Queer Eye* and somewhat differently from *Queen* (discussed below), the show remains 'underpinned by a strongly instructional, therapeutic and moralistic ethos' (Lewis, 2007: 294).

In the episode we will discuss, we are introduced to makeover-ee Selinna Tsang, a 36-year-old business development manager. Selinna, RJ informs us, 'is the only woman in a male dominated office and she insists on hiding her femininity by dressing like a man...and guess what, she's two months pregnant!'. We are then shown shots of Selinna wearing her usual work 'uniform' – a combination of short hair, dark-rimmed glasses and (what to our eyes seemed like) fairly chic, professional-style dark trousers and shirts. Selinna's 'own' assessment, though, is quite negative: 'What I wear at work is very, very boring... it's mainly black, black will make me stand out and feel more dominant.' She adds, 'We are expecting a kid now so I want to change my lifestyle.' Confirming Selinna's concerns (and in true US confessional/therapeutic style), we see her in her lounge room surrounded by friends and relatives participating in a kind of makeover 'intervention'. One (unnamed) male friend/relative 'diagnosing' her problem says, 'You have a very nice character but you're always too business...you're always too serious, you could smile more.' And her sister, conveniently echoing the 'remedy' suggested by the show's fashion 'experts' says, 'We want to see a new and improved you... still power dressing but... colourful' (Illustration 2.1).

While *Style Doctors* has a very clearly pedagogical aim, nevertheless, like *Queer Eye for the Straight Guy*, there is also a somewhat jokey, ironic edge to the show, with the two hosts, in particular, camping up their roles as 'experts'. Thus, when Selinna pronounces, 'I want to be a powerful mother who can walk into a boardroom and command my people,' Nadya, with mock serious concern, says, 'Hmmm, you know what RJ? You have to liberate this woman for the good of woman kind!' Later, at Selinna's home, where RJ is interrogating her about her wardrobe choices, he exclaims in mock horror 'they are all dark suits!' and, pulling out a jacket, says 'this must be your husband's!', while her attempts at buying more feminine clothes are met with comments such as 'Hello auntie' and 'Is this yours or the maid's?' (Illustration 2.2).

Illustration 2.1 Selinna's sister comments on Selinna's fashion shortcomings on *Style Doctors*
Source: Singapore – MediaCorp Channel 5.

While *Style Doctors* is concerned with helping women become more successful, empowered individuals, this brief discussion of the show illustrates some of the contradictory images of modern womanhood prevailing in Singaporean society. Selinna wants to dress and act in ways that reflect her identity as a powerful senior executive while also being recognized as a mother. RJ's solution is to discard her suits, which he sees as identifying her as masculine, arguing that, 'Now you're going to be a mother you should be able to celebrate motherhood with a lot of colours.' While Selinna's all-black wardrobe could be read as a marker of a late modern, globalized middle-class identity (in one scene, for instance, she is wearing a black Gap-branded t-shirt), the show attempts to negotiate the questions of individualization and femininity through returning colour to her wardrobe. The (potentially progressive) implication here is that Selinna doesn't necessarily have to wear a masculine-coded outfit, such as a dark suit, to display her 'power' in the workplace. However, despite the show's semi-playful style, its message overall is a rather unreflexive one. Rather than negotiating pregnancy,

Illustration 2.2   RJ jokes with Selinna while interrogating her wardrobe choices on *Style Doctors*
Source: Singapore – MediaCorp Channel 5.

power and the workplace, the focus of the show is on Selinna rediscovering her feminine side and shifting her lifestyle to focus on motherhood rather than work, reflecting the broader Singaporean trend (mentioned above) of abandoning the workplace after marriage and childbirth. This episode of *Style Doctors*, then, is less about freeing women from the constraints of traditional selfhood through creating a new styled identity than it is about re-traditionalizing and re-feminizing the presentation of self, reflecting a rather conservative approach to the 'problem' of femininity in the workplace.

Another show that deals, in part, with questions of identity, individualism and femininity in the workplace is Channel 8's Mandarin-language lifestyle show *Her Sense*, which aired for 17 episodes in 2008 on Mondays at 10:30 p.m. Hosts Kym Ng (a former singer turned host/actress who is known as the 'the Elder Sister of the variety genre' [综艺阿姐] of MediaCorp) and Chen Hanwei (another well-known Malaysian-born, Singapore-based MediaCorp 'artiste') introduce the latest fashion-and-beauty products and offer advice 'and even tips on how to survive office politics'. The guests on the show include Mediacorp artistes and established actors and actresses (新传媒艺人) such as Rui En, models, 'aspiring' actresses and make-up/fashion stylists, as well as the occasional ordinary Singaporean.

Although it features some makeover segments, its format is more of a magazine-style advice show than a makeover show, and its episodes include a range of segments advising guests and the audience on every aspect of self-presentation and fashion, from hairstyles to underwear to how to wear metallic fabrics. While not focused purely on working women *per se*, the show portrays its celebrity guests in the role of women who need advice, thereby articulating concerns around how one negotiates success, individualism and femininity. Episode two, for instance, highlights that 'finding yourself is the most important thing'. The individualized self that is highlighted on the show is one who cleverly uses the latest fashion styles and beauty products to empha-size her own 'strong points' – generally features of femininity, such as long legs or a slim body. As in *Style Doctors*, aspirations towards feminine empowerment are tempered by anxieties over appearing too masculine. For example, episode 8 featured a makeover of tomboyish comedy actress Patricia Mok emphasizing 'feminizing' pants and 'gen-tle' makeup. The show also offers tips on fashion and management of the self in the workplace. In episode eight, for instance, there is a seg-ment on office etiquette featuring role plays about how to manage junk email, whether to come to work if you are sick and so on. The (some-what banal) content here is of less interest than the representations of feminine labour that are visualized and naturalized in these segments, which, in contrast to *Style Doctors*, picture young women decidedly at the lower-skilled, clerical end of the labour force (Illustration 2.3).

Like *Queen*, discussed below, *Her Sense* is very much aimed at ordinary women – a focus that is reflected in episode 11 in a segment on shirts that advises the audience on how to look 'professional' at work while avoiding looking 'too powerful'. While at one level the show celebrates celebrity women and their achievements, aspirations for individualism and personal empowerment are nevertheless encouraged largely at the level of fashion choice and consumption rather than in the broader realm of life or work choices.

Singaporean media and consumer culture has to a certain extent embraced a globalized lifestyle ethos, by which we mean an ethos that assumes the self can be made and re-made via consumer and lifestyle choices and practices. On shows like *Style Doctors* and *Her Sense*, women

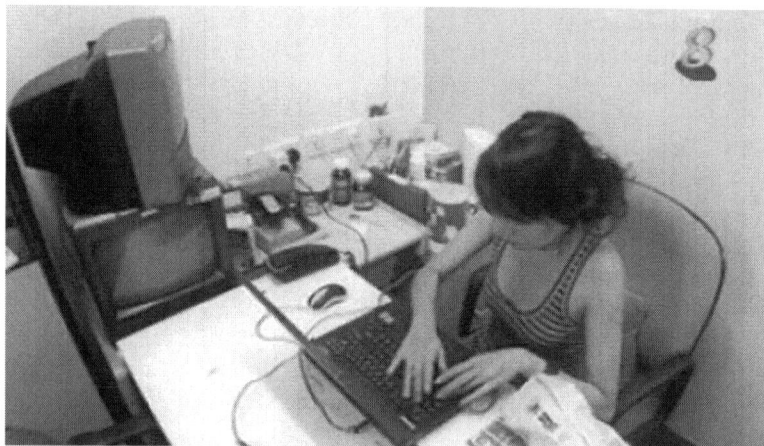

Illustration 2.3   Femininity in the workplace as depicted on *Her Sense*
Source: Singapore – MediaCorp Channel 8.

are taught that they can be a new and improved version of themselves through becoming, in a sense, experts of the self. In highly commercialized media settings like Singapore, undertaking this journey to a better self and self-knowledge invariably means internalizing the tips and techniques presented by celebrity lifestyle gurus and forms of lifestyle programming thoroughly inculcated in consumer culture. As we saw on both *Style Doctors* and *Her Sense*, however, while lifestyle media espouse goals of self-realization and consumer empowerment, on Singaporean TV such shows are highly constrained by older-style, essentialist understandings of femininity and women's roles (as carers in the home; as 'soft' counterparts to the 'hard' masculinity of the male business world).

As our brief discussion of Singapore's socio-cultural context suggests, the limited scope of the largely consumer-based images of women on lifestyle TV speaks to the specificities of a Singapore (late) modernity that is negotiating global, neo-liberal, regional and older-style Chinese patriarchal influences. More pragmatically, the conservative nature of lifestyle TV in this context also reflects the realities of producing and airing programmes in a media industry essentially owned and regulated by the government. And again, as noted above, the government has had a somewhat ambivalent relationship to questions of shifting gender roles in a post-industrial economy.

Women's socio-economic status, female individualization and Taiwan modernity

Like Singapore, Taiwan numbered among the four 'Asian Tiger' economies that underwent rapid industrialization and economic growth post-1960. Since the mid-1990s, a new wave of economic restructuring has seen Taiwan's economy shift away from industrial manufacturing towards the service sector (Directorate General of Budget, Accounting and Statistics, 2010: 16). In addition, Taiwan has also seen huge social transformations post-1987, with the revocation of martial law, the rise of democratic politics, and the intensifying linkage into transnational media, cultural, financial, commodity and labour circuits. Indeed, Taiwan's 'compressed modernity' appears to offer an exemplary site for investigating the transformation of older forms of social identity, including gender.

Chang Kyung-Sup and Song Min-Young (2010) have recently proposed that in South Korea, due to the stubbornly persistent character of the patrilineal family in compressed modernity, families have become the principal carrier of social risk. This has resulted in an increased burden on women, leading to women's collective, pragmatic choice to reduce the scope of extended family life and relations as the family becomes functionally overloaded – a phenomenon they describe as structural individualization without ideological individualism. Interestingly, their study finds that these tendencies are somewhat mirrored in both Japan and Taiwan (Chang and Song, 2010: 541).

Taiwan's accelerated economic transformation has been underwritten by women's labour. Ping-chun Hsiung (1996) illustrates how since the mid-1960s, economic growth was achieved largely by means of small, export-oriented factories run by individual families who literally conducted manufacturing and assembly work in the living rooms of their apartments, enabling married women to contribute (unpaid) to production while looking after children. Thus, Hsiung notes, 'the satellite factory system represents *the latest version of the Chinese family* – a locus where capitalist logic and patriarchal practices intersect' (Hsiung, 1996: 13, emphasis added). Hsiung's work illustrates a formation of industrial modernity that is significantly distinct from the formations analysed in Euro-American contexts, where the separation of the family from the economic sphere has been seen as a key element in the definition of modernity, and the labour market has been understood as the motor of individualization with the concomitant shrugging off of family ties (Beck and Beck-Gernsheim, 2002).

Turning to the present, we note the currently rather high rates of women's education and workforce participation in Taiwan (86 per cent of women between the ages of 18 and 21 were enrolled in tertiary education in 2008); and ongoing increases in the labour participation rate (49.6 per cent of women over the age of 15 in 2009, compared with 66.4 per cent of men; women's participation rate increased from 46 per cent in 1999); and the female–male earnings ratio (79.8 per cent in 2007: significantly higher than South Korea or Japan) (Beck and Beck-Gernsheim, 2002: 54–84; Directorate General of Budget, Accounting and Statistics, 2010). Women's rate of return to work post-child-rearing appears lower than in Singapore (in 1996, 63 per cent of once-employed mothers between 25 and 34 years of age had either returned to work post-child-rearing or had an uninterrupted career) (Yu, 2009: 28–30).

The question of women's autonomy in sexuality and relationships is not easily accounted for by means of statistics (Huang, 2008), but it is worth noting that the official figures show a declining marriage rate and a trend towards delayed marriage and childbearing. A significant increase was noted in unmarried women between 35 and 44 years of age between 1998 and 2008 – from 8.4 per cent to 15.8 per cent – along with a relatively high mean age for first marriage – 28 years old – and a marked trend towards later childbearing (Directorate General of Budget, Accounting and Statistics, 2010: 6–7). There remains a general tendency, however, for women to marry men of higher socio-economic status. In Taiwan, as in Singapore, the divorce rate has increased very significantly over recent years, growing from roughly 14 per cent in 1985 to around 37 per cent in 2008 (Directorate General of Budget, Accounting and Statistics, 2009; Tso, 2009).[2] A robust and influential public discourse critiquing older-style patriarchal and hetero-marital ideologies has been present in Taiwan since the late 1980s, with strong feminist and lesbian, gay, bisexual and transgender (LGBT) social movements blossoming as part of the explosion of social and civil movements following the lifting of martial law (Martin, 2003).

In relation to employment, although women's workforce participation is increasing, as in Singapore, women are over-represented in certain areas: they predominate in the sales, service and clerical jobs that increase as the services sector expands (Zveglich et al., 2004: 858). As Anru Lee observes in her ethnographic study of labour and gender politics in Taiwan since the economic restructuring that commenced in the late 1980s, while an influential discourse constructs service-sector work as the route to upward social mobility for young working-class women in Taiwan, the reality of such work is often very different, with a depressing prevalence of low-paid, dead-end jobs, highly demanding emotional labour and long and irregular hours (Lee, 2004: 59–60). Lee notes, however, that these disadvantages can be a trade off for certain advantages in white- or pink-collar work, including greater symbolic capital attached to office work than to manual labour (Lee, 2004: 60). As we will see, it is precisely this generation of young women, who either already work in Taiwan's expanding service sector or may be encouraged to aspire to do so, that our TV example, fashion-and-beauty show *Queen*, addresses.

Joining the 'office tribe' and 'marrying into a grand household': Aspirational femininity on lifestyle TV in Taiwan

Despite its highly developed lifestyle and consumer culture, in Taiwan the concept of lifestyle TV is far less entrenched than in Singapore. If we search for locally produced, non-fictional, Chinese-language programming instructing its viewer in stylized consumption and related skills pertaining to living in a late capitalist, consumption-oriented society, we find such content dispersed throughout an array of other genres. These include the very popular Japanese-style variety genre, and it is within this genre that we find the programme *Queen* (女人我最大).

Queen is a high-rating variety-style show produced by the moderately popular cable TV channel TVBS Entertainment. *Queen*'s success has spawned a monthly beauty magazine of the same name, while three mainland Chinese versions of the programme were launched in different regional markets in 2009–2011 by agreement with TVBS. In 2010, product sales from the programme's website, plus sales of the magazine, reputedly generated revenue of NT$350 million (over US$12 million) (Wang, 2010). Screened in Taiwan on weeknights from 9 to 10 p.m. with multiple repeats, *Queen* offers tips on feminine-coded topics like fashion, beauty and shopping. The show unfolds on a pink-themed set with the high level of post-production effects and 'friendly' comedic mode of address that characterize the Japanese-style variety-show format.

The programme is structured around two main groups plus the hostess. First, a panel of semi-regular young female hostesses composed of young media starlets are positioned as stand-ins for the 'ordinary girls' imagined as the programme's audience. A common scenario features the starlets 'choosing' an outfit (or beauty regime, etc.) that is deemed inappropriate and mocked by the hostess, then corrected by the fashion-and-beauty experts. This panel – called the 'women's

Illustration 2.4   Queen: Classmates of the 'women's corps' – Performing 'ordinary' young femininity
Source: Taiwan – TVBS Entertainment.

corps' (女人軍團) – is addressed as 'classmates' (同學). Their lively girlish clamour and appellation as 'classmates' seem designed to evoke a circle of friends with whom the target viewer can identify on her journey towards a successful adult social life: this is a specifically feminized version of the sense of 'collective *uchi*' (inside) that is central to the Japanese wide-show mode of address (Holden and Hakan, 2006: 105–107) (Illustration 2.4).

The classmates are given instruction by the second group – the 'experts' addressed as 'teacher' (老師) or 'class head' (班長); these include a regular pool of well-known hair, make-up and fashion stylists (most of whom, in a *Queer Eye*-type turn, perform a recognizable form of televisual gayness, though their sexuality is not openly discussed), plus one-off special guests. All of this is presided over by middle-aged popstar/comedian anchorwoman Lan Xinmei (addressed as 'elder sister Xinmei' 心湄姐). Adopting, at times, quite ribald humour to poke fun at the panel and at herself, Lan Xinmei wears edgy high-fashion outfits and plays the comic foil but also acts as the older, wiser woman holding it all together.

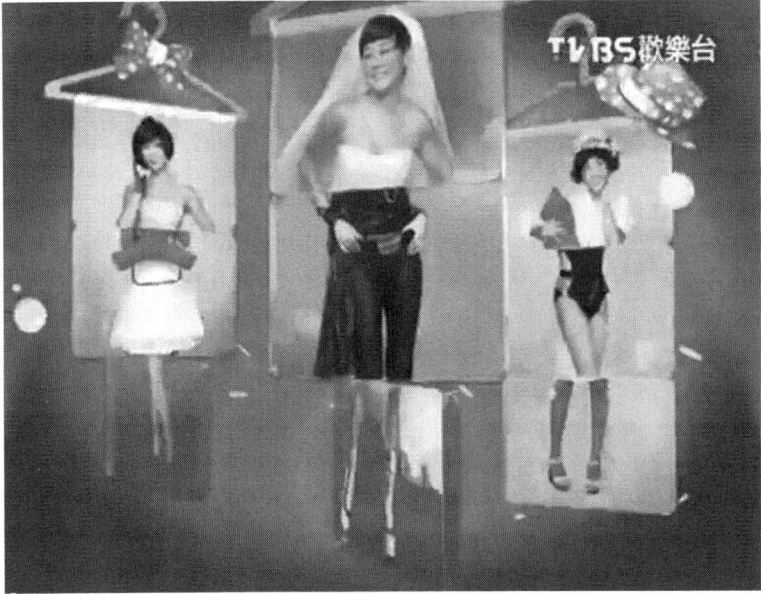

Illustration 2.5   Queen: Title sequence – Malleable, individualized feminine identity
Source: Taiwan – TVBS Entertainment.

In its project of developing forms of gendered selfhood equipped with the skills required for negotiating the perils of life in late capitalism, *Queen* clearly highlights individualized models of femininity. The title sequence, for example, is structured around the image of a set of flip-cards mixing and matching the top and bottom halves of Lan Xinmei dressed in five different styles. The multiple images and the flip-card metaphor certainly suggest the idea of malleable, individualized feminine identities, albeit constrained within the paradigm of conventional, fashionable femininity (Illustration 2.5).

We will analyse some examples from several 2010 episodes of the programme that relate closely to one of its central projects: teaching the techniques that are required for the accumulation of social capital and, ultimately, upward class mobility. A dominant theme in the programme is one of becoming a 'lady' (貴婦 , 千金 , 名媛, etc.) – a form of class-aspirationism that the programme teaches is achievable through (a) calculative consumption (fashion, hair and beauty products); (b) 'marrying into a grand household' (嫁入豪門); and (c) the careful management of work. Our first example is taken from episodes focusing on the skills required to negotiate paid employment; our second example relates to class aspirationism – something that the programme links with both consumption and marriage.

A regular theme for *Queen* concerns work: how to get it, and how to present oneself appropriately for it. In these episodes, viewers are encouraged to pursue 'respectable' work in the service sector – as shop assistants, secretaries, personal assistants and so on – members of the 'office tribe' (上班族). On 26 June 2010, the theme was 'Skills for a Successful Job Interview', and the special guest was a suit-clad male director of the Ren Li Bank. In the makeover section, the starlets' inappropriate choices of interview wear for service-sector jobs are transformed under the guidance of regular stylists Youqun and Kevin. The young women are transformed from looks reminiscent (in Sister Xinmei's mocking words) of a bar hostess and a saucy secretary with her eye on the boss, into be-suited 'office ladies' resembling the pretty young personal assistants who travel with Japanese trade delegations (as one of the stylists jokes) (Illustrations 2.6–2.8).

Illustration 2.6   Queen: What not to wear to a job interview 1 – 'Saucy secretary'
Source: Taiwan – TVBS Entertainment.

Illustration 2.7   Queen: What not to wear to a job interview 2 – 'Bar hostess'
Source: Taiwan – TVBS Entertainment.

As Teacher Youqun works on their wardrobe and explains the logic of his choices, some telling advice is given:

> [For a young woman interviewing for a low-level administrative position], a blouse with frilly sleeves and filmy materials helps give the idea that one isn't too dominating. It will make a very positive impression on a male manager. He will think you're easy to be around, not too overbearing, very cute.

On the one hand, it's clear that the premise of this kind of makeover segment underlines the worker's labours of individual self-management and self-branding. There are repeated references to how attributes of the clothing selected will attach to the image that is being constructed of the individual worker herself: 'the tailored silhouette of this suit will give the impression that your work is also careful and finely designed' (26 June 2010); 'this slightly edgy outfit will give the sense that you are creative in other areas as well' (2 July 2010). On the other hand, consider the specific attributes of the 'brand' recommended for women seeking entry-level office work: pretty, cute,

Illustration 2.8   Queen: What to wear to a job interview – 'PAs from a Japanese trade delegation'
Source: Taiwan – TVBS Entertainment.

compliant and non-threatening to male employers. If the young woman worker is 'free' to create her own individual competitive advantage by creatively managing her image, nonetheless that 'freedom' turns out only to be a liberty to mould herself to fit the rather cramped confines of the space available for young, semi-skilled female workers.

Advantageous marriage is another avenue that *Queen* suggests for young women to achieve the central goal of upward class mobility. On 29 September 2010, *Queen* screened the first of a two-part special entitled 'The Ladies Are Here!' This episode set up the 'classmates' as naïve young things desperate to make themselves over into 'ladies' to increase their chances of 'marrying into a grand household'. In this they were offered as role models two special guests: socialite sisters Sun Yunyun and Sun Yingying, who modelled classy fashion and bearing that were then translated by the regular stylists into a list of tips on how to invest wisely in name-brand goods, and institute a beauty regime to produce the fine skin and alluring eyes that would increase one's chances of nabbing a higher-class man.

Episodes like this one suggest that for *Queen*, 'strategic self-fashioning' may aim as much at success in the marriage market as in the competitive labour market, which again highlights the gendered dimension of this kind of self-making and especially the ways in which that gendering links back to older-style patrilineal family structures. The Sun sisters are daughters of a major commercial family of mainland Chinese descent; their father is the scion of the Pacific Electric Wire and Cable Co. dynasty, their mother is vice-president of Yuanta Securities. They embody the contemporary ideal of the 'lady' as *qianjin* (daughter of a wealthy family). They are born to wealth and cultural privilege, whereas the task of the 'classmates' is to achieve, by means of calculative consumption, the illusion of having been born into the upper middle class to increase their chances of marrying into it ('投胎當千金, 嫁入豪門', in Sister Xinmei's words). Sun Yunyun is married to the founder of highly successful Taipei luxury shopping complex the Breeze Centre, and has her own accessories label. The Sun sisters, framed as templates of 'fashionable ladies' (時尚名媛), thus model 'good marriage' as well as high birth. The kind of sleek, cosmopolitan taste they perform is exhibited as a contrast to the girlish vulgarity of the 'classmates'. The lesson being taught on tasteful selection of name-brand goods, in particular, speaks to current social anxieties over the 'improper' (tasteless) purchase and display of these pricey symbolic items by girls and young women (Shi, 2010).

Yet interpreting this episode as a straight directive to emulate the Sun sisters' birthright of high-class habitus would be a mistake, for the set-up in this episode often reveals itself as not wholly serious. When Sister Xinmei asks the panel at the beginning, 'Who wants to become a lady?' the starlets clamour, 'Me, me!' with strong Taiwanese accents and comically exaggerated fervour. Throughout, they perform naïve vulgarity and 'getting it wrong' with a playfulness that makes being young, female and vulgar look like a lot of fun – a kind of glamour in itself (Illustration 2.4). Their collective girly chatter about shopping, collecting and wearing cute and trendy accessories, no matter how poorly selected, evokes a localist girls' public culture that seems at least partly separated from 'serious' worries about proper behaviour, one's social status in the eyes of wider society and the search for a husband. In comparison with US makeover TV analysed extensively by Brenda Weber, *Queen* differs significantly in that the 'before-body', represented here by the merry classmates, is not wholly abject but seems to remain an inhabitable and possibly even attractive subject-position. In *Queen*, full surrender to the style experts is not so harshly demanded, and emphasis seems to be placed not so much on revealing and expressing a formerly 'blocked' authentic interior self – 'you, only better' – as on offering optional possibilities for small-scale adjustments to external appearance and social behaviour (Weber, 2009: 1–35).

This episode too, then, reveals an area of ambivalence and contradiction. Just as on the topic of work, women are induced both to subject themselves to a rigidly gender-hierarchical corporate context and to see themselves as individual agents forging their own unique brand, so in this episode they are induced both to aspire to economic security through marriage and to see themselves as freewheeling individuals immersed in a culture of girlish independence and fun via consumption; both to aspire towards advancing their social and cultural capital and class status and to revel in the joys of being vulgar and having 'no idea'. Indeed, *Queen* can be seen as fractured throughout by a similar tension: between aspiration towards improvement (moral improvement; class betterment; taste education) and a spirited revelry in contemporary local girls' culture with all its supposed 'flaws'. In particular, the democratizing address of the comic genre enables mockery of all the images presented, not just the 'before' versions in the makeover segments (recall the example discussed above, where post-makeover a trace of the ridiculous seems to remain in the classmates' sudden and total transformation into 'PAs from a Japanese trade delegation'). In the tension between the pedagogical construction of the ideal 'late modern girl' and the deconstruction of this ideal through comedy, *Queen* enacts a structural ambivalence about the whole project of social aspirationism that appears to be its own central directive.

Conclusion

Our analysis in this chapter has focused on the contradictions between the rhetoric of reflexive, choice-based selfhood that the Singaporean and Taiwanese programmes promote, and the structural constraints on this emergent, late modern feminine self in the context of ongoing gendered social and economic inequities. As we have tried to show, these are contradictions that the programmes themselves explore and illuminate.

In the case of the Singaporean programmes, such contradictions are directly legible in the character of the gendered advice that the programmes offer. Despite their attempts at a lightly ironic gloss, these programmes give fairly unambiguous advice to both their participants and the viewer that a woman's ultimate fate is to return to a gender-conservative, 'soft' femininity following her sorties into the masculine realm of wage labour. At one level, these shows celebrate successful working women and celebrities, but they are also marked by con- siderable anxieties about those forms of individualism and personal empowerment that clash with older-style feminine roles, anxieties they attempt to manage through stylistic interventions at the level of fash- ion choice and the presentation of self. While the Singaporean economy may have undergone considerable liberalization, these depictions of supposed self-realization and consumer empowerment suggest that, in the social and the cultural realm, women's 'choices' continue to be somewhat constrained by older-style conceptions of women's roles in the workplace and home. In the more complex case of Taiwan's *Queen*, the disjunction between the rhetoric of choice-based individual selfhood and the actually constrained character of available formations of feminine subjecthood occurs through the programme's ambivalence about its own central project of offering women ways of 'improv- ing' themselves through individual-level choices. This ambivalence, we have tried to show, is expressed by using comedy to undermine the programme's overt pedagogical message about appropriate forms of femininity, as well as in the double-address to the viewer that, in contrast to the usual makeover, offers the untransformed 'before- body', as much as the re-made 'after-body', as an object of viewer identification.

Our analysis suggests that in Singapore, 'lifestyle advice and makeover TV' is working as a fairly globalizing genre. The importation of formats with generic characteristics that are quite clearly traceable to Anglo- American models seems also to bring with it (conservative) ideological characteristics of the feminine fashion and makeover subgenre as it has been analysed in Anglophone markets (Palmer, 2004; Wood and Skeggs, 2004; Weber, 2009). In the Taiwan example, both the programme's style and its ideological valence are more complex. Re-located within the Taiwanese TV genre of localized Japanese-style comedic variety, the fashion-and-beauty advice subgenre seems to take on a life of its own in an ideological sense as well, revealing a certain ambivalence about its own project of 'improving' women for individual competitive advantage in late modern commodity culture.

Returning to our initial question about the role of individualization in these sites, both case studies speak to the limitations of universal- izing claims in relation to identity and culture. While both Singapore and Taiwan have outwardly embraced globalized, late modern lifestyle and consumer cultures marked by degrees of individualization, nonethe- less as Ong's work on 'neo-liberalism as exception' in Asia suggests (Ong, 2006), looking beneath the surface of such social and cultural transitions, we see often highly contested, localized reworkings of modernity, consumer culture and 'new' forms of selfhood. The limitations of universalizing claims also relate to gender and the need to recognize that the default 'neutral' subject of neo-liberal individualism around the world tends to be that of the cosmopolitan, middle-class male. On feminine advice shows oriented towards late modern women, the 'problem' of the self-making woman is placed centre stage. In the Singaporean examples, the makeover narrative aims to 'solve' these contradictions by offering the feminine subject a form of malleable subjecthood, but one limited to performative, stylistic and consumer-based identities rather than fundamentally transformed social roles. The more populist Taiwan programme responds in a more ambivalent mode, implying a certain scepticism about the importance or desirability of making ordinary young Taiwanese women over into global-style neo-liberal subjects.

Acknowledgement

The authors would like to acknowledge that this chapter is based on research supported by the Australian Research Council.

Notes

1. 22,444 marriages, 2344 divorces and a divorce rate of 0.9 per 1000 residents were reported for the year 1985, whereas 24,596 marriages, 7216 divorces with a divorce rate of 2.0 per 1000 residents were reported in 2008 (Department of Statistics, 2011). The number of marriages per year has remained almost constant through the two decades, at about 23,000. Taking this median figure as constant average of the annual number marriages gives us a divorce rate of about 10 per cent for 2344 divorces in 1985 and about 31 per cent for 7216 divorces in 2008. Although government reports use the more objective variable of annual divorces per 1000 population, commentators have projected a similar overall current figure of 30 per cent of marriages ending in divorce (Seah, 2007).
2. 153,832 marriages and 21,165 divorces with an annual divorce rate of 1.1 per 1000 residents were reported for the year 1985; and in 2008, 154,866 marriages and 55,995 divorces with an annual divorce rate of 2.43 were reported (Directorate General of Budget, Accounting and Statistics, 2009). The number of marriages per year has remained almost constant through the two decades, at about 150,000. Taking this median figure as constant average of the annual number of marriages, we get a 14 per cent divorce rate for 1985 and 37 per cent for 2008. Although government reports use the more objective variable of annual divorces per 1000 population, commentators have projected a similar overall current figure of 38 per cent of marriages ending in divorce (Tso, 2009).

References

Bauman, Z. (1991) *Modernity and Ambivalence*, Cambridge: Polity.

Beck, U. (1992) *Risk Society: Towards a New Modernity*, London: Sage.

Beck, U. (1994) 'The Reinvention of Politics: Towards a Theory of Reflexive Modernization', in U. Beck, A. Giddens and S. Lash (eds) *Reflexive Modernization: Politics, Tradition and Aesthetics in the Modern Social Order*, pp. 1–55, Cambridge: Polity.

Beck, U. and Beck-Gernsheim, E. (2002) *Individualization: Institutionalized Individualism and Its Social and Political Consequences*, London: Sage.

Chang, K. and Song, M. (2010) 'The Stranded Individualizer under Compressed Modernity: South Korean Women in Individualization without Individualism', *British Journal of Sociology*, 61(3): 539–564.

Department of Statistics (2010a) *Population Trends 2010*, Singapore.

Department of Statistics (2010b) *Yearbook of Statistics Singapore 2010*, Singapore.

Department of Statistics (2011) *Statistics on Marriages and Divorces 2010*, retrieved from www.singstat.gov.sg/pubn/popn/smd2010.pdf, accessed 28 June 2011.

Directorate General of Budget, Accounting and Statistics (2009). *Statistical Yearbook of the Republic of China*. Taipei, retrieved from http://eng.stat.gov.tw/lp.asp?CtNode=2815&CtUnit=1072&BaseDSD=36&xq_xCat=02, accessed 28 June 2011.

Directorate General of Budget, Accounting and Statistics (2010). *Women and Men in R.O.C. (Taiwan): Facts and Figures*, Taipei, retrieved from http://eng.stat.gov.tw/lp.asp?CtNode=1619&CtUnit=769&BaseDSD=7&mp=5, accessed 15 June 2011.

Giddens, A. (1991) *Modernity and Self-Identity: Self and Society in the Late Modern Age*, Cambridge: Polity.

Haspels, N. and Majurin, E. (2008). *Work, Income and Gender Equality in East Asia: Action Guide*, Bangkok: ILO (International Labor Organization).

Holden, T. and Hakan, E. (2006) 'Japan's Televisual Discourses: Infotainment, Intimacy, and the Construction of a Collective *Uchi*', in T. Holden and T. Scrase (eds) *Medi@Sia: Global Media/Tion In and Out of Context*, pp. 105–127, London: Routledge.

Hsiung, P. (1996) *Living Rooms as Factories: Class, Gender and the Satellite Factory System in Taiwan*, Philadelphia: Temple University Press.

Huang, Y. (2008) 'Consuming Sex and the City: Young Taiwanese Women Contesting Sexuality', in Y. Kim (ed.) *Media Consumption and Everyday Life in Asia*, pp. 188–202, New York: Routledge.

Lee, A. (2004) *In the Name of Harmony and Prosperity: Labor and Gender Politics in Taiwan's Economic Restructuring*, Albany: SUNY Press.

Lee, C. (2003) 'A Study of Singapore's English Channel Television Commercials and Sex-Role Stereotypes', *Asian Journal of Women's Studies*, 9(3): 78–100.

Lewis, T. (2007) 'He Needs to Face His Fears with These Five Queers!: Queer Eye for the Straight Guy, Makeover TV and the Lifestyle Expert', *Television & New Media*, 8(4): 285–311.

Lewis, T. (2008) *Smart Living: Lifestyle Media and Popular Expertise*, New York: Peter Lang.

Martin, F. (2003) 'Introduction: Taiwan's Literature of Transgressive Sexuality', in
F. Martin (ed.) *Angelwings: Contemporary Queer Fiction from Taiwan*, pp. 1–28,
Honolulu: Hawaii University Press.

Mediacorp (2011) 'Style Doctors', retrieved from http://www4.mediacorp.sg/
contentdistribution/programme/detail.php?prog_id=147, accessed 12 March
2011.

Mukhopadhaya, P. (2001) 'Changing Labor-Force Gender Composition and Male-
Female Income Diversity in Singapore', *Journal of Asian Economics*, 12(4):
547–568.

Ong, A. (2006) *Neoliberalism as Exception: Mutations in Citizenship and Sovereignty*,
Durham: Duke University Press.

Palmer, G. (2004) 'The New You: Class and Transformation in Lifestyle Television', in S. Holmes and D. Jermyn (eds) *Understanding Reality Television*,
pp. 173–190, London: Routledge.

Redden, G. (2007) 'Makeover Morality and Consumer Culture', in D. Heller (ed.)
Reading Makeover Television: Realities Remodeled, pp. 150–164, London: IB Tauris.

Rose, N. (1996) *Inventing Our Selves: Psychology, Power, and Personhood*, Cambridge:
Cambridge University Press.

Schudson, M. (1998) *The Good Citizen: A History of American Civic Life*, New York:
Martin Kessler Books.

Seah, C. (2007) 'The Strain of Success' (10 March), retrieved from
The Star website: http://thestar.com.my/news/story.asp?file=/2007/3/10/focus/
17099899&sec=focus, accessed 28 June 2011.

Shi, Q-L. (2010) '青少女沉迷名牌 急需理財教育 (Young Women and Girls Bewitched
by Name-Brands, in Urgent Need of Education in Financial Management)',
retrieved from *Lih Pao* website: www.lihpao.com/?action-viewnews-itemid-
8021, accessed 15 March 2010.

Tso, N. (2009) 'Why Has Taiwan's Birthrate Dropped So Low?' (7 December),
retrieved from *Time* website: http://www.time.com/time/world/article/0,8599,
1945937,00.html, accessed 28 June 2011.

Wang, Y. (2010) '老總請吃飯大戶藍心湄不習慣', retrieved from *Yahoo News* website:
http://tw.news.yahoo.com/article/url/d/a/101218/2/2j7tg.html, accessed 18
December 2010.

Weber, B. (2009) *Makeover TV: Selfhood, Citizenship, and Celebrity*, Durham: Duke
University Press.

Wood, H. and Skeggs, B. (2004) 'Notes on Ethical Scenarios of Self on British
Reality TV', *Feminist Media Studies*, 4(2): 205–208.

Yu, W. (2009) *Gendered Trajectories: Women, Work, and Social Change in Japan and
Taiwan*, Stanford: Stanford University Press.

Zveglich, J., der Meulen, V. and Rodgers, Y. (2004) 'Occupational Segregation and
the Gender Wage Gap in a Dynamic East Asian Economy', *Southern Economic
Journal*, 70(4): 850–875.

3
Young Women and Everyday Media Engagement in Muslim Southeast Asia

Pam Nilan

This chapter explores the engagement of young women in Muslim Southeast Asia with everyday media culture provided by online and mobile phone technologies. Young women in Indonesia and Malaysia not only consume the media culture products and experiences on offer, they use the medium of technology to constitute their subjectivity within various discourses that pertain to both the real and the virtual world – if the two can indeed be separated. This mediated engagement with new information and communication technologies involves young Muslim women in a creative enterprise that is also a form of control over their changing lives in the journey towards female adulthood. Young women in Muslim Southeast Asia are able to connect instantly with local, regional and global media resources for reflexivity and self-imagining, but there are contradictions and ambivalences in their framings of self. The discursive regime of the female self, which is embodied in the regulatory practices of Islam, emphasizes the strict moral behaviour of teenage girls and young women, producing anxieties at the intersection with ideals of individualized modernity.

Setting the scene

The following two profiles of young Muslim women in an urban setting in Central Java, Indonesia, in late 2007, illustrate the range of identity representations for young women in Muslim Southeast Asia:

The first young woman, Emmy, is 19 years old. She is waiting for the bus to go and meet her boyfriend. From a middle-class Muslim family, she is studying tourism and information technology. She is wearing a frilled miniskirt, a sleeveless hooded sweatshirt and sandals with platform soles. She has short, curly black hair. She is wearing make-up and perfume, and carrying a *Burberry* handbag. Her mobile phone is a bright acid green.

The second young woman, 21-year-old Hidayat, is shopping with her friends nearby. Also from a middle-class Muslim family, she is study-ing engineering at university. A pious girl, she is wearing a long and voluminous black dress, shoes, socks and a large, enveloping black headscarf showing just her face. She is carrying a dark handbag with-out a logo, but she is wearing *Calvin Klein* glasses. She also has a bright, acid-green mobile phone. Hidayat does not have a boyfriend. Her marriage will be arranged by her parents. But she says, smiling, that if she doesn't like their choice of husband, she will not be obliged to marry him.

There are young Muslim women like Emmy and Hidayat everywhere in Indonesia. Their different lifestyles and identity claims perhaps disguise how much they have in common. Both come from middle-class Muslim families. Both are studying at university. They use global brand name products and they have exactly the same mobile phone. Notably, neither of them will marry against their wishes, even though Emmy obviously has greater choice in the matter of a future partner. Yet at the same time, differences in representation of self are obvious.

In a similar vein, Bahfen (2008) offers the following profile of a young Muslim woman in Malaysia:

> From her profile on *Friendster.com*, it can be seen that 20-year-old student Uffa hails from Pahang. She wears a headscarf and lists her hobbies as shopping, eating, sleeping and travelling. Uffa's favourite television shows are *Smallville*, *Roswel,* and the Thai drama series *The Princess.* Her favourite movies include *Pirates of the Caribbean* and the Indonesian teen romance *Eiffel I'm in Love.*

(24)

The profile of Uffa demonstrates two important points. First, social-networking sites like *Friendster* are popular with young Muslim women in Malaysia, although it should be noted that *Facebook* had eclipsed the popularity of Friendster and other social-networking sites in both Malaysia and Indonesia by 2010. The second point is that Uffa's media favourites come from both Western and Asian sources. English is the second language of Malaysia, so English-language popular culture sources are more readily accessible to young women than in Indonesia. Yet at the same time, Uffa also favours a Thai television series and an Indonesian teen film. These consumption choices position her emphatically as a transcultural mediary, connecting with regional and global media resources for reflexivity and self-imagining.

All three of the young women glimpsed above are defining themselves as both Muslim and modern along a continuum of identity representations. They use the medium of technology to express and reflect their identities as Asian women undertaking the somewhat precarious journey towards female adulthood. They clearly engage with local, regional and global media resources for reflexivity and self-imagining, but we also see contradictions and ambivalences in their framings of self. The idealized female self embodied in the regulatory practices of Islam exemplifies morally circumspect behaviour for teenage girls and young women, in opposition to many of the discursive features of independent personhood in individualized late modernity.

Young Muslim women in Indonesia and Malaysia

In the past two decades Malaysia has seen much more rapid economic growth than Indonesia, although Indonesia is fast catching up. In both countries, the extension of post-compulsory education, the expansion of the urban middle class, a delay in the age of marriage and a growth in consumerism have driven some marked transformations in the transition of many young women to adulthood. Whereas once a girl's life was more or less mapped out for her according to the traditional female role in the family, this is no longer the case for a great many young women. They complete secondary education, engage in paid work, set up their own bank accounts, choose whom they will marry (Jones, 2010), use contraception and move around independently. The double-income nuclear family with two or three children and a mortgage is now the urban norm, driving the trend for 'partnership' marriages, which favour the autonomy of women.

Jones (2010) argues that the predominantly Muslim countries of Malaysia and Indonesia have historically had low divorce rates, due to traditional systems of arranged marriage and polygamy. The process of modern industrialization in the twentieth century saw divorce rates initially rise sharply because divorce represented an escape from unsatisfactory arranged marriages. The divorce rate then fell at the end of the twentieth century as the trend for 'free-choice' and double-income 'partnership' marriages meant that this escape route was no longer so necessary. More recently again, divorce rates have been rising in both countries, driven in part by the relative economic independence of women. Divorce rates rose first in the Muslim population of Singapore, then Malaysia, then Indonesia, following the different rates of economic growth in those countries.

Rinaldo (2011: 48) maintains that two 'global flows' are crucial for understanding the contemporary gender order for Muslim women in the Indonesian context: 'the Islamic revival and transnational feminism'. As she points out, both discourses offer normative messages about female rights and equality, and encourage women to reflect autonomously on both submission and emancipation. However, increased responsibility for individual choice in the transition of young women to adulthood may also mean increased insecurity about the legitimacy or otherwise of choices made.

The set of complex shifts in subjectivity that many call individualization is not constituted as more or less the same process everywhere. There are many cultures in the world where the process of individualization is either not as far advanced as in Western countries, or it has taken a different form in late modernity. It is acknowledged that the experience of contemporary youth transitions in most of the globalized world is now characterized by increased risk perceptions (Beck, 1992; Wall and Olofsson, 2008) and elements of reflexivity in the constitution of subjectivity (Threadgold and Nilan, 2009). Yet these useful interpretive concepts need to be delinked from homogenizing assumptions about detraditionalization (Giddens, 1991) and highly individualized choice (Brannen and Nilsen, 2007) when talking about young women in Muslim Southeast Asia. In this region, increased individual autonomy and freedom for young women do not necessarily imply the wholesale repudiation of tradition, or the withering of religious belief, or even the waning of trust in the institution of marriage and extended family support. It is questionable whether the transitions of young women to adulthood in Indonesia and Malaysia can or should be framed using the Western notion of a strongly individualized 'choice biography' (du Bois Reymond, 1998; Brannen and Nilsen, 2007), for example. The decisions made by individual young women reflect not just their personal aspirations; they are also the outcome of family negotiations that incorporate local cultural influences encoding traditional discourses (Setyawati, 2008). Collective values remain highly salient in both Indonesian and Malaysian cultures. Extended family ties offer kin support mechanisms that can bolster the resilience of young women in dealing with the anxieties engendered by the intersection of Muslim values with ideals of individualized modernity. Young women in Muslim Southeast Asia conduct both socializing and the representation of self in relation to a strong public discourse of moral propriety and gender separation in contemporary Islam. Yet at the same time they make implicit and explicit claims to be engaged with discourses of late modernity (Ansori, 2009).

Revitalized Islam

The shaping force of a revitalized Islam in the region has resulted in increased family and community constraints on the behaviour and activities of young Muslim women in Indonesia and Malaysia. Almost 50 years ago an Islamic resurgence started to become influential in Indonesia (Brenner, 1996; Howell, 2001). Around the same time a similar revitalization of faith began in Malaysia (Camroux, 1996). Dhume (2008) notes that around that time girls on university campuses in Indonesia took to wearing the headscarf. The same historical observation has been made of Malaysia (Nagata, 1995). Resurgent Muslim groups 'vigorously attacked the new freedoms of sexual expression in media and society, explicitly targeting women' (Hatley, 2008: 2). The regulatory force of Islam as a discourse about public piety in the behaviour of women has long been evident in both countries. Women cover the parts of their body known as the *aurat* with a headscarf, and by wearing clothes that cover their arms and legs. 'Veiling' of this kind serves as a symbol of an Islamic modernity:

> Women themselves, in situations of relative freedom, have often adopted the veil not so much because they had to but because it had become the normative socio-religious practice of their community.
>
> (Parker, 2008: 5)

Writing of Indonesian Islam, Parker (2008) proposes that the Muslim clothing prescription operates to ontologically separate 'good' women from women who might be morally suspect. The advantage for young women who choose wear it is that they can operate independently in the public space while preserving their respectability. In multicultural Malaysia, adherence to Islam displays 'Malay ethnicity' (Bahfen, 2008: 8), so dressing piously and wearing the headscarf also prioritizes ethnic identity, as well as signalling female virtue.

Another aspect of moral regulation in revitalized Islam is the insistence on the separation of the sexes. Islam provides a wealth of judgements and pronouncements on the dangers of mixed-sex socializing, for girls in particular. The phenomenon of young unmarried and unrelated women and men socializing is a source of pervasive moral panic (Nilan, 2008; Parker, 2009; Smith-Hefner, 2009). The great fear is that unregulated male–female contact might encourage 'free' (premarital) sex, which is a sin – *zina*. The constant adjustments made by the mainstream political parties in Malaysia and Indonesia to accommodate pressure from Muslim groups that are urging ever-more moral regulation of women – and greater prohibition of contact between unrelated people of different sexes (Tanuwidjaja, 2010) – indicates the popular strength of these two regulatory discourses. Rules for socializing are quite different for Muslim male and female youths in Indonesia and Malaysia, with boys permitted far greater freedom (Smith-Hefner, 2005).

At the same time, though, cultures are never static. Since the late 1980s there has been a considerable growth in modern Muslim 'cool' in Indonesia and Malaysia. Barendregt (2008: 161) maintains that this new emphasis on trendy Muslim modernity in Southeast Asia 'relates Islam to a modern world of lifestyle, talk shows and fashion', while still 'challenging the notion that the only way to be modern is through a Western model'. As indicated above, in contemporary Southeast Asia the constitution of the middle-class urban individual is moving towards the paradigm of an entrepreneurial, reflexive self (Beck, 2000), capable of independent action and autonomous behaviour. This late modern discourse of the self is far from incompatible with contemporary discourses of Islam available through multiple media sources. For example, it can be argued that the main feminist discourse in Indonesia at present is coming from Muslim women's groups. As Wieringa (2009: 17) points out, this persuasive discourse advances claims for female equity and public representation, 'built around the reform of Islam along gender sensitive terms, incorporating women's rights, such as those contained in the UN Women's Charter, CEDAW [Committee on the Elimination of Discrimination against Women] and the Beijing Platform of Action'. Yet these claims do not address the matter of enforced female modesty and segregation.

Media and technology

Since the 1990s there has been prolific growth in media forms and flows in Asia. Kim (2010: 28) argues that this recent profusion of media has seen 'new imaginations, new choices and contradictions'. The contemporary Asian media landscape 'generates a critical condition for reflexivity, engaging everyday people' in imaginative social practice. Like young people all over the world, young middle-class women in Muslim Southeast Asia are techno-savvy and highly conscious of the possibilities. They have grown up with mobile phones and the Internet. The new technology ensures that they are in touch with the mediated dissemination of 'taste cultures' to youth worldwide in the fields of consumption, entertainment, interactive games, fashion and the cult of celebrity. The virtual spaces made available through mobile phone and Internet technology enable communication, information, sharing and networking. Relevant to the Southeast Asian region, Lim (2003: 274) maintains that the 'convivial medium' of the Internet is now central to everyday informal communication. Through the Internet, young Muslims in the region can, in theory, connect with the youth cultures and agendas of a world brought closer by the pressures of globalization (Nayak, 2004). Yet we know that most information and communications technology (ICT) communication for young people is not with strangers or in new fields, but serves as an extension of their existing interpersonal relationships and interests (Geser, 2007). While the technology is global, practices and interpretive discourses are local. In both Indonesia and Malaysia great emphasis is placed upon political and religious discourse about the moral dangers of ICT technologies for young people, and for young women in particular.

The mediated gender discourses that Indonesian and Malaysian Muslim women have most ready access to are: first, those promoted by the State; second, local Muslim cultural traditions; and third, global meta-discourses such as Arabic Islam and Western culture – the latter including diverse discourses on sexuality. Young women access these discourses through the media, especially the Internet, TV and film, radio and print media. Malaysia has stricter censorship laws than Indonesia, and there are frequent attempts to restrict Internet access. In the last five years, mobile phone technology has become more sophisticated, allowing greater access for young women to messages and ideals of gender. Discourses on hyperfemininity and sexualized femininity circulate in the global mass media, yet so too do paradigms of Muslim female modesty, segregation and containment of sexuality. Locally, the moral double standard on sexuality for male and female young people remains virtually unchanged. Moral and religious pressure on young women in Muslim Southeast Asia means that for the most part their current patterns of sexual behaviour and partnering have not come to approximate the Western model of contemporary unfettered intimate relationships discussed by Beck-Gernsheim (2002) or earlier by Giddens (1992).

Mediated female Muslim identities

Even so, Muslim women in this region enjoy relatively high levels of social and personal freedom in contrast to women in Middle Eastern countries (Bennett, 2005). Noor (2007: 6, original emphasis) points out that 'Malay and Indonesian women have *always* played a prominent role in social life, in all areas ranging from culture to economics, religion to politics.' As we saw in the profiles of three young women at the beginning of this chapter, identity discourses on both Western sexualized culture and militant Islamic asceticism are strong in Malaysia and Indonesia, and beckon young women in two opposite directions. So it is not surprising that some choose to constitute themselves as Islamist radicals:

> There are practically no Islamist movements in Southeast Asia today – be they of the moderate, modernist, progressive, fundamentalist or even militant variety – where women are absent or deliberately excluded from membership and participation. Every single major Islamic party in the political mainstream in Indonesia and Malaysia, including the Partai Keadilan Sejahtera (PKS) of Indonesia and the Pan-Malaysian Islamic Party (PAS) boasts of having a women's wing with thousands of members, all of whom actively participate in the internal politics of their parties and go to the streets canvassing support during elections. What holds true for the mainstream Islamist movements and parties of Southeast Asia also holds for the myriad of underground radical religio-political movements in the region.
>
> (Noor, 2007: 6)

As the example above implies, new communication and information technologies mediate dialogic discourses that drive the constitution of different kinds of Muslim female identities. In part they do so by providing sources of information and forums for discussing two of the key issues of the day as they affect women: the censorship of pornography and the polygamy debate.

Studies by Hatley (2008) and Rinaldo (2011), among many others, show how young Indonesian Muslim women are divided on these two issues. The situation is very similar in Malaysia (Tong and Turner, 2008;

Moll, 2009). Taking the polygamy issue as an example, it seems that pious young Muslim women in Indonesia cannot agree on the topic. When the charismatic celebrity preacher Aa Gym took a second, much younger, wife, his popularity, which had been particularly high among young women, plummeted (Hoesterey, 2008) – which meant a fall in lecture attendance and diminished book and DVD sales. Yet many young Muslim women activists at the time stridently defended polygamy as a sanctified Islamic ideal that makes provision for male sexual needs. Rinaldo (2011: 54) points out that polygamy has 'become grist for Indonesia's pop culture mill', contrasting the popular films *Ayat-Ayat Cinta* (Verses of Love – 2008), which seems to offer a positive view, with *Berbagi Suami* (Love for Share – 2006), 'which harshly condemned polygamy'. Following the release of these films, Indonesian blogs and social networking sites filled rapidly with comments from women arguing each side of the debate. We are reminded that cyberspace is a domain in which gendered identities are asserted and negotiated constantly (Clerc, 2000).

As the example indicates, the possibilities of cyberspace have seen a rich development of varied female Muslim viewpoints in Indonesia and Malaysia: 'the Internet allows a transnational flow of perspectives and interpretations that facilitates the articulation of a wider Islamic identity' (Bahfen, 2008: 40). Barendregt (2008: 160) argues that cellular phone technology enables young Indonesians to be 'modern, mobile and Muslim'. Texting facilitates socializing without face-to-face contact (Goggin, 2006). For example, flirting and courting can be carried out by text and email without ostensibly flouting the religious regulations against mixed-sex socializing. Moreover, since the Internet eliminates barriers of time and space (Harvey, 1990), young Muslim women in Malaysia and Indonesia, who would otherwise be isolated from each other, can engage in virtual communities using the fact that the respective country languages *Bahasa Malaysia* and *Bahasa Indonesia* are variants of the same basic language. The kind of virtual communities constituted through social networking sites and blogs are not only about female Muslim identities in the political or theological sense, though. They also operate as 'fan' communities where young Muslim women negotiate as a group their relationship to bands, musicians, actors and celebrities, especially those regarded as exemplifying Muslim values, such as Muslim boy bands *Snada* and *The Fikr* (Indonesia), as well as *Raihan* and *Rabbani* (Malaysia).

In the next two sections of this discussion, the independent, dialogic possibilities of the Internet and the mobile phone for young women in Muslim Southeast Asia are illustrated by some ethnographic data collected in Central Java, Indonesia, in 2007.

Online engagement and texting in Internet cafés

Virtual mobility and autonomy

In the region of Central Java, being urban and modern is increasingly defined in terms of technological innovation that allows virtual mobility (Barendregt, 2008). Yet these new technological possibilities engender fear and anxiety in contemporary Indonesia and Malaysia about the apparently amoral sexualities with which the new media is discursively associated. Young women are adept at finding ways of having fun socializing with boys while maintaining public piety – and non-physical communication is an ideal way to accomplish such a balance. Slama's (2010) study in Central Java found that online social networking between young Indonesians to be a favoured means of communication for expressing ideas and emotions beyond the surveillance of family, and young women were frequent users. Anonymity and relative privacy in the virtual space allowed them to behave within the broad norms of Muslim propriety, even while searching for potential romantic friends across the country. One 15-year-old girl interviewed by Slama (2010) revealed that while she would be shy talking to a boy in person she feels free to be herself when communicating with a male online acquaintance. Young women can also discretely use the Internet to find out information about sexual health and reproductive matters. There is a paucity of formal sex education in Indonesia, so many young people rely on the mass media and visit 'health' sites online to get information (Harding, 2008). The need for anonymity and privacy online means that many young women, especially teenage girls, use Internet cafés. For teenage schoolgirls, visiting the local Internet café on the way home from school with a group of friends provides a safe opportunity to undertake forms of multimedia engagement that constitute both socializing and media consumption at the same time.

Observations in an Internet café – Central Java

The following observations were made by the author in 2007 in an Internet café located near several Muslim secondary schools in Solo, Central Java. School had just finished.

> Junior high students (. . .) arrived quickly in single sex groups of three to six, buying snacks and drinks as they crowd in. Latecomers wait

outside, chatting, for terminals to become free. As the teenagers fill the room, the noise and body heat level instantly increases in the small space packed with terminals in tiny booths. Stools are whisked out of booths and tussled over as groups of three, four and even five try to crowd into the same terminal. Although a few are looking for information relevant to their schoolwork, most take turns to check their emails or social network postings. Boys play online games as friends look on and wait their turn. While waiting, the young people send and receive texts on their mobile phones, showing their friends and talking and laughing as they do so. Should an email or posting of interest be found by someone, there is a shout and his or her friends all gather in to look at the email and comment, even contributing ideas for a possible reply. The sound of many music clips on YouTube being played at once raises the noise level even further.

At a terminal along the back wall, a group of four boys has accessed a celebrity website for the sexy girl band *Dewi Dewi*. Their hit *Dokter Cinta* (Doctor Love) is the ring tone for one of the boys and he plays it as they examine photos on the site together, whispering and laughing. At a terminal along the side wall, schoolgirls wearing ankle-length school uniforms and headscarves search for music clips of Ustad Jefri Al Buchori – the singing Muslim preacher. Soon Jefri's hit song *Yaa Rasulullah* can be heard. It is clear that certain boys and girls in the room are emailing and texting each other, although they do not physically connect. There are covert looks, loud whispers and syncopated giggling as interaction flows back and forth in physical space, phone texting space and online space. By late afternoon the junior high-school students have gone and an older age group occupy the Internet café.

Having fun and preserving propriety

There are a number of relevant points to be noted about the description above. First, around two-thirds of the teenage girls in the space were wearing the Muslim headscarf, and they were having a lot of fun together after school in a non-supervised mixed-sex setting. For Muslim high-school girls their lives revolve around balancing piety, propriety and fun (Parker, 2009). The local Internet café in daytime hours is a public/private space in which it appears this balance can be achieved through technologically mediated interaction. Second, they demonstrated fluid multimedia engagement. They used not only the computer terminals but also their mobile phones to communicate across time and space, sending texts and emails at lightning speed, and sometimes simultaneously. Finally, the Muslim schoolgirls' choice of a celebrity website: Ustad Jefri Al Buchori – the trendy singing Muslim preacher – indicates the paradigm of Muslim 'cool' discussed above. Spending time with a group of friends in a local Internet café after school meets the need to briefly escape from family surveillance into the wider realms of youth culture.

Furuholt and Kristiansen (2007) studied 270 student users in Yogyakarta, Central Java, of whom a third were female. Younger students were after 'entertainment and socializing, such as through chatting, games etc'. A later study in Semarang, Central Java, found that high-school students used the Internet for about nine hours a week on average, mostly outside the home and always with friends. A third indicated that communication was their main motive, and most reported an entertainment motive (Widyastari et al., 2009). Similar observations were made by Rathore and Alhabshi (2005) in Malaysian cybercafés. Here 41 per cent of users were students and just over a third were female. It was common to spend one or two hours every weekday afternoon in the cybercafés. Costs were low, and there was multipurpose use: 'emailing, chatting, and surfing, and while doing all this, being able to listen to online music'. A reported further benefit was the strengthening of social bonds with friends. Liu (2009: 173) found similar patterns in Internet cafés *(wangba)* in China, confirming yet again that the primary purpose for young people is a combination of socializing and entertainment. The young Chinese were there to 'entertain themselves, play games, listen to music, watch movies, chat and so on, not to work'. Liu found that they came with friends, seldom alone. They claim that they have 'nowhere else to go'. In urban China the commercialization of leisure activities has resulted in the shrinking of affordable youth leisure space (Liu, 2009: 174–175). The same observation may also apply to city-dwelling youth in Muslim Southeast Asia.

In the context of rapid urbanization in developing Asia, the attraction of the Internet café for young Muslim women in Indonesia and Malaysia lies partly in the compelling play of media and communication channels that such places allow. In European research on communication between older teens it is concluded that: 'Today, almost all close interpersonal relationships have to be analysed as hybrid multimedia processes that combine primary face-to-face gatherings with phone calls, text and image transmissions' (Geser, 2007: 23). The mobile phone and the Internet are not anchored to the space of the Internet café where face-to-face socializing is taking place, but allow access to the polyvalent space of the global network. Rathore and Alhabshi (2005) are concerned that the Internet café allows Malaysian teens access to pornography and gambling. However, according to the observations made above in Indonesia, neither the time of day nor the situation was conducive to accessing such sites. In Indonesia teenage girls are not associated with a taste for pornography and gambling. Furthermore, they operated in groups, not as individuals. This was collective situated practice, with all the accountability and surveillance that accompanies joint decision-making. Their joint purpose for the hour was to socialize, to have fun and be entertained. The mobile phone and the Internet facilitated the realization of these goals. As for the moral dimension of their social practices in the Internet café, this was constituted through what they did not do. Groups were single sex, not mixed, so there was no physical contact. It seemed that they kept to a selective set of entertainment and networking sites. Realistically, with so many peers looking on, surveillance and accountability was high, with retribution sure to follow later if they strayed too far from the bounds of respectability.

Mobile phone possibilities

According to Barendregt (2006), using the text-message function on mobile phones is a significant social practice for young Indonesian women in late modernity. The mobile phone 'seems at the same time to be an anchor in a society that is constantly in flux and increasingly mobile in character. Its portability roots a mobile identity.' Like the phenomenon of online social networking, the 'new cellular possibilities' of the mobile phone provide not only a sense of anonymity and privacy but also the desirable cachet of 'cool' (Barendregt, 2006: 20). There is no way of judging the content of texts and emails sent and received during the interactions observed in the Internet café in Solo, nor the nature of social network postings, but it is assumed from observed reactions that at least some communications were exchanged flirtatiously between groups of teenage girls and boys in the Internet café. It is possible to read this in terms of the gap between public conduct and private interaction that mobile phone technology inflects (Garcia-Montes et al., 2006: 72). The young men and women were not publicly in physical contact, but there was a great deal of private communication between them. In short, they were maintaining propriety in the public sphere by staying in separate single-sex groups, while in the dimension of technologically mediated personal communication they were having lots of fun together.

Observations of mobile phone-mediated socializing in a shopping mall

Just as teenage Indonesian schoolgirls visit the local Internet café on the way home from school with a group of friends for 'safe' socializing, so they also visit the local shopping mall to achieve the same goals. The following observations made in a large shopping mall in Solo, Central Java, in 2007, illustrate the possibilities and constraints. The observations were made during the fasting month of Ramadan late on a Saturday afternoon:

> A group of five girls aged about 16 – three wearing the headscarf, two bare-headed – pass a group of six slightly older senior high-school boys examining a range of computers displayed on the ground floor. The girls obviously know who the boys are because they start laughing and talking more loudly as they move slowly past to take the escalator. The boys pretend to ignore them. The girls stop on the floor above, crowding around a kiosk selling handbags which offers a view of the ground floor. After about five minutes the group of well-groomed boys, wearing t-shirts, runners and low-slung jeans, takes the escalator. As soon as they move, the girls move too, taking the next two escalators up to a shop which sells jewellery and knick-knacks. Four of the girls examine the necklaces and bracelets on display while the fifth girl is busy sending text messages, some of which she shows to her friends. After circulating around once or twice on the floors below, the group of boys ascends to the same floor. Two of them are texting as they ride the escalator. They walk slowly past the girls, who are still in the jewellery shop, and go into a trendy young men's clothing shop – a *distro* – on the other side of the mezzanine. Text messages are still being sent.

After about ten minutes, the boys take the escalator up to the next floor. They wander slowly through the games arcade. The girls, in high spirits now, leave the jewellery shop and take the escalator up to the same floor, where they inspect plush children's toys in a stall opposite the entrance to the games arcade. Two of the boys then play a game not far from the entrance where they compete in shooting at targets, noisily cheered on by their friends and singing along with the Muslim *nasyid* song (*Allah Maha Besar*) being belted out by the live band downstairs. The girls more or less drop the pretence of looking at fluffy animals to observe the target-shooting game from a distance. As it comes to a close, one girl looks at her watch and shepherds her friends over to a table in the food court. They sit down and all begin to text or play with their mobile phones, continuing to chat. Some 10 or 15 minutes later, the group of boys saunters over and occupies a table not far away. By this time it is only a few minutes to the end of the daily fast. All the tables outside the food outlets on the top floor of the mall are fully occupied by young people. The level of chatter and laughter gets louder and louder until the live music ends suddenly and a sonorous amplified drumbeat comes to end the fast.

The girls break their fast with bottles of iced tea, while the boys drink coca-cola. The live band has started playing popular rock favourites. As soon as they have all eaten, some of the boys start to call out to the girls, who seem to ignore them while texting furiously. The boys, like the girls, are showing text messages to each other and laughing. This kind of interaction – the boys paying attention to the girls who pretend to ignore them – goes on for about 30 minutes more, then the same girl who had led the way to the table gathers her friends and proceeds downstairs. All five girls are picked up outside the mall in a van, probably driven by a family member. The boys walk around for perhaps 15 minutes more, then take the exit themselves, driving off in twos on motorbikes.

Public conduct and private interaction

Some salient points can be noted in the description above. First, the extent of mobile phone texting in the observed mall interaction was intensive, enhancing and supplementing what was going on in the physical space, similar to the Internet café. Second, there is no way of judging the content of all texts sent and received in the interactions observed, but it is assumed from reactions that at least some, if not most, of the text messages were exchanged flirtatiously between the group of young women and the group of young men. It is possible to read this in terms of the gap between public conduct and private interaction that mobile phone technology inflects (Garcia-Montes et al., 2006: 72). The young men and women were not publicly in physical contact, but there was a great deal of private communication between them, the nature of which we can only guess at. In summary, they were carefully negotiating the discourses of moral propriety while indulging in the pleasures of mild flirting. In short, they were maintaining propriety in the public sphere by staying in separate single-sex groups, while in the dimension of technologically mediated personal communication, they were having lots of fun together.

It is useful to consider the situated practice of young Muslim women waiting out the daily Ramadan fast with friends in the space of the mall as encoding a distinctive late modern discourse on religious orthopraxy. The mediated subjectivity that they demonstrate and share with boys during the holy month of Ramadan is constituted within a moral discourse of piety, but at the same time with the moral legitimacy (Liechty, 2003) of being middle class, implicitly 'modern, honourable, and decent' (Ansori, 2009: 92). The young women observed in 2007 achieve public propriety within the new conservative religious discourse of Indonesia while having lots of interactive, even flirtatious, fun through the capacities of mobile phone technology.

As the examples above imply, for young Muslim women who make collective use of ICT technologies in semi-public spaces, different media spaces and forms are layered over each other. This layering through technology and media transforms and recombines elements of identity, facilitating not only reflexivity and self-imagining but also contradictions and ambivalences in framings of self.

Conclusion

This chapter has explored some ways in which young women in Muslim Southeast Asia engage with the everyday media culture provided by online and mobile phone technologies, especially the Internet. Young Muslim women in urban Indonesia and Malaysia use ICT autonomously and independently to communicate, consume and represent themselves in both the real and virtual world. In their mediated multiple representations of identity and framings of self they move, often somewhat precariously, between discourses on moral virtue and having fun.

Although the constitution of their subjectivity does seem to be more individualized than previously, collective values remain highly salient in both Indonesian and Malaysian cultures, and the discursive effects of revitalized Islam are deep and widespread. Young women in Muslim Southeast Asia conduct both socializing and the representation of self relative to a strong, and often enforced, local discourse of moral propriety and gender separation in contemporary Islam. Yet at the same time, the values of the rapidly expanding middle classes in both Indonesia and Malaysia have emphasized a dual-income, 'partnership marriage' that implicitly positions young women as future-focused, entrepreneurial and in control of their lives.

References

Ansori, M. (2009) 'Consumerism and the Emergence of a New Middle Class in Globalizing Indonesia', *Explorations: A Graduate Journal of Southeast Asian Studies*, 9: 87–97, available at: http://scholarspace.manoa.hawaii.edu/handle/10125/10713, accessed 21 December 2010.

Bahfen, N. (2008) 'Online Islamic Identity and Community in Australia and Three Neighbouring Countries', unpublished PhD thesis, University of Technology, Sydney.

Barendregt, B. (2006) 'Between M-Governance and Mobile Anarchies: Pornoaksi and the Fear of New Media in Present Day Indonesia', European Association of Social Anthropologists (EASA) Media Anthropology Network e-Seminar, available at: http://www.philbu.net/media-anthropology/barendregt_mgovernance.pdf, accessed 10 June 2011.

Barendregt, B. (2008) 'Sex, Cannibals, and the Language of Cool: Indonesian Tales of the Phone and Modernity', *The Information Society*, 24(3): 160–170.

Beck, U. (1992) *Risk Society: Towards a New Modernity,* London: Sage.

Beck, U. (2000) *The Brave New World of Work*, Cambridge: Polity.

Beck-Gernsheim, E. (2002) *Reinventing the Family: In Search of New Lifestyles*, Cambridge: Polity.

Bennett, L. (2005) *Women, Islam and Modernity: Reproductive Sexual Health in Indonesia*, London: Routledge.

Brannen, J. and Nilsen, A. (2007) 'Young People, Time Horizons and Planning', *Sociology*, 41(1): 153–160.

Brenner, S. (1996) 'Reconstructing Self and Society: Javanese Muslim Women and The Veil', *American Ethnologist*, 23(4): 673–697.

Camroux, D. (1996) 'State Responses to Islamic Resurgence in Malaysia: Accommodation, Co-option, and Confrontation', *Asian Survey*, 36(9): 852–868.

Clerc, S. (2000) 'Estrogen Brigades and "Big Tits" Threads: Media Fandom Online and Off', in D. Bell and B. Kennedy (eds), *The Cybercultures Reader*, pp. 216–229, New York: Routledge.

Dhume, S. (2008) *My Friend the Fanatic: Travels with an Indonesian Islamist*, Melbourne: The Text Publishing Company.

du Bois-Reymond, M. (1998) 'I Don't Want to Commit Myself Yet: Young People's Life Concepts', *Journal of Youth Studies*, 1(1): 63–79.

Furuholt, B. and Kristiansen, S. (2007) 'Internet Cafés in Asia and Africa – Venues for Education and Learning', *The Journal of Communication Informatics*, 3(2), available at: http://ci-journal.net/index.php/ciej/article/viewPDFInterstitial/314/352, accessed 13 December 2009.

Garcia-Montes, J. M., Caballero-Munoz, D. and Perez-Alvarez, M. (2006) 'Changes in the Self Resulting from the Use of Mobile Phones', *Media, Culture & Society*, 28(1): 67–82.

Geser, H. (2007) 'Patterns of Multi-channel Communication among Older Teens'. Soziologisches Institut der Universität Zürich, University of Zurich, available at: http://socio.ch/mobile/t_geser4.pdf, accessed 31 December 2009.

Giddens, A. (1991) *Modernity and Self-Identity: Self and Society in the Late Modern Age*, Cambridge: Polity.

Giddens, A. (1992) *The Transformation of Intimacy: Sexuality, Love and Eroticism in Modern Societies*, Stanford: Stanford University Press.

Goggin, G. (2006) *Cell Phone Culture*, London: Routledge.

Harding, C. (2008) 'The Influence of the "Decadent West": Discourses of the Mass Media on Youth Sexuality in Indonesia', *Intersections: Gender and Sexuality in Asia and the Pacific*, Issue 16, available at: http://intersections.anu.edu.au/issue16/harding.htm, accessed 20 May 2011.

Harvey, D. (1990) *The Condition of Postmodernity: An Enquiry into the Origins of Cultural Change*, Cambridge: Blackwell.

Hatley, B. (2008) 'Hearing Women's Voices, Contesting Women's Bodies in Post-New Order Indonesia', *Intersections: Gender and Sexuality in Asia and the Pacific*, Issue 16, available at: http://intersections.anu.edu.au/issue16/hatley.htm, accessed 20 May 2011.

Hoesterey, J. B. (2008) 'Marketing Morality: The Rise, Fall and Rebranding of Aa Gym', in G. Fealy and S. White (eds), *Expressing Islam: Religious Life and Politics in Indonesia*, pp. 95–112, Singapore: Institute of Southeast Asian Studies.

Howell J. (2001) 'Sufism and the Indonesian Islamic Revival', *Journal of Asian Studies*, 60(3): 701–729.

Jones, G. (2010) 'Changing Marriage Patterns in Asia', Asia Research Institute Working Paper 131, Singapore: National University of Singapore, available at: http://www.ari.nus.edu.sg/docs/wps/wps10_131.pdf, accessed 2 March 2011.

Kim, Y. (2010) 'Female Individualization? Transnational Mobility and Media Consumption of Asian Women', *Media, Culture & Society*, 32(1): 25–43.

Liechty, M. (2003) *Suitably Modern: Making Middle Class Culture in a New Consumer Society*, New Jersey: Princeton University Press.

Lim, M. (2003) 'The Internet, Social Networks and Reform in Indonesia', in N. Couldry and J. Curran (eds), *Contesting Media Power: Alternative Media in a Networked World*, pp. 273–288, Boulder: Rowman & Littlefield.

Liu, F. (2009) 'It Is Not Merely about Life on the Screen: Urban Chinese Youth and the Internet Café', *Journal of Youth Studies*, 12(2): 167–184.

Moll, Y. (2009) ' "People Like Us" in Pursuit of God and Rights: Islamic Feminist Discourse and Sisters in Islam in Malaysia', *Journal of International Women's Studies*, 11(1): 40–55.

Nagata, J. (1995) 'Modern Malay Women and the Message of the Veil', in W. Karim (ed.), *'Male' and 'Female' in Developing Southeast Asia*, pp. 101–120, Oxford: Berg.

Nayak, A. (2004) *Race, Place and Globalization*, Oxford: Berg.

Nilan, P. (2008) 'Young People and Media in Muslim Southeast Asia', in Y. Kim (ed.), *Media Consumption and Everyday Life in Asia*, pp. 45–58, New York: Routledge.

Noor, F. (2007) 'Women in the Service of the Jundullah: The Case of Women Supporters of the Jama' ah Islamiyah of Indonesia', Paper for the workshop *Female Suicide Bombers and Europe*, organized by the International Institute for Strategic Studies (IISS), London. 12 March 2007, available at: http://www.iiss.org/EasySiteWeb/getresource.axd?AssetID=2335&type=full&servicetype=Attachment, accessed 3 April 2011.

Parker, L. (2008) 'To Cover the *Aurat*: Veiling, Sexual Morality and Agency among the Muslim Minangkabau, Indonesia', *Intersections: Gender and Sexuality in Asia and the Pacific*, Issue 16, available at: http://intersections.anu.edu.au/issue16/parker.htm, accessed 20 May 2011.

Parker, L. (2009) 'Religion, Class and Schooled Sexuality among Minangkabau Teenage Girls', *Bijdragen tot de Taal-, Land-en Volkenkinde [BKI]*, 165(1): 62–94.

Rathore, A. S. and Alhabshi, S. M. (2005) 'A Case of Urban Cyber Cafés in Malaysia', *Information Technology in Developing Countries*, 15(1), available at: http://www.iimahd.ernet.in/egov/ifip/apr2005/article3.htm, accessed 30 December 2009.

Rinaldo, R. (2011) 'Gender and Moral Visions in Indonesia', *Asia Pacific: Perspectives*, 10(1): 44–60.

Setyawati, L. (2008) '*Adat*, Islam and Womanhood in the Reconstruction of Riau Malay Identity', in S. Blackburn, B. Smith and S. Syamsiyatun (eds), *Indonesian Islam in a New Era: How Women Negotiate Their Muslim Identities*, pp. 69–93, Melbourne: Monash University Press.

Slama, M. (2010) 'The Agency of the Heart: Internet Chatting as Youth Culture in Indonesia', *Social Anthropology*, 18(3): 316–330.

Smith-Hefner, N. (2005) 'The New Muslim Romance: Changing Patterns of Courtship and Marriage among Educated Javanese Youth', *Journal of Southeast Asian Studies*, 36(3): 441–459.

Smith-Hefner, N. (2009) ' "Hypersexed" Youth and the New Muslim Sexology in Java, Indonesia', *Review of Indonesian and Malaysian Affairs*, 43(1): 209–244.

Tanuwidjaja, S. (2010) 'Political Islam and Islamic Parties in Indonesia: Critically Assessing the Evidence of Islam's Political Decline', *Contemporary Southeast Asia*, 32(1): 29–49.

Threadgold, S. and Nilan, P. (2009) 'Reflexivity of Contemporary Youth, Risk and Cultural Capital', *Current Sociology*, 51(1): 47–68.

Tong, J. K-C. and Turner, B. S. (2008) 'Women, Piety and Practice: A Study of Women and Religious Practice in Malaysia', *Contemporary Islam*, 2(1): 41–59.

Wall, E., and Olofsson, A. (2008) 'Young People Making Sense of Risk: How Meanings of Risk Are Materialized within the Social Context of Everyday Life', *Young*, 16(4): 431–448.

Widyastari, D., Shaluhiyah, Z. and Widjanarko, B. (2009) 'The Influence of Internet Exposure on Adolescents' Sexual Attitudes: A Study among Secondary School Students in Semarang, Central Java, Indonesia', from Proceedings of 3rd International Conference on Reproductive Health and Social Sciences Research 2009, Mahidol University, Bangkok, available at: http://www.ipsr.mahidol.ac.th/ipsr/InterConference/Download/Final_Proceedings2009.pdf, accessed 21 May 2011.

Wieringa, S. (2009) 'Women Resisting Creeping Islamic Fundamentalism in Indonesia', *Asian Journal of Women's Studies*, 15(4): 30–56.

4
'Just a Slogan': Individualism, Post-Feminism and Female Subjectivity in Consumerist China

Sue Thornham and Feng Pengpeng

At first sight, the fashion magazines found in today's urban China are not very different from their Western counterparts. Indeed, the Chinese versions are often franchises of Western magazines. France's Hachette Filipacchi Medias has published a Chinese version of *Elle* since 1988 in partnership with Shanghai Century Publishing – initially a government-sponsored publishing house that was corporatized in 2005. Hearst Magazines International followed with *Cosmopolitan* in 1998, via a partnership with a Beijing-based, part-government-owned partner, Trends Magazine. Other franchises have followed (*Harper's BAZAAR* 2001, *Marie Claire* 2002, *Vogue* 2005) so that there are now more than a dozen Western titles, and over the last 10 years these have been joined by both Chinese franchises of Japanese brands (*Oggi* 2001, *ViVi* 2006) and by the development of home-grown titles. *Rayli* has been published by the China Light Industry Press since 1995, although it acquired major shareholders Gruner + Jahr in 2006; *iLook* has been published by the independently owned China Interactive Media Group since 1998. Advertising spending in magazines has been growing at an average of 33 per cent annually (Borton, 2004), with total revenues of US$5.5 billion in 2002 (*China Daily* 5 November 2003). As Xiaoping Li has commented: 'The fashion model has become the ultimate archetype of beauty, dominating the iconography of women. Fashion and fashion models are essential to the manufacturing of both modern women and modern lifestyles.' (1998: 80).

The result is that the crowded news stands of Chinese cities have a very different appearance from that described by Perry Johansson less than 10 years ago:

News stands in Chinese cities hold large numbers of titles geared towards female readers, and with few exceptions almost all of them are published by the official All China Women's Federation.

(2001: 96)

It is a startling shift, this 'saturation of Chinese cultural space with Western presence' (Schein, 1994: 148). If we look more closely, however, there are differences between these magazines and their Western counterparts. In her study of British fashion magazines of the late 1990s, Janice Winship identifies in them a mode of self-reflexive advertising very different from the repetitive images of conventional female beauty described by Anne Cronin a few years earlier (Cronin, 2000). It is a mode inaugurated by the Wonderbra campaign of 1994, which operated within what Winship calls a '*double* regime of signification' (2002: 34, original emphasis). On the one hand, it references a 'feminist awareness' in its appeal to an ironically amused female spectator; and on the other hand, it continues to invite precisely the male gaze on which it so clearly comments. It is this provocative and ironic play that Angela McRobbie identifies as characteristic of a post-feminist cultural space that emerged in the 1990s, a space that proclaims both the 'success' of feminism and, in its self-conscious appeal to a playful, ironic and visually literate – but not feminist – female spectator, declares it a thing of the past (McRobbie, 2004, 2009). However, writing recently about the images in post-feminist Western fashion magazines, McRobbie has identified in these newer images a far more disturbing 'semihallucinatory' quality (2007a: 7). The models now seem inaccessible, unreal, post- or perhaps simply non-human. These most recent images are a long way from the provocative and playful self-reflexive irony of the Wonderbra series and the campaigns that followed. They would appear to belong, as McRobbie suggests, to a more uneasy post-feminism, presenting us with a femininity that knows itself to be, in Beverley Skeggs' words, 'impossible ... uninhabitable' (1997: 102). No longer playful, they seem instead haunted, their seductive quality more Baudrillard's 'attraction of the void' (1990: 76–77) than Winship's invitation to a playful and knowingly ironic pleasure.

In the Chinese fashion magazines the promises are much less equivocal. 'Variously demure, coy, provocative and seductive' (Hooper, 1998: 171), the models smile appealingly to camera, their changes of outfit signalling the different identities that comprise their lives. Dressed for work or leisure, demure or smilingly successful, they pose before a male audience glimpsed at the edges of the frame. Elsewhere they are positioned, with no suggestion of irony, in front of the ideal images to which they, and we the readers, are assumed to aspire – their appearance almost, but not yet quite, matching the ideal represented in the shop window mannequins behind them. Yet these images, apparently so much less troubling in their embrace of a passive and conventional femininity, are no less the site and focus of complex identity negotiations than their Western counterparts are, and the femininity they display – despite its seeming lack of reflexivity – is no less impossible. To understand how such images function in today's urban China, the following discussion will move between an analysis of the magazines themselves, and extracts from the interviews we conducted with young women in Guangzhou about their magazine reading.

Following the completion of an initial questionnaire by 39 female students at Zhongshan University, Guangzhou, eight group interviews were carried out in March and April 2007.[1] The 24 young women we interviewed were all students aged between 20 (second-year undergraduates) and 24 (final-year Masters' students). This age group positions them historically in a number of ways. All were born in the post-Mao era, and for them there was an absolute historical divide between the 'now' that they inhabit and the 'then' of their mothers, with the Cultural Revolution (1966–1976) forming the fault line between the two. As one interviewee said, 'They [were] in a communist society... but we're the first generation in the new China.' The interviewees were also born in the era of the single-child policy, inaugurated in 1979 with the aim of fast-tracking China's modernization by producing a generation of 'First World' children (Fong, 2004). Although not all were in fact single children, most were. While many families in rural areas still risk punishment in order to have a son,[2] in the 'progressive' cities like Guangzhou an only daughter becomes the focus of parental expectations. These students are thus products of a fiercely competitive education system in which gender difference is not recognized. This is a legacy not only of the Mao years, when gender equality (or sameness) became official state policy, but also of the emphasis on 'individual success' that came with the 'opening up' (*kaifang*) of China in the post-Mao era – and to get into a high-ranking university like Zhongshan you have to be at the very top.[3] Now, however, this group are nearing the end of their time as students and looking outwards, towards employment, and here too things are distinctively different from the past. They are part of the first generation to have to compete for jobs (rather than being assigned them, as happened up to the mid-1990s), in a social context in which gender difference, officially denied in their school years, seems suddenly very pronounced. All of those interviewed thought it much harder for young women than for young men to compete in the labour market, many were conscious of discriminatory employment practices, and all felt the situation in which they find themselves to be wholly new, 'It's a different age now and everything is different.'

Interpretive strategies

So in what way is this femininity – that they now feel they must learn to inhabit – 'impossible ... uninhabitable'? And how, if at all, might we connect it to the post-feminism of Western popular culture? To try to answer the first question, we can turn to the interpretive repertoires[4] through which these students discussed the images they found in the magazines. The two most prominent groupings form a familiar, and highly contradictory, pairing.[5] The first is that of 'use': the students persistently stressed the 'use value' of the magazines[6] :

> *Ai*: I enjoy reading magazines because, the first they are useful for what, er for me. For example I want to buy some new dress in this summer and what can I buy? What is the fashion? I will read the magazine and find the answer.
>
> *Pan*: I will read some useful parts and some important parts, for example they will tell you how to make you like er elegant er a career woman er in modern times. They can tell you how to make your skin beautiful, how to dress very gracefully. I think they're very useful.

But this is always accompanied by an insistence on the second key interpretive grouping: 'daydream' or 'fantasy' – an escape from the real world that is at the same time a half-believed vision of a future 'real'. Bao, a 24-year-old postgraduate student, said:

> I always look at the colourful pictures just to relax. They are always so beautiful. Never to read very closely, never to read carefully. I never read carefully because I er for me, you know the economics for me is not very good, so I have no money to buy these clothes, to buy these decorations, so I always look at these pictures, all so beautiful. Maybe one day I will have enough money and enough time to choose and to buy these things but er I think for me just now ... I think it's just a dream, yeah it's a dream.

Here Bao explicitly denies the use value of the magazines but she nevertheless hints at a half-imagined future ('Maybe one day...') in which her fantasy might be realized. In the responses of other students, these two groupings – use and dream – come together more firmly in a 'dream' (the word appears in almost all of the interviews) of a future that is characterized by self-realization, career success and a focus on appearance. It is a future that will be, above all, different from their mothers' lives, which are seen as defined by sacrifice, but the very choices that mark it as new and exciting ('I will have enough money and enough time to choose and to buy these things') are also experienced as a form of gender regulation. Here Bao explains the attraction of a particular image:

> Because my head is not very high and I'm a little fat [laughs] so I want myself to lose weight so I always mm and when I read these magazines I will see so many models, so beautiful and with so, so great build.

The 'dream' is of an ideal image, an absolute beauty – these models are quite simply 'perfect' (Li: 'They have perfect face, perfect figure'). But it is also a dream of activity, success, control:

> *Ai*: And why I say it is a dream is because sometimes you know when we read we will think 'Wow, the model is so slim and I want to become her' and sometimes in the magazines I read, it often tells us about the life of the model and what they will do in their spare time and what books they read and I think this will let me feel er when I read about their lives I want to become the active one in my life. I want to be active in my life like models.

This contradiction between a recognition that this is dream and an insistence that the dream can nevertheless be lived emerges repeatedly in discussion of the images. They are seen to be fantasies, wholly constructed (Jia: 'I think the figure of the model we see from the magazine is not her real figure'), and yet there is a repeated insistence that they are also real. Uncomfortable, Jia immediately qualifies her original statement. She continues:

> I mean in the, at first they just use a model, they just use girls that didn't exist in the real world but in recent years I think these magazines just find some real girls on the street, they just, they are the same as us... so the magazine just give us a clue that you can do that, you can achieve it.

Invited to pick out examples of these 'perfect' images, one group chose a fantasy advertising image (A) in which a semi-naked Western woman, encircled by mobile phones and trailing stardust, looks back at us over her shoulder, her golden hair blowing in the breeze. A second group selected the image of a young Chinese teacher (B), complete with white-board and pointer, smiling at us over the heads of her class of adult male students. While the first clearly corresponds to the notion of 'dream' and the second to that of 'use', the contradiction between the two is reconciled by the concept of 'success':

> *Hong* [Image A]: They're all so cool, so it just happens in my dream. I love her hair...Long, cool, it's cool....I think it's a successful woman.
> *Mei* [Image B]: Because I don't think this...woman is beautiful but kind of pretty, maybe a little handsome I think, more like a er, not like a housewife or that kind of girl that is hoping for love.... Some kind of career – a career woman. I like her image.

For Ai, quoted above, the notion of the 'active model' provides not only a fantasized ideal in which the contradictory aims of (idealized) image and individual achievement are successfully reconciled but also a figure to identify with and provide the 'motivation for me to work hard to let myself have the life that I want'. Fashion, beauty and their associated luxuries here become signifiers of independence and hard work; the markers of 'a life of one's own' (Beck and Beck-Gernsheim, 2001) and an identity successfully achieved.

Such an association of ideals of self-actualization and a Westernized consumer lifestyle is relatively new in China – a result of what Li calls 'the national need for modernization' that accompanied the adoption of a market economy in the 1990s (1998: 87). It is a development, argues Li, in which 'the refashioned "modern woman" ' performs a central symbolic role, creating 'the illusion of an affluent modern China and women's emancipation' (*ibid.*). For Angela McRobbie, this refashioned figure has become the 'global girl', whose modernity is expressed in 'her new found freedoms, her wage-earning capacity, her enjoyment of and immersion in beauty culture and in popular culture, and in her pleasing and becoming demeanour' (2009: 88). Although she lacks the ironic or aggressive qualities of her Western counterparts, argues McRobbie, she functions, like them, to pre-empt critique: feminist and postcolonial analyses can be rendered 'obsolete' through the celebration of a self-produced feminine individuality. For many of the students we interviewed, then, the belief that they will succeed in affording the luxuries advertised as long as they work hard is bound up with a belief in the power to become 'self-made'. Consumption as success is an outcome of individual ability, character and, above all, self-determination. Asked which models they wished to look like, they were uneasy with the question. They did not want to 'look like' any of them, they said. They wanted to learn from them: 'I do not think we want to copy them. We just want to get advice, get information from them like what kind of clothes are presently popular. . . . I do not think we should use the word "copy" ' (Rong); 'I think it is not useful to look like, but I can get some information to make my appearance better, . . . more professional' (Fang). Self-realization and self-determination are repeatedly emphasized, however contradictory the arguments may become. The following is an extract from an interview with three undergraduate students:

> *Zhang*: When I look at them, I know they are models. Different jobs, so different life goals. But if it is just the appearance, the faces, I think everyone wants herself/himself to be as beautiful as they are. . . .
>
> *Wang*: We want to be similar to them in personality, or in mentality. We do not focus on the faces. We want to know how sophisticated they are.
>
> *Interviewer*: But all these are print pictures. How can you know their personality and their mentality?
>
> *Yang*: We do not want to look like them because they are too far away from the reality. They are illusionary. . . .
>
> *Zhang*: When you look at them, you know this is not how they look like in their daily life. Their clothes are sponsored by some company, and they have designers to put on make-up for them. They purposefully pose their body and their faces this way. It is monotonous. It looks fake. They are like walking hangers. I do not want to be like them. . . . [But] if I read it, I will really want to buy some new clothes.
>
> *Interviewer*: You want to buy clothes to make yourself look like them?
>
> *Zhang*: I must go shopping quickly.
>
> *Wang*: People want to change their image, and make themselves more beautiful. [Laughs] Everyone thinks that way.

As this conversation develops, the insistence that the models are merely exemplars of success – to learn from in the process of self-realization and self-improvement – shifts first to a more decisive rejection of the commodified and illusory quality of their appearance and then, amid embarrassed laughter, to an acknowledgement that they do provide fantasized ideal images for the students. For Bao, a postgraduate student from a poor rural background, the dream of a fantasized self-transformation is similarly a dream of independence and success. But in her responses, both are acknowledged to be fragile and experienced self-consciously as 'dream':

> *Bao*: Yeah I will have my dream. If I lose my dream and I just want, I just want to be a housewife I think I will lose my, I will lose myself. For finance I will depend on my husband. It's so terrible, you know, if your financial [position] is not very is not independent you will depend on him. So no, a short time is OK but after a long time he will lose ∗∗∗ [trans: look down upon][7] look down on me so I think it's so horrible, but I, so I still have my dream.

Beauty ideals

The most difficult aspect of these images to address in interview was the fact that they are overwhelmingly white or 'whitened' and yet, in the students' view, completely Chinese. The relationship between whiteness and femininity has a long and complex history in China, which can only be sketched here. In court paintings ranging from the Tang dynasty (eight–ninth century) to the Qing dynasty (seventeenth century), white skin is identified with aristocratic femininity. Classical Chinese literature frequently refers to ice, snow, jade and cream – all of which identify ideal feminine beauty with whiteness and purity (Li, 1998). With the Republic of 1912 and its embrace of 'modernization as westernization' (Edwards, 2002: 620), the images become more complex, as whiteness becomes associated with both modernity and Western sophistication.[8] In post-1949 China, however, China's women were to be liberated as workers 'in the struggle to build a great socialist country' (Mao, 1955), so that whiteness becomes 'evil whiteness', a 'capitalist colour'.

With China's 'opening up' in the 1980s and 1990s, whiteness returned as an acknowledged ideal, again associated with modernity and Westernization but now characterized by the intensified emphasis on image and consumption brought by exposure to a globalized Western consumer culture. Perry Johansson writes of this period that the images of women 'changed towards emphasizing glamour, individualism, and hedonism', citing as an example an advert for cleansing cream in which a fashionable and sexualized Asian woman stands in front of a 'fancy, European-style hotel' evoking 'associations of the flashy lifestyle of the international jet-set' (2001: 98). Writing at the end of the 1990s, however, Johansson identifies a shift towards 'self-orientalizing' advertising images in which Chinese models in traditional costume combine 'stereotypical, Orientalist representations' with a seductive appeal to a male gaze. Through this attempted 'repatriation' of consumer culture, he argues, adverts offered an image of Chinese femininity that embodies a global 'modernity' and reaffirms traditional gender roles (2001: 112, 119).

Yet in today's magazines, white Western(ized) faces and tall, thin Western(ized) bodies dominate. Adverts for skin whiteners were the single most frequently occurring advert in the magazines we surveyed.[9] In their responses to these images, the students' definitions of beauty emphasized thinness (Chang: 'a slim waist and long legs'); skin that 'should be white, [or] very fair' (Ai); 'very big eyes, ... very good skin, very small lips, and very small and straight noses' (Juan). Models or actresses whose eyes are 'small ... slant (trans.)', they said, 'fit the Western imagination [of Chinese women], but not our evaluation' (ibid.). Many of the students talked about the popularity of cosmetic surgery, particularly double-eyelid surgery, both with Chinese models and among their own acquaintances.

At the same time, however, they insisted that this makes the women not only more beautiful but also more authentically Chinese. In the following extract, Ai's irritation at Western assumptions was typical:

I think in China what we think is beauty is different from the old days but in Western eyes it's the same, and they think Chinese people ∗∗∗ [trans: Yes, the single eyelid] and their eyes are like this and small mouth. They think Chinese are like that, that is the beautiful Chinese woman, but in China I don't think so. Many girls like the eyes and higher nose so that is the reason why they go to have some operations on their face.

For these students, beauty seemed both a universal and a transparent quality – a combination of 'inner' and 'exterior' qualities – and nationally specific. They are critical of a perceived Western orientalism that displays as exotic and different those Chinese models who fit Western stereotypes of a pre-modern Asia:

Wen: I think Westerners have a very strange impression about the Chinese. They think Chinese people have eyes like these [uses her fingers to make slanted eye shape. All laugh]. They think maybe tall, big eyes, straight nose not Chinese.

The ideal with which they counter this stereotype, however, is one conceived on the model of the Western image ('slim waist and long legs', white or fair skin, large eyes with double eyelids, 'very small lips, and very small and straight noses'). So, on the one hand, 'Western' ideals of beauty represent a standard of modernity to which these young women wish to lay claim – older Chinese actresses are rejected because they 'just look like some ... ancient people. Their eyes are very ... very ... small, slant' (Juan). On the other hand, China, they insist, has its own standards of beauty that stand in opposition to the globalizing ambitions of the West:

> *Yang*: I think these Western models stand for a globalized standard of what beautiful should be like. They have that cultural advantage. Or it is not cultural, it is an economic advantage. Then the Westerners sum up their ideas of what is a beauty, and then they have a universal standard. They put that standard here.... The new standard of beauty says that you have to be tall if you want to be beautiful. In the traditional Chinese view, slenderness and small build was thought beautiful.

The argument is not new. Johansson (2001) describes the debates of the early 1990s in *Women of China* (*Zhongguo Funü*), the official magazine of the Women's Federation, on the question of how a specifically Chinese version of contemporary female beauty might be defined. Modern Chinese women, it was argued, should on the one hand lose the 'masculine' characteristics they had acquired during the Mao era, becoming both 'beautiful and well dressed' like Western women and once more expressing their natural 'female beauty' (*nüxing mei*). On the other hand, they should exhibit a 'soft and gentle' femininity seen as a specifically Chinese quality quite unlike the nature of Western women (2001: 107–108). For the young women we interviewed, however, the question remains urgent and immediate. Chinese and Western models, they insist, 'are very different' (Yang), and it is a specifically Chinese version of beauty that they wish to emulate. Yet in the acknowledgement that 'people want to change their image, and make themselves more beautiful' (Wang), voiced by the same group of students a few minutes later, it is the Western model of beauty to which they refer.

Some students did refer to the concept of a specifically 'Eastern' beauty. In these instances it is Japan that serves as the imagined ideal through which they seek to reconcile an aspiration towards a global 'modernity' identified with the West with the reaffirmation of a specifically Asian identity. The concept of Eastern or Chinese distinctiveness is one that is central to the advertising campaigns of Japanese producers. Beverley Hooper notes that Shiseido cosmetics are advertised as suiting the characteristics of 'Eastern' skins (1998: 187), and current adverts for Pola's Whitissimo range similarly claim to provide readers with a 'brilliant face like the white orchid' with products containing extracts of the Chinese herb Sophora. It is this assumed difference in physical characteristics that the students emphasize in defining a specific 'Eastern' quality. Chinese women, they argue, have a different body type (smaller breasts, shorter legs) and different skin, so they need different models, different styles of make-up and different fashions. Against the West's attempt to impose a 'universal standard' of beauty and fashion, they assert an Eastern difference that, through its identification with Japanese modernity, can at the same time incorporate what Louisa Schein calls an 'imagined cosmopolitanism'.[10] Many young Chinese women, said Pan, 'want to make themselves look like the Japanese girls because they think that they will be very popular.... So they don't eat much, they even go hungry'. Japanese models, then, embody the ideals of thinness, fair skin and modernity identified with Western models while preserving a specifically 'Eastern' identity.

(Post-)feminisms and loss

Let us return to our earlier question, then, of how, if at all, we might relate these images and responses to the post-feminism of contemporary Western popular culture – a post-feminism that the magazines themselves seem to gesture towards but not quite embrace. In her discussion of the images of Western fashion magazines, McRobbie writes of the rigidity of their photographic conventions. These are images that feel, she argues, 'pregnant with undirected and impossible desire, always just and no more caught within the frames of the pictures and somehow held at bay'. They 'visualize the disturbance which accrues from the interplay of desire with constraint', haunted by an 'unavowable loss' (2007a). It is a striking analysis, and although we do not want to follow McRobbie entirely here,[11] we do want to draw on aspects of her account. Reflecting on these Chinese magazines and some of their readers, it seems that the sense of loss here is just as palpable. In particular, then, we want to use McRobbie's idea that it is the 'something lost, that remains somehow out of reach or unspeakable' (*ibid.*), which the fashion image works both to contain and to compensate for, and that the 'something lost' is feminism.

Chinese feminism is a complex subject. According to Tani Barlow (1994: 255), the generic category 'woman' does not appear in Chinese until the 1920s. *Nüxing*, meaning 'woman' (as in man/woman, woman as subject, woman as agent, etc.) is a neologism that appeared in the aftermath of the revolutionary May Fourth Movement of 1919. It was replaced in the Mao era by *funü*, a state-generated term that described – or produced – 'woman' as a social or political category, like *gongren* (worker) or *qingnian* (youth). Thus the Chinese Communist Party-led 'women's liberation' of the Mao era has been much criticized for its erasure of sexual difference in the imposition of a notion of gender-equality that was in fact gender-sameness – what Dai Jinhua calls 'the liberated woman as defined by revolutionary (male) norms' (2002: 119). But *funü* has itself been replaced in post-Mao popular discourse with a return to *nüxing* – and this is the term that is used in the contemporary fashion magazine. What this means is that the notion of the 'strong' or 'liberated' woman is hopelessly compromised in contemporary Chinese discourse, and linked with notions of revolution, state control and a refusal of difference. *Nüxing* promises a return to a 'femininity' equated with modernity but construed as essentialized sexual difference. As such it is easily co-opted by a (Western-style) consumerism that identifies women, and women's 'empowerment', with consumption (Gill, 2007). That *'feminism'* can be translated by two terms, *nüquán zhǔyì*, ('theory/doctrine of women's power'), or *nüxing zhǔyì*, ('theory/doctrine of the female gender'), with the first now 'loaded with negative connotations' (Ko and Zheng, 2007: 7), and the second aligning itself with femininity, indicates just how problematic the Mao years have rendered any notions of a women's social or political identity or movement.

There is a loss here, then, that the students' constant sliding between a dream of the perfect appearance (and the commodified Western nature of that appearance) and a dream of autonomy and control gestures towards but cannot quite grasp. Chinese women, they recognize, are discriminated against as a group, but the individualized and individual-izing strategies that function to authorize them as subjects (as *nüxing* rather than *funü*) can offer neither an explanation nor a solution. Indeed, asked to look further forward, to how they see their future, the conflicts seem insuperable. This is Bao again:

Maybe after you get married you will, I will, you will have children yeah, you will have a family and your husband's family and my family. My family and my husband's family is 2 families and I think er his parents and my parents have to look after and to take care of them so I think this is so, many many things have to do with and then er, for me I think, when I was little I want to be a career woman but I think after I get married there is *so* many things [M: housework] and housework to do and then after I do these I have to do the, my job and now I think maybe the housework er can, my husband can do the half and I can do the half of it. This will be better but I think just now I think it's just a dream. You know in the culture he says the women to do the housework. You say 'I'm a feminist' but it's just [laughter] ∗∗∗ [trans: slogan] just a slogan. In real life you can't do this, just a slogan yeah.

For these young women, continuity with an older Chinese feminism (as *nüquán zhǔyì*) is impossible, because that lies behind the impassable barrier of 1976. But the new (imported, Western) feminism (*nüxing zhǔyì*) is not only 'just a dream', as Bao says, but also a dream hopelessly entangled with an individualism and consumerism that are both desired and mistrusted. The impossibility of even thinking of that older moment (and hence the present) as political is captured in this account by Ai, the most fashion conscious of the students, of her relationship with her mother:

> *Ai*: Because your skin, if your skin is very good and when your age is getting old but you don't look very old it will make you be happier. And I will send my mom some skin care things and sometimes she thinks that is unnecessary, but this time when I talk to her again and again now she cares about herself more. And I think it's very important for a woman....
>
> *Interviewer*: So she wasn't as interested in fashion as you then, when she was young?
>
> *Ai*: No. They have their fashion at that time, for example the trousers like this and when, in China at that time they will ∗∗∗ [trans: the Red Guard, you know, the Red Guard are young people] yeah they wear those very clothes and in that time they think that is fashion. Although everybody seems the same, but they think it's very fashionable.

From this young woman's post-socialist perspective, the dress of the Red Guard becomes simply 'fashion' – its political and historical meanings erased.

Conclusions

This is a very different history from that which produces the Western magazine images on which McRobbie comments. But we want to argue that there are important connections here. Cut off, co-opted or made-over, both feature a feminism that has been rendered inaccessible. The loss, it seems, is not so much that of an object of desire, as McRobbie in part suggests, as of a historical and political 'space', and of the subject position that might inhabit it. Indeed, to call it 'loss' is to risk obscuring the very active processes – of global capitalism, its media and cultural industries, its political cultures, and our own active complicities – that erase it. One conclusion we would draw from this research, then, is to re-emphasize the always uncomfortable and difficult tension that researchers in feminist cultural studies must, in the face of what McRobbie (2007b: 734) calls 'consumer global citizenship', somehow maintain between an insistence on historical and cultural specificity and a recognition of commonalities.

On the one hand, these magazines look the same as they do in the West, but they are not exactly the same – and both the social and symbolic histories into which they are inserted and the discursive repertoires within which they are received, though they intersect and converge at key points, are far from identical. On the other hand, the sense of loss and melancholia that McRobbie identifies, and associates with post-feminism, is a feature of both cultural spaces. For the young women we interviewed, a specifically Chinese feminism was inaccessible, while its Western counterpart was compromised by its entanglement with femininity and consumerism. So when Western feminists examine the images and narratives that constitute the cultural space of post-feminism, it is important that they do not see them as part of an internalized historical shift specific only to the West – evidence, perhaps, of a shift to 'late modernity' manifest in the reflexive individualism of a Western post-feminism. Worse still would be to see this shift as a kind of (Western, but hence 'universal') liberation. Rather, we need to hold in co-present tension the historical specificity of the political histories that are thus obscured and rendered inaccessible and the globalized nature of the economic and cultural processes through which, in the name of empowerment, this erasure is effected.

Acknowledgement

This chapter has previously been published in *Feminist Media Studies*, 10(2), 2010, and appears here with the permission of the publisher.

Notes

1. The students were interviewed by both of us, and spoke in a mixture of English and Chinese, with Feng translating where necessary. In the transcripts that follow, the students' English is occasionally modified in the interests of clarity. The students' names have been changed.

2. Of the students we interviewed, all who were not from single-child families came from rural areas.
3. A recent study notes that the school performance of girls in China is now better than that of boys, and that more girls than boys are awarded scholarships based on their academic performance. (Wen, 2005)
4. Edley and Wetherell define an interpretive repertoire as a 'recognizable routine of arguments, descriptions and evaluations distinguished by familiar clichés, common places, tropes and characterizations of actors and situations' (2001, p. 443). See also Hermes (1995).
5. Janice Winship's 1987 *Inside Women's Magazines* characterizes women's magazines as a combination of 'survival skills and daydreams' (1987: 1–15).
6. In the transcripts that follow, the students' English is occasionally modified in the interests of clarity, and their names have been changed.
7. In the transcripts, ∗∗∗ indicates speech in Chinese. Feng's translation – supplied during the conversation – follows in square brackets.
8. Barlow et al. (2005) describe the emergence in the 1920s of the international figure of the 'Modern Girl', whose 'cultivation of a svelte body and prescribed application of whitening creams or tanning lotions' emerged through 'the international strategies of corporations and the mass media as well as transnational ideologies of consumption, individualism and emancipation' (2005: 247).
9. According to *The Guardian* dated 6 August 2006, skincare products represent between 40 and 60 per cent of all healthcare products sold in China. Website accessed at http://www.mg.co.za/articlePage.aspx?articleid=279928&area=/insight/insight__international/.
10. She defines this as 'an imagining of mobility through the consumption of foreign objects and media and through the potential for global access implied by the "opening" policy.' (1994: 159)
11. For McRobbie, the losses are of, first, (following Judith Butler) the same-sex love object, and second, the feminism that would have made both possible and legitimate such object-desire.

References

Barlow, T. (1994) 'Theorizing Woman: *Funü, Guojia, Jiating* (Chinese Woman, Chinese State, Chinese Family)', in A. Zito and T. Barlow (eds), *Body, Subject & Power in China*, pp. 255–289, Chicago: University of Chicago Press.
Barlow, T.E. et al. (2005) 'The Modern Girl around the World: A Research Agenda and Preliminary Findings', *Gender & History* 17(2): 245–294.
Baudrillard, J. (1990) *Seduction*, trans. Brian Singer, Basingstoke: Macmillan.
Beck, U. and Beck-Gernsheim, E. (2001) *Individualization*, London: Sage.
Borton, J. (2004) 'Magazine Licensing Red Hot in China', *Asia Times Online*, 16 December, available at: http://www.atimes.com/atimes/China/FL16Ad01.html, accessed 5 August 2008.
China Daily (2003) 'Foreign Magazines Facing China's Newsstand Fever', *Business Week Magazine*, 5 November, [online] available at: http://www.chinadaily.com.cn/en/doc/2003-11/05/content_278774.htm.
Cronin, A. (2000) *Advertising and Consumer Citizenship*, London: Routledge.

Dai, J. (2002) 'Gender and Narration: Women in Contemporary Chinese Film', trans. Jonathan Noble, in J. Wang and T. Barlow (eds), *Cinema and Desire: Feminist Marxism and Cultural Politics in the Work of Dai Jinhua*, pp. 99–150, London: Verso.

Edwards, L. (2002) 'Narratives of Race and Nation in China: Women's Suffrage in the Early Twentieth Century', *Women's Studies International Forum*, 25(6): 619–630.

Fong, V. (2004) *Only Hope: Coming of Age under China's One-Child Policy*, Stanford: Stanford University Press.

Gill, R. (2007) *Gender and the Media*, Cambridge: Polity.

Hooper, B. (1998) ' "Flower Vase and Housewife": Women and Consumerism in Post-Mao China', in K. Sen and M. Stivens (eds), *Gender and Power in Affluent Asia*, pp. 167–193, London: Routledge.

Johansson, P. (2001) 'Selling the "Modern Woman": Consumer Culture and Chinese Gender Politics', in S. Munshi (ed.), *Images of the 'Modern Woman' in Asia*, pp. 94–122, Richmond: Curzon Press.

Ko, D. and Zheng, W. (2007) *Translating Feminisms in China*, Oxford: Blackwell.

Li, X. (1998) 'Fashioning the Body in Post-Mao China', in A. Brydon and S. Niessen (eds), *Consuming Fashion: Adorning the Transnational Body*, pp. 71–89, Oxford: Berg.

Mao, T. (1955) *The Socialist Upsurge in China's Countryside*, Chinese ed., Vols. I and II, from *Quotations from Mao Tse Tung*, online edition (2000), available at: http://www.marxists.org/reference/archive/mao/works/red-book/ch31.htm.

McRobbie, A. (2004) 'Post-Feminism and Popular Culture', *Feminist Media Studies*, 4(3): 255–264.

McRobbie, A. (2007a) 'Illegible Rage: Young Women's Post-feminist Disorders', available at: www.lse.ac.uk/collections/LSEPublicLecturesAndEvents/events/2007/20061204t1746z001.htm.

McRobbie, A. (2007b) 'TOP GIRLS? Young Women and the Post-Feminist Sexual Contract', *Cultural Studies*, 21(4): 718–737.

McRobbie, A. (2009) *The Aftermath of Feminism*, London: Sage.

Schein, L. (1994) 'The Consumption of Color and the Politics of White Skin in Post-Mao China', *Social Text*, 41: 141–164.

Skeggs, B. (1997) *Formations of Class and Gender*, London: Sage.

Winship, J. (1987) *Inside Women's Magazines*, London: Pandora

Winship, J. (2002) 'Consuming Women: Winning Women?', in S. Miles, K. Meetham and A. Anderson (eds), *The Changing Consumer: Markets and Meanings*, pp. 25–40, London: Routledge.

Part II

Competing Regime of Signifiers: Representation and Production

5
Women and Sexual Desire in the Japanese Popular Media

Alexandra Hambleton

There are many ways in which the Japanese mainstream media discuss, depict and wrestle with issues of female sexuality. This chapter focuses primarily on the case of women's magazine *anan* and TV programme *Yoru Bijo*, both of which purport to provide information about sex and pleasure to female consumers. In 1984, the Japanese women's magazine *anan* began the tradition of publishing a yearly 'sex special' and in 1989 grabbed headlines with the cover 'Become Beautiful through Sex' (*sekkusu de kirei ni naru*). Since then the magazine has continued to push the boundaries of social acceptability with a wide variety of erotic content and an ongoing sex survey of their readers that gauges changing concepts of sexual norms and perversions. Similarly, local TV production *Yoru Bijo* (Night Beauties), running from 2004 to 2007, dedicated weekly episodes to advising female viewers about pornographic videos, magazines and even love hotels that they may enjoy. Both *anan* and *Yoru Bijo* are examples of the rising number of magazines, TV programmes, books and other media about sex that are increasingly marketed to a female audience in Japan.

In the post-war period, women's social roles have undergone a rapid transformation. The image of the 'good wife and wise mother' (Sato, 2003) has been replaced by that of the career woman, who is working and playing for pleasure. This chapter addresses the significance of discussions of sex and sexual norms in media that are aimed specifically at a female audience. As women's bodies and sexual behaviour have traditionally been symbolic sites of nationalist traditions (Sinha, 2004), media purporting to cater to women's sexual desires and needs offer a fascinating window through which to examine the changing role of women in Japanese society, their shifting relationship with the media and the way in which their desires may be manipulated for the benefit of the nation. Exploring *anan* and *Yoru Bijo* as examples of mainstream media featuring information about sex and sexuality for women, this chapter will describe the changes that *anan*'s yearly sex special issue has undergone and how the magazine ultimately plays a prescriptive role in readers' lives. Similarly, *Yoru Bijo* reads as an advertorial programme, encouraging the consumption of various products as a way for female viewers to explore their sexuality. Both examples demonstrate that, according to the mainstream media at least, women in contemporary Japan are expected to find their identity not as independent sexual beings but as consumers, in order to maintain the status quo in contemporary consumer society.

Women as wives, mothers, workers, consumers and individuals

1976 to 1985 marked the UN Decade for Women – a period during which Japan was put under considerable pressure from the international community to provide better legal infrastructure to support women in their quest for social advancement and equality. In the wake of the introduction of the Equal Employment Opportunity Law (EEOL) on 1 June 1985, there was great hope that the door to equal participation in the workforce for women would open and great changes would take place. Instead, due to a number of factors, social and workplace roles remain strongly gendered. Today, women constitute 42 per cent of the workforce but comprise 67.9 per cent of part-time workers (Japan Institute for Worker's Evolution, 2003). Women are employed in less than 10 per cent of management positions, and less than 15 per cent of politicians are female. As Brinton (1994: 2–3) explains: 'the Japanese educational system and labour market have developed historically in ways that disadvantage women in economic terms', leading to 'a high level of gender differentiation and stratification in the economy'.

While in comparable economies women now make up more than 50 per cent of university graduates, the disparity between men and women in Japan begins early, with only 40 per cent of the total undergraduate student population in 2006 being female. This figure continues to fall, with women constituting less than 20 per cent of postgraduate students. More telling, however, is not what percentage of students overall is female, but how many choose to go to the country's top universities. The proportion of female students at the University of Tokyo and the University of Kyoto – Japan's most esteemed universities – is around 20 per cent and 24 per cent, respectively. As these universities often provide pathways to career positions within the government, the bureaucracy and prestigious companies in Japan, a lack of female graduates indicates a problem that is greater than educational inequalities. In the year 2010, the percentage of university graduates able to find a job immediately after graduating fell to 68.8 per cent, the lowest since comparable data became available in 1996. Despite hope in recent years that Japan's ageing population would mean education and employment conditions for women would improve out of necessity, due to ongoing economic concerns this situation has yet to arise.

The gap between men and women continues to widen as graduates enter the workforce. Fujimura-Fanselow (1995: 125) explains that despite the expansion of education and employment opportunities providing Japanese women with greater choices, 'that freedom of choice is greatly circumscribed by a variety of social structural as well as attitudinal constraints'. She goes on to outline such constraints: biases against women in the workplace, lack of childcare facilities and persisting norms and expectations of women's roles in both the home and society. Yu (2009) examines similar barriers, focusing her study on cultural factors, as well as inadequate childcare provisions for working women in Japan. In fact, while estimations vary, the Ministry for Health, Labour and Welfare reported in 2010 that there were more than 40,000 children on waiting lists for childcare places around the country. Additionally, Japanese corporations have created a two-tiered system in response to the 1985 EEOL law, in which full-time workers are divided into career track (*sōgōshoku*) and regular (*ippanshoku*) streams upon entering a company. The long hours, compulsory transfers to branches around the country and even overseas, and the general dedication required of career-track workers has created a situation in which many female workers, who hope to balance work and family, choose regular employment and the career track remains a predominantly male domain.

As can be understood from the studies above, women continue to face pressure in the fields of education and employment, as traditional attitudes about the place of women in society remain strong. However, despite such pressures, the gains women have made are substantial and increasingly women are choosing to put their energy into their work, rather than family. The divorce rate in Japan more than doubled between 1970 and 2000 as attitudes shifted, and even more significant has been the falling marriage rate. The effects of this shift can also be seen in Japan's now notably low birth rate of around 1.3 – well below replacement levels. While the average age of marriage in 1970 was 24.2 for women and 26.9 for men, by 2008 this had risen to 28.5 and 30.2, respectively. However, according to Retherford et al. (2001: 65), late marriage is responsible for only half of Japan's fertility decline since 1973. The remainder can be attributed to smaller families, and women and men choosing not to marry or have children at all. As a result, a new kind of discourse surrounding women has appeared in the media. While the kind wife and mother figure remains ubiquitous in TV dramas, advertising and magazines, the figure of the young, fashionable and, most importantly, financially independent woman has also found a place in the media landscape of Japan.

While women remain marginalized in higher education, the workforce, politics and other spheres of power, despite (or perhaps as a result of) their often marginalized roles in society, young women are frequently described as powerful consumers in Japan. In fact, it is young, unmarried women in their 20s – *anan*'s prime demographic – who often have the highest disposable income as they work full time but continue living with their parents. Kelsky (2001: 85) describes such women as commanding 'a high level of expendable income, derived from their secretarial "office lady" (OL) positions in Japan's corporations, combined with often company-mandated residence in their parents' home'. Although it is less common in recent years for companies to insist that workers remain living with their parents, for practical and financial reasons workers often do, contributing little to the family finances and spending a large proportion of their income on fashion, play and travel. It is these white-collar women that most women's magazines target, marketing a lifestyle and accompanying accessories to readers. Skov and Moeran (1995: 5) argue that women are seen as 'key figures in Japan's consumer culture' and are the country's greatest spenders. This phenomenon is further described by Kim as women 'allowed to be, or coerced into being the primary agents of cultural consumption' (2010: 29). In fact, Tanaka has even gone so far as to describe consumption patterns as enabling women to become the 'force behind major changes in society' (1998: 128). The concept of power through consumption, however, has its critics. By claiming that consumption is 'a form of self-reflection offered to Japanese women by those media targeted directly at them' (1995: 5), Skov and Moeran question the idea that consumption leads to greater social power and ask instead whether women actually compensate for their subordination and lack of participation in politics and industry by participating fully in consumer culture – the one sphere of public life to which they have full access.

It is often argued that Japan is a case that demonstrates that modernization does not necessarily take the same path as

Westernization, and that while the two are interrelated they do not always have to occur together. Despite similarities between Westernization and Japan's modernization in the fields of technological development and industrialization, social change has taken a very different route. Japan's modernity can be very much characterized by the boom in consumer culture (Clammer, 1995) as led primarily by female consumers. Visual and mass culture, as seen in the medium of magazines and TV in Japan, provide a window through which to examine the phenomenon of modernity in Japan and what it means in particular for the desires and lifestyles of Japanese women.

Even today, women in contemporary Japan are provided with very few avenues outside of consumption through which to explore their identities, make authentic life choices and experience individualization. As Kim (2010: 32) explains, 'Japanese women are among the world's best educated but most under-utilized'; a frustrating position in which to be. While many are striving to take on increasingly public roles in society, the 'either/or' culture of the Japanese employment system, in which one must choose life as a career worker or as a wife and mother, leaves little room for women to make choices, explore their authenticity or achieve fully individualized lives. The following sections explore how, despite seemingly open attitudes to sex in the mainstream media, enjoying one's own sexuality is not perceived as a freeing, self-actualizing experience but as a consumer product to be bought and sold within narrowly defined patterns of consumption.

Positioning *anan* in the women's magazine market – Sex, desire and consumption

anan is one of the highest-selling women's magazines in Japan, and it is available at news stands and bookstores around the country with a circulation of around 200,000 copies each fortnight. Launched in March 1970 as *anan ELLE JAPON*, the magazine was originally a sister publication of popular French fashion magazine *Elle*, and was marketed to a demographic of female readers in their late teens and twenties. The magazine currently publishes two issues a month and has shifted from being a publication primarily focused on fashion to more of a lifestyle publication for young women, featuring articles on everything from clothing and make-up to fortune-telling, travel, movies, manners and, of course, love and sex. Each issue focuses on a particular theme, such as fortune telling, popular desserts from around Japan, or the latest spring make-up trends. Since 1984, *anan* has released at least one 'sex special issue' each year. According to *anan*'s – editor-in-chief Kumai Masahiro, the sex special issue sells up to three times more than regular issues (AERA, May 2010) and is widely publicized and discussed in other mainstream media upon publication every year.

Information on sex, sexuality and the more euphemistically named 'sexual hygiene' (*sei no eisei*) for women has been around for centuries in Japan. As far back as the twelfth century Buddhist texts entitled 'A Companion to Solitude' (*Kankyo no Tomo*) linked enlightenment to women's pleasure (Pandey, 1995). In her examination of discourses of masturbation and women's sexual practices and the texts that describe and educate about them, Walthall (2009: 1) even goes so far as to suggest that 'talk about sex dominated popular culture in early modern Japan (1600–1868)'. However, it has been in the last century, in line with the development of the publishing industry and increased literacy rates, that most women, not just those from privileged backgrounds, have been able to access information about sex and sexuality through more mainstream means. As Sato (2003) and Frühstück (2003) explain, early women's magazines often provided sex information under the title of education for a population of women burdened with the responsibility of providing the next generation of citizens for the pre-war Japanese state. However, it was not until the post-war period, and more specifically the 1980s, that mainstream magazines featuring information about sex began doing so in a way that regularly mentioned desire and pleasure alongside typical topics such as filial duty, health and contraception. *anan* was a leader in this trend.

Since 1972 *anan* has been releasing occasional issues dedicated to love and sex, including issues with cover titles such as 'Erotic Feelings' (*erochikku na kibun*) in April 1984 and 'I Want to Know about Other People's Sex Lives!' (*hito no sekkusu ni tsuite shiritai*) in April 1989. However, it was the April 1989 issue 'Become Beautiful through Sex' (*sekkusu de kirei ni naru*) that created the biggest splash. The cover of the issue featured a cartoon woman, with neither a particularly Japanese nor Western face, wearing a very short pair of unzipped shorts, topless with one gloved hand covering her breasts and the other sitting suggestively on her hip. The subtitle reads 'Even more suggestive and bold, for all women, the sex special issue' (*sara ni kiwadoku daitan ni, subete no josei ni okuru, sekkusu daitokushū*). The issue featured almost 100 pages of advice on how to achieve a body worthy of being seen naked, as well as stories in which readers tell stories of how sex helped them lose weight and cure acne – complete with graphs and a doctor's analysis. There were also articles about contraception, sexually transmitted diseases, erotic short stories and feature interviews with celebrities discussing what kinds of sexual activity they most enjoy. Matching the content, on each page there was information about products, including prices and where they could be purchased, for readers to buy and use in their quest to adhere to the magazine's advice. The 'Become Beautiful through Sex' series continued until 2000, with each issue following a similar structure and pattern.

anan's special issues all view women's sexuality through a typically male gaze. Women are told to have sex to achieve beauty, not pleasure. They are told that it is white underwear, more than any other colour, that will arouse men, and they are instructed that to be desirable (to men) they must alter their own bodies through exercise and grooming, as well as learn about how best to satisfy male desires. The first issue even featured a double-page spread of interviews with men about the 'bad sex manners' they find unforgivable (*konna sekkusu manā yurusenai!*). More recent issues have become increasingly prescriptive, featuring surveys that examine just what is 'normal' and 'abnormal' sexual behaviour – clearly demarcated and presented in graph form for easy comprehension.

The tone of *anan*'s special issues shifted somewhat in the late 1990s with the focus falling less on beauty obtained through sex, and more on what men desire directly. Issues during this era included those entitled 'The Kind of Women Who Hold Men Captive' (*otoko o toriko ni suru onna to wa?*) in 1997 and 'I Want To Be the Kind of Woman Men Chase' (*'otoko ga oikaketakunaru onna' ni naritai*) in 2000. As the content became less directly centred on beauty and more focused on catching the attention of men by being attractive and sexy, the tone of the special issue began to focus increasingly on how readers could pleasure their boyfriends or partners, rather than find pleasure in sex themselves.

Closely examining 30 years of sex special issues, the most surprising discovery is that contrary to expectations, it is older issues that are more explicit and confrontational than more recent issues. Special issues of *anan* in the 1980s often employed graphic cartoons of women masturbating and couples in various sexual positions, as well as erotic photographs accompanying each article. On page 31 of 'Become Beautiful through Sex: Part 2' (April 1990), young female adult video stars pose topless, smiling happily for the camera. Page 105 features a large photograph of a grinning bondage mistress holding a whip as the accompanying article describes her product recommendations for readers interested in trying sadomasochistic practices at home. The issue even discusses homosexuality, telling readers that even their own boyfriend may have homosexual tendencies and giving them advice on what to do should such an issue arise. In contrast, more recent issues appear somewhat restrained in their content, with the articles about sexually transmitted diseases and contraception remaining, but less graphic content discussing potentially taboo topics such as sadomasochism and homosexuality.

The biggest shift, however, can be found in examining the subjects of the photographs featured in each year's special issue. In stark contrast to the artistic photographs of non-Japanese couples in various stages of undress featured in the first 10 years of the special issue, more recent issues have evolved to include erotic photographs of mainstream Japanese media personalities and celebrities, including soccer player Miura Kazuyoshi in 1995 and members of pop super group SMAP – Kimura Takuya in 1998 and Katori Shingo in 1999. The eroticization of men's bodies has become a central feature of the sex special issue, as the magazine strives to outdo itself year after year by featuring the hottest male celebrity of the year on the cover, and inside in erotic pictorial features. It could be speculated that due to the symbiotic nature of the Japanese entertainment industry, the magazine has had to reign in taboo content in order to receive permission to use such celebrities in its features, although it is difficult to establish such connections conclusively.

Since the first celebrity male nude picture-feature in 1991, apart from the appearances of actress Yonekura Ryōko in 2004 and actress/singer Tsuchiya Anna in 2008, all other special-issue main pictorials have featured male Japanese celebrities, photographed pin-up style. Ishiguro's 2009 work on female models in fashion magazines explains that in the 1990s, a paradigm shift occurred in the type of 'ideal body' depicted in women's magazines – from that of a Western face on a Western body, to a Japanese face on a Japanese body. In *anan*, however, the ideal body is that of the Japanese male – pictured alone in the 1990s and then increasingly with a Western female model in the 2000s. While in the 1980s Japanese women were depicted nude, or in sexual poses, in the 1990s and 2000s the role of sexual object has increasingly fallen on males, augmented with non-Japanese females in a variety of sexual, yet ultimately benign, poses. This shift has for the first time positioned men's bodies as a commodity; yet another product for women to consume, supposedly for their own pleasure. In recent years, each fortnightly issue of *anan* has featured a one-page nude photograph of an 'ordinary' (not celebrity) man, entitled 'male nudes' (*otoko no hadaka*). The page features the man's age, profession, height, weight, blood type and place of birth, along with a short interview with the participant. In *anan* men's bodies are now commoditized and consumed with passion, and female readers are encouraged to gaze upon the male body for their own pleasure. As Beggan and Allison (2009: 446) explain, 'Whereas traditional, male-oriented pornography treats women as objects and men as subjects, for-women pornography is intended to afford women the subject role as spectator and men the object role as target of female gaze.' In contrast, Coward (1984: 26) argues that 'Female desire is to some extent the lynch pin of a consumerist society...Everywhere female desire is sought, bought packaged and consumed.' She explains that in a 'sexually divided hierarchical society' pleasure is 'tied to positions of power and subordination' (1985: 106). Providing erotic pictorial features of famous men, *anan* invites women to feel empowered and modernized through the consumption of the male body; an act that ultimately requires them to once again participate in contemporary society in very much the way that they have been for the past century – as consumers. The mainstream media have positioned a women's issue through the lens of male sexuality and dominance, overlooking the agency and autonomy of women and instead positioning them solely as the primary consumers in contemporary Japanese consumer culture.

Yoru Bijo – New medium, same message?

Broadcast weekly from 2004 to 2007, the cable TV show *Yoru Bijo* (Night Beauties) contained similar subject matter to *anan*'s yearly sex specials. It also featured the in-depth examination of a viewer's letter each week, exploring problems as diverse as breast size, erectile dysfunction and marital affairs. In between studio-based talk sessions, the show also featured various weekly segments, including adult store staff recommending pornographic videos for female viewers, advertorials featuring love hotels, and an erotic photo session with an aspiring young female model posing in various stages of undress. Women's magazines have a long history of marketing lifestyles and desires to their consumers, with sex and sexual pleasure being a large part of such 'lifestyle choices'. On TV, however, it has always been more difficult to discuss sexuality because of stricter content regulations. *Yoru Bijo* circumvented standard taboos in two ways: first, by taking advantage of its local TV status, and second, by broadcasting only in a very late night timeslot. A producer of *Yoru Bijo* (who wished not to be identified) explained the motivation behind the programme:

Japan is currently confronting a period of great change when the meaning of love in the contexts of family, marriage and dating is being reassessed. As producers and creators we both aim to make people happy at this time, and we take our responsibilities seriously. Until not long ago Japanese society was extremely closed when it came to sex. However, in this era of increasing openness, I feel that there are many young people who are moving in the wrong direction. I hope that an attitude of healthy, enjoyable sex will take root in Japan.

The producer undoubtedly takes their job seriously, and put a great amount of thought into their explanation. However, despite the discourse of 'healthy, enjoyable sex', the programme clearly emphasizes the consumption of sex-related products and the female form throughout. When the concept of a healthy sex life is discussed, the focus falls on what products might be of use. Despite the producer's intentions, the programme is somewhat irrelevant to young people who may be just beginning to form their sexual identities.

Similar to later issues of *anan*, *Yoru Bijo* is once again clearly created with male pleasure in mind. The hosts of the programme dress in sexy attire, and studio discussions are centred on how to maintain a happy sex life with the satisfaction of the male partner central to the conversation. Similarly, the erotic photo session featuring a young, semi-nude model each week can also be read as appealing to a male audience. Both *Yoru Bijo* and *anan* are media products created by men with a supposed female audience in mind. However, examining both texts it can be observed that complicated messages about female sexuality and women's limited roles in contemporary consumer society abound.

Mainstream or raunch?

When I first saw *Yoru Bijo* on late night TV and noticed the special sex issue of *anan* on news stands, I briefly considered whether they could be examples of 'raunch culture' or 'fishnet feminism' (Charles Pearce, 1999). This is a form of so-called female empowerment in which it is claimed that increasingly prevalent expressions of female sexuality in the media and wider culture are an example of how successfully feminism has allowed women to free themselves from oppression and feel empowered to express themselves sexually. However, detractors warn that such sexual expression remains as a sign that women are still very much valued for their appearance and sexual attractiveness rather than the other ways in which they participate in and contribute to society (Levy, 2005; Dines, 2010), and that female sexuality is still presented in the media through the prism of masculine normative sexual expectations. I found myself wondering if *anan* and *Yoru Bijo* were just further examples of the explosion of raunch culture reaching into the Japanese market and competing with the 'good wife and wise mother' (*ryōsai kenbo*) ideology for a way in which to define and limit women's roles. However, this explanation fits uneasily in the Japanese context. If anything, the content of *anan* has become less, not more, explicit in recent years, despite a shift towards depicting Japanese male bodies for pleasure and consumption (as opposed to female bodies). Instead, the magazine has treated female sexuality very much as a product, one which can be marketed and sold in a capitalist marketplace. One of the most telling articles written about *anan*'s sex special issue, entitled 'Sex: From Hidden Existence to as Everyday as Makeup', commented that as women's magazines changed throughout the 1970s and 1980s, 'sex' became just another feature alongside staples such as fashion and make-up (*Mainichi Shimbun*, 2000). The article points to *anan* as being a sensation initially, but maintains that as the market became filled with similar content it ceased to shock. Instead, selling sexuality became mainstream.

Sato (2003: 37) describes the position of the 1920s 'modern girl' as she featured in magazines as a 'sex object', part of a social trend described as 'nothing more than consumer-oriented hedonism' in a time in which it went against social mores to behave in such a way. 'Modern girls' were criticized for their promiscuity, for enjoying their sexuality and for embodying values out of step with the state's preferred *ryōsai kenbo* ideology. In contemporary Japan, however, *anan* and *Yoru Bijo* embody not subversive values but those very much in step with state ideology – the encouragement of consumption. Clammer (1997) argues that magazines both sell and become commodities in themselves. In this case, both *anan* and *Yoru Bijo* sell the image of the 'contemporary modern girl' as one who is not only sexually available but who also has a 'useful' sexuality that is not to be feared by men or the state but rather celebrated as it opens up new markets for her as a consumer. Within the context of *anan* and *Yoru Bijo*, women's sexuality and pleasure become commodities, packaged so as to remain safe rather than subversive.

Within this context, magazines no longer play the role of products and actors of social change as they did in pre-war Japan (Frederick, 2006). Instead, they safely maintain social norms (Felski, 1995). Women remain the protectors of a new traditional culture in this way, maintaining the capitalist system through the ever-expanding consumption of new markets, including their own desires and sexuality. In describing the contemporary world of pornography, Akagawa (1996: 175) discusses an 'enormous market of sexual desire'. Media about sex for women in Japan can be seen as a continuation of this market, pitching consumerist desire through the lens of sex and sexual freedom. Skov and Moeran (1995) argue that women may be using their power as consumers as a substitute for real social power. The mainstream media position women to consume, and *anan*'s sex special issues are no different. Every aspect of sexuality is held up as an item for consumption, every problem has a solution that can be solved by the purchase of another product, and even the body becomes available to consume and enjoy. *Yoru Bijo* tells viewers that there is a wide collection of DVDs, love hotels, sexy lingerie and other sex-themed products on the market for them to purchase and use to aid them in mending or fulfilling their sexual desires. Pleasure is explicitly linked to consumption as sexuality is commoditized and the media prescribe to readers exactly what they must do to be good at sex, obtain a boyfriend and be successful, modern women.

Examining *anan* and *Yoru Bijo* one could be forgiven for thinking that Japanese women have come a long way from the 'good wife wise mother' discourse and have found a space to articulate and celebrate their own pleasure and desires. However, as Yano (2002: 150) explains, 'A woman is, by definition, one who is socially embedded as daughter, lover, wife, mother. She is always part of a larger human unit.' Sexuality operates similarly. Foucault has argued that the body is never free from valuation and power relations (1978), and that sexuality is consistently placed in a social context, laden with value judgements and expectations. The media do not operate outside these contexts, but rather play an ongoing role in perpetuating and strengthening ideas of womanhood and sexuality.

Conclusion

Charles Pearce (1999: 272) argues that the idea of 'gender' has been replaced with the construct of 'sexuality' on the online battleground of third-wave feminism. Examining *anan* and *Yoru Bijo*, the expectation is that women will view their sexuality through the male gaze and adapt their consumption patterns to match. In the case of the mainstream media at least, women's desires are created, constructed and manipulated for the benefit of the capitalist state. The mainstream media have to some degree hijacked women's sexuality, repackaged it and marketed it to female consumers. This sexuality can then be 'correctly' consumed within clearly demarcated 'safe' boundaries that do not threaten to subvert the status quo.

This chapter addresses only the media, overlooking readers and their place as agents within Japanese society. In a discourse analysis such as this, however, it must be acknowledged that readers will ultimately construct and create meaning in their own right (e.g. Morley, 1980; Radway, 1984; Ang, 1996). For those for whom the mainstream media holds little appeal, the Internet has provided an avenue through which to create and participate in new media that are sometimes vastly different to the mainstream. Similarly, the recent popularity of sexually explicit 'boys love' comics among adult women (Malone, 2009; Mori, 2010) demonstrates that a small, yet growing, group of women have found mainstream depictions of their sexuality and sexual desires lacking and are searching for alternatives. As Malone (2009) explains, 'Given the pervasive lack of such equality in real society, the immediate popularity of *shōnen ai*, or boys' love themes, reflected Japanese girls' rejection of their sexuality as a commodity in the patriarchal structure.' Ultimately it is this area that will be of most interest in future research – the arena in which Japanese women may be exploring their individualization most, as they consume and create media on their own terms.

References

'Is This Erotic? Are You Sexual? *anan* and the Famous Sex Issue (*kore w ero? anata wa ikeru? anan wa sekkusu kai no katsuma bon)'*, *AERA Magazine*, May 2010, Tokyo: Asahi Shimbun.

Akagawa, M. (1996) *Freedom of Sex/Freedom from Sex (sei e no jiū/sei kara no jiū)*, Tokyo: Seikyū Publishing.

Ang, I. (1996) *Livingroom Wars: Rethinking Media Audiences for a Postmodern World*, London: Routledge.

Beggan, J. K. and Allison, S. T. (2009) 'Viva *Viva*? Women's Meanings Associated with Male Nudity in a 1970s "For Women" Magazine', *Journal of Sex Research*, 46(5): 446–459.

Brinton, M. (1994) *Women and the Economic Miracle: Gender and Work in Postwar Japan*, Berkley: University of California Press.

Charles Pearce, K. (1999) 'Third Wave Feminism and Cybersexuality: The Cultural Backlash of the New Girl Order', in M. Carstarphen and S. Zavoina (eds), *Sexual Rhetoric*, Westport: Greenwood Press, 271–281.

Clammer, J. (1995) *Difference and Modernity*, London: Routledge.

Clammer, J. (1997) *Contemporary Urban Japan: A Sociology of Consumption*, Oxford: Blackwell.

Coward, R. (1984) *Female Desires: How They Are Sought, Bought and Packaged*, London: Paladin Books.

Coward, R. (1985) *Female Desire and Sexual Identity. Women, Feminist Identity, and Society in the 1980's*, Amsterdam/New York: John Benjamins Publishing Company.

Dines, G. (2010) *Pornland*, Boston: Beacon Press.

Felski, R. (1995) *The Gender of Modernity*, Cambridge: Harvard University Press.

Foucault, M. (1978) *The History of Sexuality Volume I*, New York: Random House.

Frederick, S. (2006) *Turning Pages: Reading and Writing Women's Magazines in Interwar Japan*, Honolulu: University of Hawaii Press.

Frühstück, S. (2003) *Colonizing Sex: Sexology and Social Control in Modern Japan*, Berkeley: University of California Press.

Fujimura-Fanselow, K. (1995) 'College Women Today: Options and Dilemmas', in K. Fujimura-Fanselow and A. Kameda (eds), *Japanese Women: New Feminist Perspectives on the Past, Present and Future*, New York: The Feminist Press 125–154.

Ishiguro, J. (2009) 'Westernized Body or Japanized Western Body: The Desirable Female Body in Contemporary Japanese Women's Magazines', in B. Turner and Y. Zheng (eds), *The Body in Asia*, Oxford: Berghahn Books 97–112.

Japan Institute for Worker's Evolution (2003) *The Situation of Working Women*, retrieved 01 December 2010, from http://www.jiwe.or.jp/english/situation/situation2003.html.

Kelsky, K. (2001) *Women on the Verge: Japanese Women, Western Dreams*, Durham: Duke University Press.

Kim, Y. (2010) 'Female Individualization?: Transnational Mobility and Media Consumption of Asian Women', *Media, Culture & Society*, 32(1): 25–43.

Levy, A. (2005) *Female Chauvinist Pigs: Women and the Rise of Raunch Culture*, New York: Free Press.

'The 20th Century as Depicted in Women's Magazines/1 Sex: From Hidden Existence to as Everyday as Makeup (joseishi ni egakareta 20seiki/1 sekkusu ura no sonzai kara okeshō to onaji nichijō e)', *Mainichi Shimbun*, 12 December 2000, Tokyo: Mainichi.

Malone, P. (2009) 'Home-Grown Shōjo Manga and the Rise of Boys' Love among Germany's Forty-Niners', *Intersections: Gender and Sexuality in Asia and the Pacific*, April 2009, retrieved 12 December 2010, from http://intersections.anu.edu.au/issue20_contents.htm.

Ministry of Health, Labor and Welfare Japan Official Website 1 October 2010, retrieved from http://www.mhlw.go.jp/stf/houdou/2r9852000001419l.html.

Mori, N. (2010) *Women Reading Pornography – Women's Sexual Desires and Feminism (onna wa poruno wo yomu – josei no seiyoku to feminizumu)*, Tokyo: Seikyū Publishing.

Morley, D. (1980) *The 'Nationwide' Audience: Structure and Decoding*, London: BFI.

Pandey, R. (1995) 'Women, Sexuality, and Enlightenment: Kankyo no Tomo', *Monumenta Nipponica*, 50(3): 325–356.

Radway, J. (1984) *Reading the Romance: Women, Patriarchy, and Popular Literature*, North Carolina: University of North Carolina Press.

Retherford, R., Ogawa, N. and Matsukura, R. (2001) 'Late Marriage and Less Marriage in Japan', *Population and Development Review*, 27(1): 65–102.

Sato, B. (2003) *The New Japanese Woman: Modernity, Media and Women in Interwar Japan*, Durham: Duke University Press.

Sinha, M. (2004) 'The Promiscuous State: The Contributions of Political History', *Journal of Colonialism and Colonial History*, 5(3).

Skov, L. and Moeran, B. (1995) *Women, Media and Consumption in Japan*, Surrey: Curzon Press.

Tanaka, K. (1998) 'Japanese Women's Magazines: The Language of Aspiration', in D. Martinez (ed.), *The Worlds of Japanese Popular Culture*, Cambridge: Cambridge University Press.

Tanaka, Y. (1995) *Contemporary Portraits of Japanese Women*, Westport: Praeger Paperback.

Walthall, A. (2009) 'Masturbation and Discourse on Female Sexual Practices in Early Modern Japan', *Gender and History*, 21(1): 1–18.

Yano, C. (2002) *Tears of Longing: Nostalgia and the Nation in Japanese Popular Song*, Cambridge: Harvard University Press.

Yu, W. (2009) *Gendered Trajectories: Women, Work and Social Change in Japan and Taiwan*, Stanford: Stanford University Press.

6

Move Freely: Single Women and Mobility in Taiwanese TV Advertising

Ping Shaw and Chin-yi Lin

Images of femininity in Taiwan have traditionally been limited to domestic settings that revolve around the roles of wives and home-makers. The social space for women to display their capacities or move freely was highly restricted. In a critical sense, space functions as a social construct by naturalizing the given, gendered power relations, which further means the exclusion of women from the public sphere. However, with the enhancement of female status that goes in line with economic development, Taiwanese women today seem to have gained greater mobility. Apparently, they have not only more space to travel in but also the ability to drive motor-powered vehicles. These changes have resulted in female liberation from restricted private domains and some degree of freedom to control their lives, as women can work outside, accumulate capital and become a growing force in socio-economic terms.

Technology, as a manifestation of power that has historically been used to control the environment, usually connotes a male-dominated order, and women have traditionally been considered incapable of engaging with state-of-the-art technologies. Technology can facilitate the mobility that is correlated with the implicit gender relations so engrained in Taiwanese patriarchal culture. Vehicles are exemplary in this regard, as they often functioned as indices of masculine power. The socially constructed assumption that women are technologically ignorant can be seen as a reproduction of traditional gender relations (Wajcman, 1996). Therefore, the challenging yet ambiguous manner in which Taiwanese women today are represented with respect to techno-logical devices – especially vehicles – in the media and cultural domain is the focus of exploration in this chapter.

Since Taiwan started its modernization in the 1960s, the growth of consumerism has promoted the purchase and use of industrial and tech-nological products by the general public. One can sense how vehicles have become popularized in Taiwan simply by examining the ever-growing ownership rates of cars and motorcycles, which have almost become household items for most Taiwanese today. Taiwan's indus-trialization has helped promote the participation of female labour; Taiwanese women – most conspicuously, young women – have grad-ually entered into the wage-earning workforce. According to Taiwan's Council of Labour Affairs, the percentage of women in the workforce has increased from 39.1 per cent in 1978 to 49.6 per cent in 2009 (Taiwan Council of Labour Affairs, 2010). Taiwanese women appear to break away from their traditional roles as mothers and caregivers. With the mass promotion of education and the more professional division of labour, educated and skilled women are increasingly participating in the labour market and seek to assert their socio-economic capacities (Cheng, 1999). Taiwan's younger generation, especially young females, have increasing purchasing power (Gao, 2008), and they are catching up with their male counterparts and receiving more attention from advertisers (ZenithOptimedia, 2008).

On the contrary, as Taiwan's economy evolves and female labour par-ticipation rises, the nation's birth rate continues to decrease, and the average age of marriage and the divorce rate increase constantly. The phenomenon of late marriage has been viewed as a burgeoning 'social problem' that needs to be addressed in the public sphere (Wang, 2005), as young women increasingly delay marriage to pursue work and eco-nomic power. More than 30 per cent of Taiwanese women aged 30–40 are unmarried, with 25 per cent of women aged between 35 and 40 remaining single. This significant rate is second only to France (Lang, 2010).

The increasing number of unmarried single women is developing into a stand-alone segment in terms of purchasing power. Many adver-tising agencies are aware of the growth potential and consumption capacities of these economically powerful single women, and so tact-fully adjust their strategies to model appropriate consumer images (ZenithOptimedia, 2008). TV advertisements are social discourses that attempt to respond to these changes in women's lives (Leiss et al., 1990; O'Barr, 1994). As women increasingly participate in the workforce and

late marriages become more prevalent in contemporary Taiwan, economically viable and seemingly individualized single women represent
an emerging social trend that draws public attention and academic
research. Newly emerging and individualism-oriented images of single
women are being constructed on Taiwanese TV advertising, and these
changing images of femininity appear to break away from traditional
gender stereotypes by evoking individuality and consumerism.

Individualization is one of the main concerns to which many contemporary social theorists have paid attention (Giddens, 1991; Beck, 1992;
Bauman, 2001; Beck and Beck-Gernsheim, 2002). Increasing globalization has made the flow of desire more possible and contributed to the
formation of a stronger self-identity, while local restrictions and family
bonds seem not as overwhelming as they used to be. Through the experience of increased freedom, female individualization has emerged as
one of the major trends worth noticing in the West and globalizing
urban Asia. This individualization process demonstrates an increasing
reflexivity, self-surveillance, self-monitoring and awareness of female life
trajectories (Kim, 2010). With the newly gained access to female role
models, which are sometimes based on the Western media and lifestyle
of individualization, single women in urban Asia can acquire a sense of
imagined freedom by reflexively identifying with the modern consumer
culture and alternative lifestyle depicted by the media.

The media, with the power deeply rooted in what people take for
granted in their cultural community, should be explored in detail to
understand the dialectical construction of cultural identities. It is a crucial arena, where emerging signs of female individualization wrestle and
negotiate with the local customs and social norms. With its innovative
character and interlocking relationship with capitalism, the media can
create a virtual world where alternative social, cultural and symbolic
relations can be established by Asian women and a new kind of self and
lifestyle can be defined in everyday life (Kim, 2010).

This chapter thus attempts to understand how mediated self-identity
in the media can possibly influence the way that single women in
Taiwan see themselves in contrast to their traditional roles, and in
particular how TV advertising articulates and responds to women's
growing desires for mobility, freedom and self-expression. Based on
semiotic analysis, this study explores how single women are variously
represented in relation to vehicles, such as cars and motorcycles, on
Taiwanese TV advertising, and also how technology and gender are
being constructed socially and discursively. Media images and readings may involve the 'given' gendered assumptions based on a shared

Table 6.1 TV advertisement samples

Broadcasting year	Vehicle	Brand	Advertisement theme
2007	Motorcycle	KYMCO	Pretty cherry (Cherry)
2008	Motorcycle	Yamaha	CUXI Royal Academy
2009	Motorcycle	KYMCO	Tokyo Fashion Adviser (Many)
2009	Motorcycle	Yamaha	My Smart Style (Ciao)
2010	Motorcycle	Yamaha	CUXI Kingdom
2007	Car	Mitsubishi	Returning Home
2009	Car	Volvo	Be Real Me (S40)
2010	Car	Yulon	Cartoon Life (M'car)
2010	Car	Volvo	Reunion (S80)
2010	Car	Cathy	Independence

local culture; thus, critical attention can be given to the exploration of existing power structures and social ideologies as part of the process of constructing meaning. The analysis in this chapter draws on the sampling of 10 TV advertisements, dating from 2007 to 2010, where single women were represented with vehicles. Five advertisements used cars, with the remainder featuring motorcycles, as listed below for analysis (see Table 6.1).

Mobile experience as single female individuality

In the past, vehicles in Taiwan were commonly used to display masculinity, largely because only men were in paid employment and able to afford these technological devices. Cars were relatively rare and expensive, which often made them status symbols. Men used vehicles to demonstrate their mobility and to express their socio-economic status and distinction. However, as vehicles have become more available to women, the meanings they convey have diversified. Beyond social status, the associations between masculinity and mobility have become subtle and complex. In an attempt to cater for modern women, whose growing labour participation engenders economic capacities, new images have been developed by the advertising industry. From the sampled advertisements above, it is apparent that single women are the main focus rather than mere decoration – appearing as leaders in campus life (as in *CUXI Royal Academy*), fashion models (*Tokyo Fashion Adviser* and *CUXI Kingdom*), travellers (*Be Real Me*), princesses (*Cartoon Life*), and white-collar professionals (*Returning Home*). Single women are represented as decision-makers with full autonomy and competence, modelled as successful icons and willing to purchase expensive items to experience individuality, mobility and freedom.

For example, for the KYMCO Many – a petite scooter with bright colours and trendy designs – the advertisement emphasizes that the headlights sparkle like diamonds and the cushion is patterned like luxury bags. The single female character appears as a stunning fashion model who quickly attracts the attention of photographers. With her high heels, designer dresses, fancy earrings and bags, she is the epitome of beauty, confidence and dominance – and a celebrated socialite whom even men have to look up to. The advertisement ends with a sign of female success, as she takes the lead in a convoy of male and female riders.

The M'car advertisement features a dreamy young girl expressing the freedom she experiences in her small 'cute' car animated as a cartoon character. With its white base colour and black pattern, the car looks like a cute panda, but the car in effect shields the driver from the harsh realities of life. It represents a colourful and cartoon-like fairytale that is characteristic of the imagination of younger people, whose imagined freedom away from social responsibilities allows them to live temporarily in an enchanted world marked by individualistic identity. It can be said that the car is portrayed as the pleasure principle on wheels by which women can seek pleasure and avoid pain (Hark, 1997).

Wang (1993) found that in the past, most advertisements in America and Taiwan depicted women in stereotypical gender roles. For instance, young women were seldom shown in the workplace, and voice-overs were mostly read by men as they were considered to be more authoritative and persuasive. When travelling by car, women were expected to sit dutifully in the front passenger seat next to their husbands. Being a good wife and mother was the socially constructed calling for women (Chen and Shaw, 2008). However, with their growing economic status, women begin to demand new role models other than just mothers, homemakers and caregivers.

In these advertisement samples, almost all of the female characters are shown as free and confident while driving or riding – literally, taking the helm. For example, the single female driver in the Volvo S40 advertisement is depicted as free while driving, with her long hair trailing in the wind. She even sings and glances in the rear mirror at the reflection of the male scooter riders who look small and rather ridiculous. These males left behind signify female success and independence. She then parks her luxury car in the countryside, removes her high heels and walks on the grass under a bright blue sky. The female voice-over says, 'I want it. I feel free.' In her own space, she can have control and choose her own destination. The luxury car is expressive of female autonomy and empowerment.

The Cathy advertisement employs similar visual cues. A plainly dressed single woman keeps asking while shopping, 'Can I just buy one?', but the whole business culture appears unfriendly and unresponsive to single women. Thus, she turns to her car to drive away and enjoy her freedom at a riverbank, watching the sunset alone and eating an apple. The car represents an instrument through which single women can escape temporarily from the established heterosexual hegemony of marriage. The mobile experience is a marker of single female individuality. Technology is a medium of power that users can display externally (Lin, 2004). Representations of the modern 'new woman' in Taiwan, with their rising economic status, demonstrate newly gained power and freedom through the operation of technological devices.

Mobile home

On the other hand, it is also clear that some vehicles, especially cars, are implicitly portrayed as metaphorical homes where family members can meet and share emotional intimacy. The narrative in the Mitsubishi advertisement, for example, is conveyed in this familial and nostalgic fashion. A female child is shown growing up in the country, where her father always takes her home safely on the back seat of his bicycle. It then shows her as a white-collar professional woman working in a city and she now has a car of her own. When she whizzes through the familiar neighbourhood in her silver and adamant car, the implicit message is that the vehicle is a substitute for the reliable and protective father. Yet this is framed in a subtle way to suggest the continuity of tradition and family insofar as a little girl should always be protected by her family (more specifically, by her father). The car is then an extension of the traditional family structure in modern life. The car is a symbol with both metaphorical and functional meanings (Wernick, 1991). When a car is designed to be used by a 'complete' family, it transforms into a so-called mobile family, and the assumed pattern behind the design is of a nuclear family. This is shown by how the seats are arranged in the car, with the father taking the wheel, the mother next to him and their children in the back seat. However, while stereotyped as 'complete', the traditional nuclear family has undergone a dramatic transformation in contemporary Taiwan.

Such variations in family patterns are already occurring, as manifested in the Volvo S80 advertisement, for example. Three females (one single mother and two grown-up daughters) are shown in this spacious luxury car. The middle-aged single mother is driving the car. They share girls' talk just as they do at home, effectively recreating their home inside the enclosed space of the car. The black car looks classy and sophisticated, while the bright and clean interior creates a feeling of warmth and comfortable family life. As one of the daughters (the storyteller) enters the car, she stretches in a clear display of relaxation. The voice-over says: 'Although the time we live separately is much more than our time together, I cherish every second of being together.' The younger daughter in the back seat feels so safe that she soon falls asleep, while the advertisement encourages the viewers to believe that the family is well protected by the car's ACC+CWAB technology (an auto-braking system). The female voice-over says: 'There are too many beautiful things in life more important than Volvo. That's why we choose Volvo S80.' Powerfully creating the 'mobile home' metaphor, the advertisement suggests that the family is secured by the car as it offers necessary shelter and emotional intimacy.

But what is particularly notable in this advertisement is that the driver is a middle-aged single mother; such representation is far different from traditional car advertisements in Taiwan. Middle-aged single mothers were rarely shown behind the wheel on TV advertising in the past. They were extremely under-represented, if not non-existent. Volvos are generally considered to be luxury cars that only successful and white-collar male professionals can possibly afford. It is extremely rare for a middle-aged single mother to be represented as being successful and driving the 'mobile home' of the luxury car. The father-absent 'incomplete' family highlighted in this advertisement is uniquely atypical.

These differences in representation reflect and also articulate the social changes that are happening in Taiwanese society. Advertising agencies are aware of these changes and adjust their strategies accordingly, such as depicting the family unit without a father at centre stage. Single women are shown as autonomous and able to control their own life course, which is a notable breakthrough in terms of pluralistic representations. Single women without male company can still display confidence and capabilities by driving technological devices. Yet, if one takes a closer look at the way in which the family is represented, it is possible to find that the absent father is actually substituted by the car itself. In the Mitsubishi advertisement, the car takes the single young female home safely. In the Volvo S80 advertisement, the car protects the single females from harm with the latest technology. Hence, one can still get the connotation that a family without a father (thus unprotected) is seen as defective because it is not safe; but it should be, and can be, made complete and safe by the car, as the advertisements signal.

Feminization of vehicles

Vehicles may appear as neutral technologies, yet they are in reality highly gendered and carry specific connotations. As Wajcman (1996) suggested, the very definition of technology has a male bias and the association of technology with masculinity is the result of social construction. Technological devices can be viewed as signs that have a great impact on gender identity, as control over vehicles often displays masculinity. However, from the advertisement samples above, one can notice some interesting changes in female representations with vehicles. Instead of masculinity, feminine characteristics are stressed and promoted as new marketing strategies targeted at female consumers. In these advertisements, young women are implicitly associated with fashion, art and aesthetics, and vehicles themselves are even feminized in response to a growing sense of female identity.

In the Many advertisement, both the female and the scooter are referred to as a fashion model adorned with fancy designs and vibrant colours. Similarly, in the CUXI advertisement the female character and the scooters are shown as visually pleasing fashion models that appear on the catwalk. In these advertisements, single females are still portrayed as eye-catching sex objects for the male gaze. In the Volvo S40 advertisement, the monologue reads like a poem expressing the inner emotions of a single woman. When the car is parked, the driver takes off her high heels and enjoys coffee with the door half-open. She conveys a mixture of art, style and independence – a kind of individualist aesthetic lifestyle.

In the M'car advertisement, the cartoon-like settings are transgressing and transformative. The opening sequence shows a conveyor belt on which a female baby grows into a girl, and then a woman, who then grows sick and old and is 'dumped' at the end of the belt. However, a cartoon character that represents the female model jumps off the belt. While falling, she plays the guitar. Fantastic adventures begin as soon as she reaches the ground, driving in the M'car. Her voice-over says, 'Mother said life is about trivial chores. I say life is like a lollipop.' This single female demonstrates a small act of resistance; instead of playing expected normative female roles, she would rather jump off the given track (conveyor belt) and choose a cartoon-like life of her own. The collage of pictures is imbued with rich colours and a playful sense of imagination, where pop art and pleasurable fantasies are created. Pleasure and fantasy are important notions in understanding how ordinary women identify with, and closely relate to, popular media texts (Modleski, 1982; Blackman and Walkerdine, 1996; Walkerdine, 1997). As Modleski (1982) argued, these are not simply escapist fantasies designed to pacify women, but fictions that engage with 'real problems' in women's constrained lives in complex and sometimes contradictory ways. They characteristically offer temporary or symbolic solutions. In this advertisement, the cartoon-like life that the single female desires can be realized through the M'car. By means of the pleasure derived from her fantasies, she can symbolically create her self-identity in relation to the car and resist the hegemonic pressure from normative female roles. The young female and the car demonstrate transformative, mobile and playful femininity.

Traditionally, the advertising of cars and motorcycles was mostly targeted at males, and thus the stressed features were speed, power and social status. In the CUXI kingdom advertisement, some differences are discernible between male and female riders. The man is shown wearing a leather jacket, looking cool/emotionless and riding a black CUXI with a necktie pattern, whereas his female counterpart is portrayed as trendy/cute and is riding a red CUXI in a voguish pair of high-heel boots. Female riders are associated with fashion, aesthetics, amiability or some emotional appeal, which implies that men still use vehicles as a way to display power but women use them for emotional intimacy and desirability.

Vehicles and thus mobility today are becoming feminized in their symbolic representations. In the Ciao advertisement, for example, the scooter is no longer represented as cold and masculine, but personalized as a cute pet dog; when touched, it even whines for care and attention. There is an increasing tendency to associate vehicles with feminine features – a phenomenon worth noting because a seemingly new construction of identity between females and technological devices is taking place here. By using and identifying with these allegedly feminized, cute and attractive vehicles, single female consumers may acquire a mediated self-identity, while being as adorable and desirable as these scooters is a sign of female freedom and individuality. These 'given' feminine qualities are re-featured and promoted as desirable values that are objectified in the scooters and can be obtained simply by consumption.

With many conventional feminine elements being included in these current advertisements, an ambiguous image of the modern 'new woman' is taking form because of growing female purchasing power. Construction of the 'new woman' is a process of ongoing negotiations that involve both modern and traditional values, responding not only to current social changes but also to common cultural values. The advertisers brandish conventionally feminine characteristics, yet at the same time, the freshly minted 'new woman' image must also look powerful and independent. In a sense, both femininity and feminism, without their stable meanings, are appropriated and displayed by TV advertising as new discourses of female representation in contemporary Taiwan.

Conclusion

Technology is the embodiment of a culture or set of social relations, which often has a male bias; the identification between technology and masculinity is the result of the historical and cultural construction of gender (Wajcman, 1996). However, with rising female labour participation in Taiwan and the socio-economic status it appears to promote, new images of femininity (using vehicles) have been created via Taiwanese TV advertising. In a capitalistic social context, popular media construct an identity of the modern 'new woman' to resonate with middle-class single women with great purchasing power (Yang, 2004). Single women are represented with more autonomy and mobility in various ways, yet these new images are intentionally geared towards individualistic consumption. The purpose of modern advertising is to create consumers and promote capitalist consumption as a new lifestyle (Kellner, 1995). Advertising constructs a notion that consumption can resolve problems and bring happiness, while women are encouraged to create their self-identity and confidence through the possession of commodities. The method to 'be real me' (an inner voice heard in the Volvo S40 advertisement) is narrowed down to consumption. These newly emerging images somehow feature feminist qualities, such as a female model that is no longer the second sex but sexually equal and able to travel independently (Yang, 2004), but at the same time these images are also closely associated with beauty, fashion, art and feminine sensibility.

In the Many advertisement, the female character asks, 'What is charm?' Then, she confidently narrates, 'You have to be sparkling like diamonds. You have to be the centre of attention. You have to change like cosmetics. Charm is about having an unrestricted heart.' She expresses what characteristics a charming and powerful female should possess. Freedom and individuality are placed at the heart of the idea of the 'new woman', but the newly promoted femininity must also be charming and fashionable. All of these qualities are materialized and articulated in the scooter advertisement. Deeply rooted gender ideologies are still insinuated in these 'new' images. Women are shown as eye-catching fashion models whose main function is to draw men's attention and to entertain. Beauty is still the most valued asset that a single female should manage to have.

Women are still considered to be less competent in complex technologies; nearly all the female-tailored scooters stress their one-touch design and ease of use, while functional features such as speed, power and mechanics are never emphasized but fashion/design is prioritized. It is assumed that women do not have a mechanical aptitude, so the 'looks' of technological devices are what matter to them. The cultural assumption that men dominate technologies reproduces the established power relations, reinforcing the stereotype of women as (technologically) inferior and incapable. As Hall (2003) noted, media text is an arena where social, political and ideological forces struggle for hegemony in the process of to-and-fro negotiations. Advertising is an arena where many new and old values are competing for dominant representations. Even though advertising is infused with new ideas, old values remain a significant force to be reckoned with. Traditional values such as home and family still have a great impact on the newly created cultural regime of female individuality, mobility and freedom.

TV plays an important role in telling people what society is like and how gender roles are supposed to be, while transforming traditional ideologies into modern individualism and consumerism (Lipsitz, 1986). The growing desire to be a free and independent woman in contemporary Taiwan is channelled into individualistic consumption. The equating of female rights with discretionary spending power and consumption is an all-too-convenient and misleading solution to the ongoing problems of gendered structural suppression. Indeed, any calls for structural reforms aimed at the socio-political levels can be drowned out by the myth of consumerist individualism in which the 'new woman' is the focus of the cultural realm.

References

Bauman, Z. (2001) *The Individualized Society*, Cambridge: Polity.
Beck, U. (1992) *Risk Society: Towards a New Modernity*, London: Sage.
Beck, U. and Beck-Gernsheim, E. (2002) *Individualization*, London: Sage.

Blackman, L. and Walkerdine, V. (1996) *Mass Hysteria: Critical Psychology and Media Studies*, London: Palgrave.

Chen, C. and Shaw, P. (2008) 'Happy Family Car: Ideal Family Represented in Car Advertisements', *Mass Communication Research*, 96: 45–86 (in Chinese).

Cheng, B. (1999) 'Cointergration and Causality between Fertility and Female Labor Participation in Taiwan: A Multivariate Approach', *Atlantic Economic Journal*, 27(4): 422–434.

Gao, S. (1 June 2008) 'Investigation: Consumption Power of Taiwanese Young Females Cannot Be Ignored', *The Central News Agency* (in Chinese).

Giddens, A. (1991) *Modernity and Self-identity: Self and Society in the Late Modern Age*, Cambridge: Polity.

Hall, S. (2003) 'The Spectacle of the Other', in S. Hall (ed.), *Representation: Cultural Representations and Signifying Practices*, London: Sage.

Hark, I. (1997) 'Fear of Flying', in S. Cohan and I. Hark (eds), *The Road Movie Book*, London: Routledge.

Kellner, D. (1995) 'Advertising and Consumer Culture', in J. Downing, A. Mohammadi and A. Serberny-Mohammadi (eds), *Questioning the Media*, Thousand Oaks: Sage.

Kim, Y. (2010) 'Female Individualization?: Transnational Mobility and Media Consumption of Asian Women', *Media, Culture & Society*, 32(1): 25–43.

Lang, P. (2010) 'Don't Have Kids. Don't Get Married. So What?', *Common Wealth*, 440: 112–114 (in Chinese).

Leiss, W., Kline, S. and Jhally, S. (1990) *Social Communication in Advertising: Persons, Products and Images of Well-being* (2nd ed.), Ontario: Nelson Canada.

Lin, C. (2004) 'Secret to the Power of Technology', in C. Wu, D. Fu and S. Lei (eds), *Taiwan STS Reader*, Taipei: Chung-Shuei Publishing (in Chinese).

Lipsitz, G. (1986) 'The Meaning of Memory: Family, Class, and Ethnicity in Early Network Television Programs', *Cultural Anthropology*, 1(4): 355–387.

Louie, K. (2002) 'Wen-wu Reconstructed: Chinese Masculinity Hybridized and Globalized', in K. Louie (ed.), *Theorising Chinese Masculinity: Society and Gender in China* (pp. 160–166), Cambridge: Cambridge University Press.

Modleski, T. (1982) *Loving with a Vengeance: Mass Produced Fantasies from Women*, New York: Routledge.

O'Barr, W. (1994) *Culture and the Ad: Exploring Otherness in the World of Ad*, Boulder: Westview Press.

Taiwan Council of Labour Affairs (2010) *Taiwan Female Labour Participation Survey* (in Chinese).

Wajcman, J. (1996) *Feminism Confronts Technology*, Philadelphia: Pennsylvania State University Press.

Walkerdine, V. (1997) *Daddy's Girl: Young Girls and Popular Culture*, London: Macmillan.

Wang, H. (2005) 'Happy to Be DINKs or Single?', *The Money Magazine*, 221: 112–125 (in Chinese).

Wang, L. (1993) *Sex Role Portrayals in Advertising: A Comparison of Television Advertisements in Taiwan and the United States*, Master's thesis, National Chiao Tung University, Taiwan, retrieved from http://ndltd.ncl.edu.tw/cgi-bin/gs32/gsweb.cgi/ccd=ndr7nX/record?r1=1&h1=1 (in Chinese).

Wernick, A. (1991) *Promotional Culture: Advertising, Ideology and Symbolic Expression*, London: Sage.

Yang, F. (2004) 'Beautiful and Bad Woman: Media Feminism and the Politics of Its Construction', in W. Hsie (ed.), *The Dialectics of Gender and Power in Knowledge Formation* (pp. 455–486), Taipei: Tang-Shang Publishing (in Chinese).

ZenithOptimedia (2008, December) *Female Power Rules – A Female Consuming Force That Can't Be Ignored*, retrieved on 6 May 2011 from: http://www.zed.com.tw/mediabulletin/20081201/moreinfo/female%20power.pdf (in Chinese).

7
Producing Individualized Voicings for a Global Labour Force: Digitizing Agency through Social Media

Radhika Gajjala

> Conduct an Internet search on microenterprise using Google and a vast array of smiling brown-skinned women poised above their work, with children in the background, greet your eye.
>
> (Nadesan, 2010: 9)

It has been widely noted, whether as a critique or in celebration, that current forms of economic globalization require labour forces that are individualized. Often, these are individual workers uprooted culturally, materially and socially (and oftentimes even physically) from within local economies made non-functional through the direct and indirect effects of globalization. My continuing work examines how the process of individualization functions through practices in online work and play environments. In this chapter, I will focus on looking at socio-financial networks. Examples of what I refer to as socio-financial networks include, but are not limited to, *kiva.org, lendwithcare.org, novica.com, etsy.com* and *eBay*, where an online platform enables e-commerce through microtransactional abilities allowed by programs such as Paypal. These networks encourage community formation, dialogue and networking in varying degrees along with the ability for the user to sell and buy, or lend and get loans.

Each such network has different rules of engagement, and prospective sellers are screened with the use of various kinds of criteria that involve both online and offline processes. In the case of some, the offline screening for sellers is more rigid than in others. So, for instance, while *novica.com* has a rigorous process of examining the prospective seller's product in order to approve them for sale on the *novica* platform, *etsy.com* has seemingly less institutional involvement with examining the actual offline product. Policing the quality of products and the conduct of individual sellers is thus done with varying degrees of online and offline interaction between the owners/producers/managers of the portal and the users of the portal. The gatekeeping and screening processes are not easily understood unless one actually uses the online interface and also interacts offline with and through multiple online and other channels in conversation with sellers and buyers. Much of my understanding of how these differences play out is drawn from several years of ethnographic journeying to offline contexts of craft production and marketing both in rural and urban south India and elsewhere in the world. In addition, my ongoing methodology for understanding these practices involves cyber-ethnographies and 'epistemologies of doing' (Rybas and Gajjala, 2007).

The language employed in the description of these portals that enable such networks carries claims of 'empowerment'. But there is a variation in how the network is considered empowering and in the kind of individual action possible or permitted at the online/offline interface in each of these contexts. These differences occur, no doubt, partly because the basic design of online software and Web 2.0 interactivity is tested and built with very particular, situated user populations in mind. Further, the ease or difficulty of engaging in microtransactions themselves is easy or difficult based on the offline context of access to these technologies. Offline international, national and cross-cultural business and social communicative translations, banking policies, foreign exchange and trade regulations, as well as shifts in everyday practices of users that need to take place to set the stage for the possibility of individual online presence, all play a role in how access and digital divides are reconfigured within these apparently interactive Web 2.0 contexts. Thus, in the case of the third-world subaltern (rural) 'other', there are more steps and gatekeeping issues both culturally and technically, in addition to material access issues. In the case of the western-educated and comparatively materially well-off self (whether located geographically in Western and European nations or in developing world contexts), wireless technology adoption is comparatively more seamless in the context of their everyday lives. These kinds of implicit and explicit embedded hierarchies of literacy and access shape the user base for each of these socio-financial networks. Thus, for instance, networks such as *etsy.com* are accessible to a particular set of craft producer who wishes to reach a consumer market (generationally, geographically, culturally and so on), while shopping portals such as *novica.com* work with another set of craft producers who use the platform to reach global and international consumers. What is common to both, however, is that there is a socio-financial online network set up through an online platform that allows the use of micro-transactional tools for buying and selling while profiling buyers and sellers in ways that link them as a community. While *etsy.com* is mostly viewed as a leader in a now widely prevalent online and offline DIY (do-it-yourself) culture, *novica.com* is a portal set up by *National Geographic* with the aim of connecting crafts producers (mostly) from previously colonized locations to first-world collectors and art lovers. This latter logic of colonial gaze is extended in global microfinance networks set up through portals from first-world locations such as the US and the UK (e.g., *kiva.org*, *microplace.com* and *lendwithcare.org*), and the message of philanthropy is explicit.

There is also a difference in how users are profiled as 'agents' in each of these networks. To a large extent, these differences are manifested mostly because of the different degrees of access that particular kinds of users of these platforms have to the technologies and related social, cultural and technical literacy needed for the production of self online. Some of these social networks and microtransactional platforms/portals that are set up online implicitly and explicitly make claims of 'empowering' the poor of the world financially and socially, and work from a model of what Aradhana Sharma, in her anthropological study of the struggles that non-governmental organization (NGO) workers face in seeking to empower women rural India, refers to as 'neoliberal logics of empowerment' (Sharma, 2008). This logic functions through the production of pre-modern subaltern through visual and textual representations that are not just mere re-productions of previously available frames for the representation of the 'other' in print media. They mobilize a renewed discourse of agency of the subaltern through the discourse of 'empowerment and self-production' that is implicit in how Web 2.0 technologies are described as bringing the 'real' and the 'authentic' individual into the global interactive space to submit voluntary accounts of themselves – here I invoke Couldry's definition of voice as giving an account of one's self (Couldry, 2010) – through the equalizing interface of the social network online. Thus, while in actuality there are active processes and practices of both online and offline preparation of how the real and authentic self performs her identity online, a majority of socio-financial networks online actually serve to essentialize, freeze and visually immobilize subaltern 'others', while mobilizing a modern global middle class to participate in philanthropic/entrepreneurial projects made accessible to them via wireless technologies.

In the case of microfinance networks using socio-financial tools online, a distinction needs to be made between those that are produced from developing world contexts, such as those from Kenya (that use M-pesa as currency), and those from regions in India and those produced from the Europe and the US (e.g., *Kiva.org*). These former networks may raise similar or other issues to those I present through the examples from *kiva.org* that I discuss in this chapter, but they are raised differently from Western-produced microfinance networks that target lenders mostly from the westernized and urban centres of the world through their discursive and visual interface.

In this chapter I only take up the case of these global microfinance networks. Thus far I have discussed a few diverse examples of what I term as socio-financial networks, which includes craft and microfinance networks, but I must reiterate that each of these portals/platforms/networks functions differently and has different issues and embedded hierarchies. To unpack all these fully is beyond the scope of this present chapter (for more details, see Gajjala, 2002; Rybas and Gajjala, 2007; Gajjala et al., 2010; Gajjala, 2011; Gajjala et al., 2011).

This chapter will therefore discuss the mechanisms of [producing] voice, empowerment and the production of individualized global labour forces that materialize in such online social and financial networks made possible by social media technologies and microtransactional technologies such as Paypal. I will draw on feminist frameworks to examine race, ethnicity and development in connection with an ever-pervasive globalization underpinned by economic integration, media convergence and global expansion of the Internet. I do this to trace the implications of voicings (as different from 'voice' yet staging 'voice') from the margins in a global economy. In such an examination, it is important to take into account how the Internet represents a global space where rich and sustained interactions constitute cultures that impact upon global socio-economic practices online and offline through producing individualized labour forces for the global economy. The Internet and related digital technologies are the product of specific ways of thinking and are situated in particular local hierarchies of practice and production that are increasingly being named and privileged (without sufficient caution or introspection) as global and progressive. Yet, the Internet does seem to allow the emergence of a particular domain of material culture that, on the one hand, provides people with the space for enacting the empowerment of women, while simultaneously highlighting the desirability of 'female individualization', which can only occur under specific circumstances of access and literacy. We need to understand how intricate everyday practices and socio-cultural hierarchies contribute to the shaping of online identities to showcase ideal labourers and small-business owners for a global economy. However, what is invisible to the viewer desiring to be global citizen either as lender or borrower in the online microfinancial networks that I use as examples in this chapter is that such individualized global citizens are produced through hier-archies, and the process of inclusion and exclusion – gendered, raced and classed online subjectivities. Such hierarchies, even though based in virtual, visual cyber-spatial praxis, are real; for example, outsourcing due to the employment of foreign workers online if we are to become self-aware users and producers within such an individualized neo-liberal environment.

The Internet has been extensively described and celebrated as a site for marginalized voices to enter the global, to emerge in activism and protest as diverse populations gain access to this medium and its related literacies (Huesca, 2001; Owens and Palmer, 2003; Best, 2005; Pickard, 2006). Parallel to this, digital microtransactional technologies that function through the Internet have become salient tools for the production, representation and consumption at play in transnational financial exchange. This gives rise to 'e-philanthropy' networks that use the microtransactional abilities of financial tools online for fundraising and charity. In such a context, networks such as *kiva.org* and *lend-withcare.org* have adapted the use of such microtransactional financial tools, along with Web 2.0-based social networking tools, to deliver microfinance. These instruments are used in multifarious political and economic reconfigurations within the larger neo-liberal framework of governance. In this chapter, I intend to problematize the discursive processes of production, representation and consumption at play in transnational online microfinance lending sites such as *kiva.org*, and *lendwithcare.org*. Visual and textual representations on most of these socio-financial networks online, such as those that offer microcredit through online portals, serve to invite a modern global middle class to participate in philanthropic and entrepreneurial projects that are set up to empower the poor of the world financially. While there is no explicit claim of cultural, social and political empowerment, the nar-ratives on these websites – stories told by those receiving the financial assistance and reports by fieldworkers working on site – clearly imply cultural empowerment through modernization. Such e-philanthropy delivered through online social networks appears to 'give voice' to the subaltern 'other' – most often, non-western women from regions including Asia – while producing a neo-liberal model of globalization through e-philanthropy. The (in)visible online interface includes features for microtransactions of various kinds – social and financial. The so-called subaltern appears to be speaking online, giving the illusion that she is giving an account of herself individually and seems finally to have global access, while the westernized do-gooder finally has access to the marginalized 'other' who has thus far been tucked away in the dark depths of the globally unheard 'local'.

Digital technologies have thus become key instruments in the processes of globalization and modernization. These instruments are used in complex political and economic shifts and reconfigurations. In the current study, therefore, my critical attention is focused on the correspondence between the emergence of global spaces for financialization (financial transactions) through online social networking and microtransactional software. At the same time as I note the playing out of globalization processes through such technologies, I will problematize the discursive processes of production, representation and consumption at play in transnational online microfinance lending sites formed through socio-economic Web 2.0-based software. Through methods of textual analysis and visual analysis, I will analyse and discuss the social implications of the acts of mediation and representation within such networks.

Examples: Kiva and CARE

kiva.org, for instance, seems like an appealing twenty-first-century version of faith-based missionary work. As argued in a comment posted on a blog about Kiva, 'what Kiva captured so well was the immediacy our culture thrives on, seen in countless ways and now through charitable giving-instant-gratification (give, be connected, see the instant results)' (Chang, 2008). This new Internet-mediated and globalized version of the philanthropic image of the person living in global urban settings and/or in Western affluence appeals to those aspiring to be modern citizens and wishing to be seen as global citizens. It is strongly anchored in a global framework. Thus, for the sake of persuading other prospective lenders, a Kiva fellow argues that 'you're a venture capitalist when you're on Kiva [...] you are financing somebody who is an entrepreneur in the developing world'. Kiva's networking practices seek to raise social consciousness among privileged individuals with regard to microentrepreneurs in developing countries. The former can catch a glimpse of the harsh economic situation outside of their everyday reality, and can thus exercise social responsibility first-hand on *kiva.org*.

While *kiva.org* emerged as one of the first successful online-only microlending platforms and appears to implicitly lead the development of the design and practice of online microfinance networks, CARE International – a leading aid organization with more than 60 years' experience in helping the poor in Asia and the rest of the world – has also entered the theatre of global microfinance. CARE International is based in the UK – a country that is one of the world's leading trading powers and financial centres, and that has the third-biggest economy in Europe after Germany and France (Central Intelligence Agency, 2011). CARE International works in more than 70 countries worldwide, and due to their long history of providing relief to people around the world, the *lendwithcare.org* site is therefore culturally and financially located within CARE International's powerful network. In addition, the digital financial software tool provider Paypal, which also owns *eBay* (a pioneer in online consumer exchange), has its own microfinance portal called Microplace. Advertisements for this latter network appear to users of Paypal as we go about our buying and selling of consumer goods online. Images flash up to show us how, with a click of the mouse, we can be global modern citizens who empower backward and exotic 'others' in rural Asian settings to become 'individualized and global' producers and labourers. The reality of the loans on borrowers' lives is authenticated by means of virtual Web 2.0 tools. Thus, the goal of such a social-media-based visualization of the actual impact of the loans through online text and imaging is to show lenders that these loans are 'real'.

Techno-economy as theatre

In 1996, Spivak published her piece on 'Woman as Theatre', which was a commentary on the UN Conference on Women in Beijing – a conference that is a milestone as it meant that the UN was beginning to centre on 'women's concerns', albeit in problematic ways. But how does this sort of recognition acknowledge and even examine the ways in which international NGOs can benefit women who are not likely to be active participants in the social networks of liberal feminism and economic globalization? Spivak writes:

> The financialization of the globe must be represented as the North embracing the South. Women are being used for the representation of this unity – another name for the profound transnational disunity

necessary for globalization. These conferences are global theatre. There is, of course, no politics which is not theatre. But we are interested in *this* global theatre, staged to show participation between the North and the South, the latter constituted by Northern discursive mechanisms.

(Spivak, 1996: 2)

In *Subaltern Studies*, Susie Tharu and Tejaswini Niranjana ask, 'How might we "read" the new visibility of women across the political spectrum?' (Tharu and Niranjana, 1996: 232). They go on to discuss the complexities of approaching a variety of political issues using what might be referred to as a 'gender lens'. In past work, I have critiqued certain strands of cyber-feminisms and their celebration of digital technologies as tools for empowerment. I have asked, how might we read the (in)visibility of 'gender' across cyberspace? Everywhere we turn these days there is a celebration of women using the Internet or some other computer-related technology. But what are we allowed to use these technologies for and within which contexts? Why are they allowed? Who are the women allowed? Under what conditions are they allowed? Why are they under a constant state of 'being allowed'? Where and how can we locate women's agency without simultaneously noting the pitfalls when we see how this notion of woman as an 'individualized agent' is mobilized and appropriated for the production of the ideal global actor within neo-liberal global economic frameworks? At the same time, as there is this mediated visibility of 'gender' in relation to computers and cyberspace, much discourse surrounding 'new' technologies implicitly assumes the transparency of these technologies. Therefore, even as women are displayed visibly in relation to various technological contexts, the complex gendered, raced, classed, embodied – in short, the socio-cultural and economically situated – nature of technological design and practices is not acknowledged (Gajjala, 2002).

Issues related to women, technology and access always were and continue to be about access to capital. Whether we access technology for work (outside or inside the home) or for leisure, whether we feel the lack of access because of distance, culture, inadequate literacy or sexism – the issue of accessing capital is central to it. A particular techno-mediated experience is produced as a 'lack', a 'gap', or a 'need' and an obvious necessity when the technology somehow becomes important to capital flows and exchange. Why else does a particular 'technology' suddenly emerge as visible in the socio-economic sphere? Issues of globalization, women's empowerment and individualization, and the spread of microcredit transactional abilities through socio-financial online networks enhance the understanding of how such networks shift the debates around women's labour and leisure, digital technology, access and globalization. I have criticized discourses of women's emancipation in online spaces from my ongoing research at two specific global/local, rural/urban intersections (Gajjala et al., 2010). I consider this point through examples from my continuing research into craft networks and microfinance online (Gajjala, 2011; Gajjala et al., 2011).

My research over the years has examined Internet spaces in relation to offline community practice at the intersection of development and globalization, rural and urban and how they are being impacted upon by multinational economic globalization drives. I have argued that even the languages of women's emancipation in globalized media spaces are in fact recodings of familiar liberal feminist discourses interweaved with a capitalist, consumerist rhetoric of individual choice, as described in the beginning paragraphs of this chapter. These discourses of women's empowerment and the 'new' of media and of feminism perform a multicultural, 'inclusive' global village. Such a global village requires individualized labour forces that appear to 'speak' for themselves – and are able to voice legitimized modern individual subject positions. At the same time, such a global village is routed in communities of people whose image and praxis cannot be easily appropriated into the rhetoric of individual choice in consumption. Thus, for instance, while the intentions of lender groups and individuals through online microfinancial networks are selfless and well-meaning, the ways in which they are encouraged and directed towards the making 'right' choices on who to lend to – through visual and textual cues – play into the lender's own desire to be a participating and involved global citizen. In short, they become an activist through socially and politically safe practices that make altruism and selflessness 'doable' and visible to fellow community members worldwide through public staging. These right and correct choices often involve implicit and explicit assumptions coming from situated understandings of what it means to be a productive work and business owner. The westernized and educated citizen of the world has long been drawn into the ideology of the upwardly mobile individual and knows at once when she sees the image or story of such a person in formation.

Westernized individualistic values are underpinned by neo-liberal rhetoric of empowerment based on particular notions of economic development that follow a linear trajectory based on a false binary between 'traditional' and 'modern'. Such progress narratives are noticeably mirrored in the presentation of the profiles of borrowers on *kiva.org*. Profiles usually place particular emphasis on and extol the individual dimension of the entrepreneurial endeavour of the exhibited borrowers – who are most often women from non-westernized contexts including Asia. This individualizing production and discursive formation of the female entrepreneur/worker results in the downplaying and disregarding of the significant communal values woven into the social fabric of local livelihoods, and thus into their human labour and capital.

For instance, in one of the profile brief narratives, we are being introduced to Vilma Elloren from Bayawan, the Philippines, who is 41 years old, married, and has one child (http://www.kiva.org/lend/359278). Within her agricultural business, Vilma has been raising pigs for seven years and she needs a loan to buy feed and vitamins for them; the prospective lenders are also notified that her future plans include the expansion of her business. Another borrower, Ou from Prey Chor, Cambodia, who is 43 years old, married with six children, makes her living though growing rice. She is requesting her second loan from Kiva, which she will use to purchase rice seeds and to remunerate labourers to cultivate her rice crops. The short presentation highlights her gratitude for the Kiva loans that make it possible for her to further 'invest in her farming business and generate more income' (http://www.kiva.org/lend/359391). Similarly, the profile description of Ofelia Sango, a borrower from Palawan, the Philippines, who has run a fishing business for four years and needs a loan to repair her boat, emphasizes her future plan to 'save enough money to expand her business' (http://www.kiva.org/lend/359271).

Another borrower, Odgerel Jigjidsuren, who is 40 years old and living with her husband in a Mongolian yurt in Selenge Province, Mongolia, has had a vegetable and fruit trading business since 2001. She is requesting a loan to purchase more fruits and vegetables and to save some supplies for winter. Very importantly, the online profile records her expressed aspiration for the future: 'in the future we are planning to make our own grocery store' (http://www.kiva.org/lend/359389). All these profile narratives are thus suggestive of a particular construction of a westernized economic progress desideratum, namely the key objective of profit-making and the further generation and expansion of business. It is such individualizing dimensions, strategically incorporated in the profile stories, that a prospective lender can easily identify with and acknowledge.

Communities in the third-world locations that continue to thrive around 'older' livelihoods such as weaving and farming, which are not completely mechanized as they are in the West, become disrupted through such a call for individualization. Productive livelihood practices and communities thus made invisible are disrupted and drawn into hidden transnational labour forces – migrant farm labourers, sex workers, sweat-shop labourers, workers producing computer hardware and so on – upon whose social and economic immobility and lack of access to resources rests the mobility, individual-appearing choices and freedom of other layers of workforces that contribute to and benefit from multinational economic globalization.

Individual women from such communities in Asia, for instance, are produced as subaltern 'others' on the Internet and juxtaposed in relation to images of empowerment as transformation into 'individual modern subjects' through the proper consumption of goods and ideas. Yet, these subaltern 'others' must also be staged as on the verge of becoming individuals in a global workforce. For example, in a borrower profile for a young woman from Cambodia seeking a loan to buy a cow, the woman is positioned as an individual weaver woman struggling to feed her baby with what she makes from her weaving. While the actual narrative is not untrue, what this portrayal allows the Western female lender – who may herself be an individualized 'DIY' weaver, such as those to be found on blogospheres *etsy.com* and *rivalery.com* – to consider that her condition may not be all that correct. The weaving community that this borrower belongs to is strategically erased or not described – and we have no context or understanding for what the actual struggle is that this woman faces. She is staged in Western clothes, catering to a Western male gaze that views Asian women as sexualized, yet because she is carefully positioned with spinning wheel and yarn in a rural setting with a 'clean' seeming smile of innocence, she also caters to the Western female gaze. Both men and women from multiple backgrounds – those who favour alternative lifestyles to modernity in the West included – are drawn into a desire to empower and help this young enterprising Asian woman who may otherwise be forced into an oppressive life as suppressed wife/woman or sex worker. Colonial narratives about the third-world female 'other' from Asia – or rather the non-urbanized female 'other' – on the Internet happen through marketing techniques that rely on implicit assumptions of the urban and westernized viewer as they produce an Asian oppressed 'other' who has been 'liberated' through acts of techno-mediation and liberal feminist handouts. These images are produced under the gaze of the urbanized 'global and multicultural and individualized self' who, it is implicitly suggested, will liberate the oppressed 'other' through their acts of consumption.

Thus, it is possible for the urban woman consumer to maintain her dreams of suburbia, while also helping the poor and oppressed women – for example, those less fortunate than her. Of course, the irony of this kind of online marketing is that it reinstates racist and westernized patriarchies while highlighting the urban and suburban woman's post-feminist (so-called) freedom of choice and agency.

However, the contradiction of the interplay between economics and culture is that consumption patterns do indeed shape the existence or disappearance of indigenous cultures and modes of production not endorsed by the discourse of 'newness' embedded in mainstream globalization processes. In addition, the euphoric rhetoric about the impact of information and communications technology on economically disadvantaged communities, given its implicit colonial legacy, recasts 'third world' and rural women as somehow 'ignorant' in light of our high-tech information age. Thus, feminist activists and scholars wishing to use the Internet and related digital media within economic systems in order to highlight issues of concern within such communities are faced with contradictions and dilemmas that are methodological, ethical, material and lexical. Socio-financial networks such as those that offer microfinance loans through fully online formats, such as *kiva.org, microplace.com* and *lendwithcare.org,* rely on such an interplay of contradictions to raise the money needed for deserving 'others'.

The reality is that as long as 'technology' is only clearly situated in a linear narrative of 'progress' that is based on colonial discourses about the so-called non-technological 'other', and as long as markets are embedded in such technological narratives, it will be very difficult to re-route production, representation and consumption in ways that empower these not-visible populations that the liberal feminist websites are supposedly helping. We must examine closely how the processes of globalization that are embedded within current digital capitalistic modes of commerce have reshaped notions of 'technology' in ways that only certain techno-mediated practices and associated communities, cultures and ideologies are considered to be 'developed' and 'enlightened'. The rhetoric of 'modernity, individualization and globalization' has seeped into almost all of our daily practices and re-formed different ways of being by making our production, representation and consumption patterns fairly uniform. Thus, 'difference' in image and performance is substituted for difference in praxis. This difference in image in performance stands in for the authentic voice in what I call 'voicings'.

Voicings and empowerment

The ways in which the concept of 'voice' is used when writing about the empowerment of marginalized people/women in Asia invokes authenticity and immutability of voice across time and space. Therefore, I use 'voicings' to suggest the shifting nature of voice as acts of speaking occurs within various contexts. In this way I signal how 'voice' is a construct based in situated, contingent speech acts shaped through existing power hierarchies, where the marginalized speaker emerges as a speaking agent as she or he speaks through the cracks and fissures – ruptures – that occasionally or accidentally permit subaltern speech to be heard in the mainstream. After voice emerges in this manner and finds a way to carve a space for the agent, the speaker is subjected/disciplined into the existing power structure. Thus, for instance, while the Dalits of India (a historically ill-treated lower caste in Indian society) and women weavers and craft workers from various parts of Asia appear to have a voice online and in various activist venues offline and online, they are heard only when they voice their issues and concerns within frameworks that are recognizable within existing discursive logics shaped by current power hierarchies. The concept of 'voicings' as opposed to 'voice' (which suggests authenticity of representation and self-representation) allows me to examine how individuals act within communities as their subjectivities are shaped and they are produced as actors or subjects within interdependent global/local hierarchies. In asking who gets mapped out and why, I seek to understand how this happens processually and structurally. I seek to understand how 'voicings' are produced in either offline development contexts or in diverse online contexts (including development projects using online venues to facilitate their work), and under what conditions 'subaltern' speech gets heard. Thus, rather than stop at a euphoric celebration of this emergence of voice from thus-far marginalized groups, it is important to ask about the implications of these emerging voicings for the existing and emerging structures of power. Attempting to understand how voice emerges through such voicings opens up ways to examine where oppression shifts to when third-world women apparently gain a voice within the visible structures of globalization, such as the Internet and within social and financial online networks.

Globalization processes include material and discursive hegemonies produced at the intersection of the economic, the cultural and the social, and are mediated in multiple ways through old and new mediascapes. These processes feed into economic and cultural local formations. Global technospaces are produced through and are a consequence of economic globalization. For instance, digital diaspora from regions such as south Asia are a product of transnational commerce. So, the theoretical lenses for engaging these contexts continue to be developed, as I immerse myself in various (trans)rural, (trans)urban, online, offline, first-world and third-world locations. These lenses serve to pose questions and to describe how seeming contradictions contribute to situated praxis within the global–local continuum of everyday economic and communicative practices. There has been considerable celebration over how the Internet allows various marginalized voices to access the global and how empowering that is. An examination of multiple and even chaotic voicings as they emerge in these social networks allows us to highlight a different kind of disciplining role played by the technical interface and design. At the same time, as the individual begins to feel empowered by the ability to speak up and back in such networks, there is a quick and simultaneous appropriation occurring that quickly 'places' this voice into a slot that can be located and categorized as known and knowable. However, what is crucial to note here is that while appropriation occurs, there is also a certain kind of individual empowerment occurring simultaneously.

This apparent contradiction has been noted in pedagogical settings. Feminist teachers have implemented computer-mediated communication in their teaching to see if it allows women and girls an online 'voice'. In such attempts, discursive context and discursive agency are brought to bear on the writing process so that students write for self-transformation and social change. Similarly, in social networks – whether the explicitly leisure oriented ones such as *Facebook* and *Myspace*, or those formed to empower and finance individual groups from marginalized communities such as *kiva.org* – power plays out in a nuanced and complex way that allows an emerging global capitalist status quo to reassert itself, while allowing for particular formations of marginalized voices to be centred. Thus, the way in which power plays out shifts to work around these centred marginalized voices by making them seem the exception to the rule, by assigning to them some values associated with the existing mainstream or by exoticizing them.

Does this mean that the empowerment and voice gained by rural Asian and south Asian women in such a setting, whether momentary or not, should be discounted as insignificant? No, that is not what I am arguing. I am signalling the process of the emergence of multiple marginalized voices at social-network interfaces while pointing to the simultaneous re-placement of voice and identity in an emerging power structure in order to urge that we examine these shifts to understand what the paradigm and technical interface of 'network society' might mean for us socially, culturally and economically. But I am also interested in questioning whether just the fact of emerging voice in and of itself functions to empower. And if so, what expected and unexpected forms might this empowerment take and what paths, trajectories and networks might emerge? Also, what does this moment of empowerment mean for the various actors and contexts within and through which the voice emerges? This chapter has demonstrated through examples concerning the staging of Asian women borrowers on online microfinancial socio-economic networks. Where does privilege and hierarchy shift? Who and what does it oppress, and why? Online networks, built through technologies that foster quick interactive moments – through instant messaging, texting, frequent updating of status messages, continual blogging and updating – allow for instant communication that is conducive to subversive and evasive one-on-one contact that is simultaneously public and open to surveillance. Thus, the way that power plays out in such contexts is nuanced and complex. A group of teenagers may produce 'egocentric networks' on *Facebook* and *Myspace* as suggested by Boyd and Ellison (2007). But these same spaces also function panopticon-like to discipline subjectivities through uniformed practices of work and play within such networks. All these move us away from previous conceptualizations of online formations as 'community' while allowing the formation of ideal global subjectivities that work to the everyday rhythm of seemingly deterritorialized networks that are controlled through (in)visible and implicit hierarchical codes situated in transnational corporate logics.

Acknowledgements

The author would like to acknowledge Anca Birzescu, Franklin Yartey and Yeonju Oh for their help with collecting some of the data for this continuing project.

References

Best, K. (2005) 'Rethinking the Globalization Movement: Toward a Cultural Theory of Contemporary Democracy and Communication', *Communication and Critical/Cultural Studies*, 2(3): 214–237.

Boyd, D. and Ellison, B. (2007) 'Social Network Sites: Definition, History, and Scholarship', *Journal of Computer Mediated Communication*, 13(1): 210–230.

Central Intelligence Agency (2011) *The World Factbook: United Kingdom,* retrieved from https://www.cia.gov/library/publications/the-world-factbook/geos/uk.html.

Chang, C. (2008) 'Kiva Is a Menace: Why Copying the Internet Fundraising Sensation May Be Dangerous to Your (Fundraising) Soul', retrieved from http://www.socialedge.org/blogs/forging-ahead/archive/2008/12/01/kiva-is-a-menace.

Couldry, N. (2010) *Why Voice Matters: Culture and Politics after Neoliberalism,* London: Sage.

Gajjala, R. (2002) 'Introduction', *Rhizomes: Cultural Studies in Emerging Knowledge,* 4, retrieved from http://www.rhizomes.net/issue4/intro.html.

Gajjala, R. (2011) 'Snapshots from Sari Trails: Cyborgs Old and New', *Social Identities: Journal for the Study of Race, Nation and Culture,* 17(3): 393–408.

Gajjala, R., Zhang, Y. and Dako-Gyeke, P. (2010) 'Lexicons of Women's Empowerment Online', *Feminist Media Studies,* 10(1): 69–86.

Gajjala, V., Gajjala, R., Birzescu, A. and Anarbaeva, S. (2011) 'Microfinance in Online Space: A Visual Analysis of Kiva.org', *Development in Practice,* 21(6): 880–893.

Huesca, R. (2001) 'Conceptual Contributions of New Social Movements to Development Communication Research', *Communication Theory,* 11(4): 415–433.

Nadesan, M. (2010) 'Enterprising Narratives and the Global Financialization of Microlending', *Women and Language,* 33(2): 9–30.

Owens, L. and Palmer, K. (2003) 'Making the News: Anarchist Counter-Public Relations on the World Wide Web', *Critical Studies in Media Communication,* 20(4): 335–361.

Pickard, W. (2006) 'United Yet Autonomous: Indymedia and the Struggle to Sustain a Radical Democratic Network', *Media, Culture & Society,* 28(3): 315–336.

Rybas, N. and Gajjala, R. (2007) 'Developing Cyberethnographic Research Methods for Understanding Digitally Mediated Identities', *Forum Qualitative Sozialforschung/Forum: Qualitative Social Research,* 8(3), retrieved from http://www.qualitative-research.net/index.php/fqs/article/view/282.

Sharma, A. (2008) *Logics of Empowerment: Development, Gender, and Governance in Neoliberal India,* Minneapolis: University of Minnesota Press.

Spivak, G. (1996) 'Woman as Theater: United Nations Conference on Women, Beijing 1995', *Radical Philosophy,* 75: 2–4.

Tharu, S. and Niranjana, T. (1996) 'Problems for a Contemporary Theory of Gender', in S. Amin and D. Chakrabarty (eds), *Subaltern Studies XI,* pp. 232–260, New Delhi: Oxford University Press.

8
Transforming Documentary: Indonesian Women and Sexuality in the Film *Pertaruhan* *[At Stake]* (2008)

Fatimah Tobing Rony

A laughing Indonesian woman, on her day off as a caregiver, serenades her pretty girlfriend, another Indonesian migrant worker, in a karaoke club in Hong Kong....

In West Java, a little girl in a puffy red tulle dress sitting in an eagle-shaped palanquin is carried on the shoulders of four dancing young men at the festival before her circumcision.... Her pinched face, heavily powdered and lipsticked, is unsmiling....

A Chinese-Indonesian woman is lying on an examining table in a Jakarta clinic after having had a pap smear, when the elderly gynaecologist suddenly puts his hands on her bare thighs and intones the Lord's Prayer in English....

A stout, no-nonsense mother who breaks stones in the blazing sun during the day in a village in East Java, gets on a motorcycle at night to cluck at potential male clients in a Chinese graveyard at the top of a mountain....

As the above images attest, the documentary film *Pertaruhan [At Stake]* takes as its raw subject matter images of women and sexuality never before seen on screen in Indonesia. This controversial content – overseas lesbian communities, inadequate health care for women, female circumcision, AIDS and illegal prostitution – is not the only thing shocking about this film, which premiered at the 2008 Berlin Film Festival.

Produced by Nia Dinata, one of Indonesia's most famous director/ producers, and directed by five unknown film-makers who were trained in a documentary workshop, *Pertaruhan [At Stake]* reconfigures, translates, and converts the genre of the commercial feature documentary, overturning certain conventions regarding the authorial voice and subjectivity of the film-maker and his or her relation to the audience. This chapter will delineate the importance of the film in two areas: (1) its frank treatment of the transnational and globalized subject matter of Indonesian women and sexuality, which heretofore had hardly ever been broached in private discourse much less on the big screen; and (2) its divergence from the traditional form of authorship, production, distribution and exhibition of the feature commercial documentary.

What is eye-opening about *Pertaruhan [At Stake]* is how it boldly explores taboo issues such as how an unmarried woman's worth is measured in her remaining a virgin – defined as having never been penetrated, even for a necessary medical examination. This means that the college-educated transnational worker living in Hong Kong, named Ruwati, who is already in her 40s, is afraid to tell her fiancé that she needs to be examined by a doctor for a uterine tumour because it would mean that he would not be the first man to 'penetrate' her. This notion of 'virginity' also makes for a situation where any young woman who is sexually active cannot get a pap smear until she is married – another problem that is depicted in the film. Another section of the film depicts specific circumstances of female circumcision in cultures both modern and local, to control the supposed sexual wildness of women. And finally, the film gives us the portraits of two mothers who work as stone-breakers by day, and as prostitutes by night in a gang-controlled prostitution area in a Chinese graveyard in East Java.

Since the late 1970s, there have been tremendous changes in the socio-economic status of Indonesian women, due to mass education, widespread employment of women in private and public sectors, and mobility into the city, all of which have altered the family and class structure of many communities in Indonesia, both urban and rural. Like many Asian economies, the economy of Indonesia has benefited from integrating women into the labour force.[1] Studies further show that the more educated the woman, the more autonomy she tends to have.[2] As Krishna Sen has pointed out, the image of the 'working woman' has replaced the image of the housewife 'as the paradigmatic female subject in political, cultural and economic discourses in Indonesia'.[3]

There is no greater sign of the complexity of modernity in Indonesia than the popular adoption of the *krudung (hijab)* or headscarf from the

1980s to the present day, which is perceived in Europe and the US as a sign of tradition and conservatism, but is actually a multivalent sign of protest (against Suharto's regime of dictatorship before 1998) and modernity. Indonesia is the largest Muslim country in the world, but Indonesian Islam has always been a syncretic mix.

Therefore, the growth of female individualization in Indonesia involves a confluence of political, religious and cultural factors, whose signifiers of individualization substantially differ from those in the West. As in other parts of Asia like Japan, China, Korea and Singapore, Indonesian women are encouraged to become educated in order to pursue a career, while also maintaining their traditional roles of being head of the domestic household as wife and mother. What happens when we throw the condition of transnational mobility into the mix? Not all academic degrees have the same value on the market: an Indonesian woman educated abroad in Australia, the US or Europe will be successful in the corporate labour market, while someone from a less prestigious Indonesian university may have to seek work abroad in the service sector as a nanny or babysitter – a situation highlighted in the film *Pertaruhan [At Stake]*.

Youna Kim (2010) writes that, 'Arguably, female individualization has emerged as a major mode of identity formation that is now operating in a transnational flow of desire, giving rise to the experience of increased freedom, as well as increased insecurity and personal responsibility for every move.'[4] As we will see, *Pertaruhan [At Stake]* traces these modes of female individualization: from the college-educated nanny working in Hong Kong who seeks medical care even though it defies her Javanese fiancé's wishes, to the other Indonesian workers who are lesbians in Hong Kong but 'sisters' when they go home to Indonesia, to the activist who fights against female circumcision even though her father promotes it in his *pesantren* (religious school), to foreign-educated Chinese-Indonesian women returning to Jakarta and finding their access to obstetrics and gynaecology prohibited until they get married. Female individualization in Indonesia is constituted by vastly differing histories of social, economic, class and gender inequality.

Given the more conservative political climate as reflected in the recent Anti-Pornography Law of 2008 and the Health Law of 2009, which created setbacks for the reproductive rights of women, a film about women and sexuality such as *Pertaruhan [At Stake]* would seem unlikely to get made. Women trying to fight against recent setbacks like these two laws are seen as being 'immoral' and as 'girls who are out of control', explains Mariana Amiruddin, director of the Jurnal Perempuan Foundation.[5] But the producer Nia Dinata has made a career in making narrative feature films about what had been taboo subjects: *Ca-bau-kan* (2002) dealt with Chinese Indonesians, *Arisan* (2003) with homosexuality, and *Berbagi Suami [Love for Share]* (2006) with polygamy from the point of view of the wives. Since the Anti-Pornography Law was enacted, there is now even more scrutiny of her work from the censorship institution and other public organizations. She explains, 'It is difficult because when I make movies I include people of different sexual orientations.' She continues:

> For me, film is a description of social reality. In my social realm, there are homosexuals, there are Indonesian Chinese, Indonesian Indian. I meet a mix of people. Why should I only tell a story about mainstream people, mainstream religion, mainstream sexual preference?[6]

In fact, according to Dinata, the impetus for making *Pertaruhan [At Stake]* was precisely because Indonesian society was becoming less and less open, and more and more conservative, especially with the debate over and passage of the Pornography Law – which was enacted two months before the opening of the film. Because her films deal with so many critical social topics, Dinata is often invited to speak to campus groups and women's organizations and show her films, and from these meetings her eyes were opened even wider to the problems of Indonesian society. Dinata's film-making, which includes the research, the collaboration and the bringing of films to audiences, is a political intervention.

In 2007, Dinata and several other film-makers and film activists founded the Masyarakat Film Indonesia, or the Indonesian Film Society, to promote change in government legislation affecting the film industry and to protest against the Draconian closed-door policies of the Film Censorship board. That same year, Dinata produced the box office smash *Quickie Express*, a sex comedy directed by Dimas Djayadiningrat about gigolos and wealthy older women. In January 2008, *Perempuan Punya Cerita [Chants of Lotus]*, a narrative film produced by Dinata and featuring four films that were directed by Upi, Nia Dinata, Lasya Susatyo and myself, was released in major theatres all across Indonesia. Featuring stories about women and sexuality, the film was cut very heavily by censors. All but one reel of the film was cut: scenes such as a teenager smoking while wearing a *krudung* (hijab) was cut, and a group sex scene was cut so that it appears that the woman is only having sex with one boy, thus making the storyline meaningless. Nia Dinata has described the violation of the censor as a rape: to a film-maker, seeing one's film cut does feel like a violation because the scenes are literally 'cut out'. Ironically, that experience made her want to do an even more serious film, which turned out to become *Pertaruhan [At Stake]*. She explained:

> You know when *PPC [Perempuan Punya Cerita (Chants of Lotus)]* got all the censorship cuts and got all the protest then that's like the momentum for me to really do something... it's the momentum for 'yes I have to do something that is even more daring and more touching than anticipated'. It has to be documented. So that they know that these things happen. And then why do you have to close your eyes and close your ears ... because otherwise if you ignore these things, then you know... there will be more and more violations in human rights, right?[7]

Dinata's first omnibus film involving several directors, *Perempuan Punya Cerita [Chants of Lotus]*, utilized extensive field research for the stories concerning HIV/AIDS, midwifery, abortion, teenage sex and child trafficking, but cast actors. The following film *Pertaruhan [At Stake]* got rid of the whole business of casting and writing dramatic scripts, but continued the themes of women and sexuality. When asked why women were the theme of the documentary *Pertaruhan [At Stake]*, Dinata explained:

> There are many faces of Indonesian women, there are interesting multi-dimensional characters of Indonesian women, because we grew up in a very interesting and challenging society. I would always feel obliged to portray them in as complex a manner as possible, because we are not that simple, we are not one-faceted human beings, we are very unique.[8]

And when I asked her why sexuality, Dinata replied, 'Because that's the basis for anything... sexuality deals with more than the actions itself, it deals with health, it deals with your rights, it deals with so many things.' She explained, 'Because most women in Indonesia don't even know their basic rights, that your body is your decision. Health issues are your own decision.'[9] Thus, one can see that a confluence of events led to the making of *Pertaruhan [At Stake]*: the demise of the Indonesian film industry that led to the growing prominence of women, leading to the possibility of more do-it-yourself film-making; a growing maturity and stability in Dinata's film-making, with the solidity of her production house Kalyana Shira Films that could make profitable films such as the lucrative *Quickie Express* in the same year as *Perempuan Punya Cerita [Chants of Lotus]*; and a desire to protest against the growing conservative forces in Indonesia that were hampering and violating women's rights.

Pertaruhan [At Stake] was shot and edited at a remarkably quick rate. The workshop Project Change! was held in July 2008, the films were shot in October, the film was edited in November, and released on 35 mm for theatres in December 2008. Each of the four short documentary films tackles the issue set out by Nia Dinata for the workshop Project Change! – the basic human right of a woman's sovereignty over her own health and sexuality.

Although there are four distinct story segments, the feature coheres as one film. Mothers and labour and class is a key theme in this film, explicitly and implicitly. The first segment, *Mengusahakan Cinta [Effort for Love]*, directed by Ani Ema Susanti, opens with a frenetic contemporary score as we see Chinese pedestrians in the bright city streets of Hong Kong, followed by shots of Indonesian women wearing the *krudung* (hijab). The hiring of Indonesian women is explained by a Chinese woman early in the film, who declares that she wants to work, so Indonesian women are hired to take care of their elderly, children and dogs in order to make that possible. The film-maker herself, Ani, who wears a *krudung* like many of the *tenaga kerja wanita* (overseas women workers) or TKW, had worked from 2001 to 2003 in Hong Kong as a TKW taking care of her Chinese employer's ageing parents and dogs, so that she could make enough money to support her family and fund her university education. Thus the director is not an outsider: she went back to Hong Kong to film the locations and community of workers that she remembered and knew well.[10]

We first meet Ibu Ruwati (Ms. Ruwati), a middle-aged woman who was a college graduate and has been working in Hong Kong for 10 years. She explains that a teacher in Indonesia only makes 30–40 dollars a month; an intertitle explains that in Hong Kong they can make 500 dollars a month. In front of a painted portrait of that icon of ideal womanhood, Kartini, Ruwati teaches dance to other Indonesian women workers. Ruwati's desire to be the perfect wife is a distillation of the Suharto regime's successful idealization of Kartini.[11] Even though Ruwati is respected as a cultural teacher, and is college-educated, she defers to her fiancé Yanto back in Malang in Java, Indonesia.

Back in Malang, Yanto is interviewed. He is a widower and the father of a young girl whom Ruwati adores. He explains in Javanese, and it is translated into Indonesian, that his fiancé is '*masih lajang*', which means 'still unmarried', but this gets translated into English as 'pure'. '*Lajang*' (or being single) is an adjective that may be applied to both men and women. One says, '*masih jejaka*' or '*masih bujang*' (still unmarried man), '*masih gadis*' (still unmarried, literally still a young girl), '*masih perawan*' (still a virgin). The opposite would be '*telah menikah*' (already married) or '*sudah berumah tangga*' (already having a household). But here '*lajang*' or being a virgin means that no one has penetrated her vagina, including by medical procedure, a surprising definition. Ani explains that a woman must be 'perfect'. Losing one's virginity is tantamount to losing one's fundamental value:

> Even though sometimes a person is no longer a virgin because you were forced by your boyfriend or because you were raped, and there are many who were forced by their boyfriends that I researched, but they said they weren't worth anything anymore. And Ibu Ruwati I can conclude that she wants to appear 'perfect' to her fiancé. Even though she herself can explain very clearly that she is not a virgin, because she was examined gynaecologically by an instrument that penetrated her, but because their thinking is constructed by culture and by *adat* (tradition) in this way that we have to appear 'perfect', we have to offer it to our husbands-to-be, so that she didn't even want to be examined by a doctor. Even though it's about her health. Why should one have to take into account the husband-to-be, but the doctor is not taken into account? [translation mine].[12]

Equally surprising in the first film is a second story of a brash androgynous young woman named Ryantini who is in love with another Indonesian woman worker. We see Ryantini teasing and coaxing the older Chinese woman that she takes care of, walking with her through the streets of Hong Kong. Married off at 13 to a brutal man she did not love, Ryantini explains that she left for Hong Kong, leaving behind her daughter in the village, because if she was going to be a servant she might as well get paid for it.

Like 'virgin', the word 'lesbian' is another term that takes on another meaning for these overseas workers in Hong Kong, although the word 'lesbian' is never uttered. Ani explains that her friends who were not lesbian in Indonesia could enjoy being in relationships with women in Hong Kong, and in fact the film shows us Toko Abadi, a dry goods store run by an Indonesian woman where women can marry each other. Ryantini explains that her employers know her flaws, including that she likes to smoke and she likes women (*'aku suka sama cewek'*), but they tolerate it as long as it does not interfere with her work.

Tom Boellsdorf proposes an interesting notion to account for the forces of globalization. Gay and lesbian communities in Indonesia do not just adopt the Western ideas of sexuality wholesale, but 'dub' them and make them their own.

> 'Dubbing culture', then, is about a new kind of cultural formation in an already globalized world, one for which the idiom of translation is no longer sufficient. It questions 'the relationship between translation and belonging', asserting that the binarisms of import-export and authentic-inauthentic are insufficient to explain how globalizing mass media play a role in 'lesbi' and 'gay' subject positions but do not determine them outright.[13]

He explains:

> Disjuncture is at the heart of the dub; there is no prior style of pure synchrony and no simple conversion to another way of being. Where translation is haunted by its inevitable failure, dubbing rejoices in the good-enough and the forever incomplete.[14]

What is so brilliant about the notion of 'dubbing' is that it does not limit an authentic gay or lesbian subjectivity as one defined by the West: it makes room for what Boellsdorf calls 'the nonteleological, transformative dimensions of globalizing processes'.[15] Although it is perhaps a question of nuance, I would argue that the way that English is often used by Indonesians in the context of this film is more pointed in purpose than mere translation, and/or dubbing, since it is mixed with Indonesian. In *Pertaruhan [At Stake]*, the use of English (and later I will argue the form of the documentary feature film) is one of appropriation, as a form of struggle towards sovereignty over one's own body. Where Indonesian fails them, and is either too patriarchal or not complex enough, terms in English are forcefully used and underlined.

The second film, *Untuk Apa? [What's the Point?]*, directed by TV journalists Iwan Setiawan and Muhammed Ichsan, continues the themes of privacy, health, class and motherhood by dealing with *khitan*, or female circumcision, a topic that is almost never discussed in the media in Indonesia. Although the practice was banned in 2006 by the Indonesian government, it appears that support for it is growing in rural areas.

As friends, the two male film-makers proposed this subject for the workshop Project Change!, because Iwan Setiawan, who is Christian, was shocked to find out from Muhammad Ichsan, a Muslim, that female circumcision is carried out in Indonesia. Since the practice is so rarely discussed, and is confined to certain groups in certain areas of Indonesia, many Indonesians have not even heard of it. But with fundamentalism on the rise, the practice of *khitan* persists. It can take a form that is mostly symbolic, such as the rubbing of the clitoris with an antiseptic, to a form that actually entails the drawing of blood. Although *khitan* is not known to be as invasive as the female circumcision that is performed in parts of Africa, the voices of the women interviewed here who were circumcised and recall the trauma of that event, are particularly poignant.

In one of the most incredible scenes of the film, under the blaring music of a 'Rasulan' ceremony in Indramayu, West Java, fathers pay for the circumcision of their daughters with coins, according to the girls' body weight. They all look as if they are under the age of four. Dressed in bright yellow, red and pink party dresses, their faces powdered and made up with lipstick, the little girls, their small faces pinched and scared, are feted for the day, seated on bird-shaped palanquins carried by dancing young men in purple jogging suits and black *peci* hats.

This film uses several interviews to explore the theme of female circumcision. Conservative religious promoters of circumcision are interviewed and contend that it is needed for sexual control and health reasons. The personal interviews with women who have been circumcised – some of whom are mothers with daughters – are the soul of this segment, and a counterweight to these conservative supporters. Dance teacher Wangi Indriya, a graceful woman of 48, explains that as a girl she had to agree to the procedure, because if one did not do it one risked isolation, or one would be made into an enemy by those who side with *adat* (tradition). She also explains that people believe that women who are not circumcised are sexually wild.

Another woman who recounts her struggle to understand being circumcised is the Muslim activist Darol Mahmada, a member of the liberal Islamic organization Jaringan Islam. Bright, articulate and highly intelligent, Darol walks with her daughter to a *pesantren* (an Islamic religious school) to ask Darol's own father, the leader of that *pesantren*, if female circumcision is really necessary. Over montage shots of her walking with her daughter, we hear his off-screen voice explain that the point is 'to safeguard a woman's dignity', due to the fact that women have immense sexual desires.

Near the end of the sequence we see the father, Darol and her daughter together in one shot, her father prominently in the foreground. She presses him on the religious justification for *khitan*. The father replies, 'to make women equal to men. Yes women are human beings too'. Frustrated and troubled, we cut to a medium shot of just Darol, who has all of a sudden become quiet. Later it is Darol who brings home the message for this segment. She addresses the camera:

> When it starts to regulate women, I have my doubts. They always say, it's about a woman's honour. When in fact it's about the honour of the spouse.

As in the previous film, English and Indonesian are often combined in a struggle to transform definitions.

> A woman here is nobody. Women have no place. We are totally controlled. Circumcision is just another form of controlling the private territory of women.

Looking closely at what she actually says above we can see that in order to explain herself she must use both Indonesian and English. The English words 'nobody', 'control' and 'domestic space', must be used to begin to carve out a message of resistance against the local traditions of female circumcision, as perpetrated by *adat* (tradition), religion, medical institutions and a state loathe to enforce its prohibition of the practice. As Darol puts it, *khitan* in females does not do good to oneself; *khitan* in females only does good for somebody else.

The third film takes as its theme the appalling medical care that women get in Indonesia, especially unmarried women. Like the first two short films, the title for *Nona Nyonya? [Miss or Mrs?]* appears only at the end of the third film. Instead of a title we first see an intertitle that says that there are only 7000 obstetricians and gynaecologists for a population of 230 million. We also hear a doctor explain that the biggest cause of death in women is cervical cancer. Set mainly in the cosmopolitan capital city of Jakarta, several young unmarried Jakarta women explain their difficulty in obtaining a pap smear. For the most part, they are condemned by the nurses and the doctors for seeking such medical attention without a husband's approval. Nurses assume that the women seeking a pap smear have made a mistake when they have checked off 'Miss'. They are even refused a pap smear unless they can get permission from their 'future husband' because the pap smear would mean penetration by an instrument, hence a 'loss of virginity'. When one woman says that she is sexually active and has a disease, the medical staff insist that they need to see her marriage certificate. '*Sudah menikah?*' does not just mean 'are you married?', but implies, 'are you no longer a virgin?'. The essential problem is that a sexual woman who is not married is a threat to the status quo, *adat* (tradition), culture, even the nation.

A second story in this segment is that of a 17-year-old high-school graduate Kelly who is living in Bogor, a city outside of Jakarta. She is suffering from vaginal discharge but doesn't have the money or the courage to see a gynaecologist. Gynaecology is seen as being a realm for married women only. Her friends advise her not to go to a gynaecologist, 'otherwise they will think you are loose'. At the end of the film, Kelly goes to a library, only to learn from books that she indeed should be checked. A few scenes later we see Kelly walking down a dark staircase, afraid to go to the doctor.

As Ninuk Widyantoro, the director for a health foundation, declares in the film:

> Health care in Indonesia stinks. They're very inconsiderate. It's discriminative. It's abusive. It violates human rights.

She explains, 'They have no idea by not giving their patients access to knowledge, information, and fact they're pushing young girls, even the adults, into the darkness where they have to blindly look for information.' At the word '*kegelapan*', or darkness, the film cuts to Kelly's face. Like many others in *Pertaruhan [At Stake]*, Ninuk uses English to underline her points, in particular using the words 'access', 'knowledge', 'information' and 'fact' in her explanation.

The director of this segment, Lucky Kuswandi, is a young gay Chinese-Indonesian film-maker, educated in Los Angeles, who later directed the 2010 film *Madame X* – a narrative feature about a cross-dressing super-hero who fights fascistic fundamentalism. What's striking about this film is Lucky's strategic use of women working at Kalyana Shira Films as participants to get information on gynaecology practice. He explained to me in an interview that he knew that his presence as a male and with a camera would change the ways that both women and doctors would act in front of the camera, so he decided to use hidden cameras.[16] A couple of the women he enlisted were women who have worked for a long time with Kalyana Shira Films: Cinzia Rini Puspita has worked in varying capacities as line producer, assistant director and director; and

Ade Kusumaningrum has worked as a publicist. As Cinzia, who was the actual line producer for Lucky's segment, says in the film, 'I decided to experience it myself what these people have to go through.' She and another woman, Naya, carrying hidden cameras in their bags, then embark on a funny and frightening journey to get a pap smear.

The results are surprising and horrifying. The first doctor is described by Cinzia as being an old doctor with receding white hair and big ears. First he asks her if she is married, '*sudah berumah tangga?*' (literally, 'have you set up house yet?'), and when she tells him no, he asks, then how are we going to do a pap smear? His bullying includes asking her if she has a boyfriend and if they are having sex and when is she going to marry him. He also asks her if it is he or she that wants the sex. She replies, 'we both want it'. The doctor then states, 'but he wants it more than you, right?'. Cinzia tells him, '*Kebetulan kita semua butuh*' (We both want it).

Cinzia relates that after doing the pap smear the doctor then put his hands on her naked thighs and asks in English, 'Why are you doing this to yourself?' Suddenly he starts reciting the Lord's Prayer in English:

In the name of the Father and the Son and the Holy Ghost Amen. Thy kingdom come, thy will be done, on earth as it is in heaven. Is it? Give us this day our daily bread. And forgive us our trespasses. As we forgive them who trespass against us. And lead us not into temptation. But deliver us from evil. What you are doing now is evil!

Cinzia replies to him in English, and the verbal exchange is caught on the hidden camera.

Cinzia: But it's not my... I'm not evil
Doctor: Yeah your doing is evil.
Cinzia: Do I look like Satan to you?

The doctor then begins to berate her in Indonesian: 'You shouldn't have thrown it away.' He also threatens to smack her. He intones, 'God created us for a reason. To be a good person unto others. Do you consider yourself to be Indonesian? Pancasila.'

Pancasila – the five principles of the nation – was the special ideology of the Suharto regime, including the belief in one God. By invoking Pancasila, the doctor is deriding Cinzia's behaviour as against the state and as immoral. Cinzia answers his Indonesian diatribe in English, 'I want to know my health'. This scene, along with another hidden camera scene with Naya, absolutely underlines how *adat* (tradition), medicine, religion and state politics conspire to deny women their basic health rights. The quality of the hidden camera footage is poor, and the doctors' faces are obscured, but the language they use to try to intimidate the women is well recorded, and the message loud and clear.

Another person who has worked frequently for Kalyana Shira Films, the publicist Ade Kusumaningrum, also seeks a pap smear and her story serves as a counterpoint to the abuse Naya and Cinzia suffer. Her dilemma is boldly declared by her: 'I'm a lesbian and anti-penetration', but she decides to get a pap smear because her family has a history of cancer. She tells us, 'Honestly, it freaks me out to go to a gyno. My head is already clouded with anti-penetration. I can't even digest the idea. But on the other side I really want to know my health.'

Her gynaecologist, a woman, is competent and professional, and does not chastise her. The section is funny because we see her effervescent but flustered partner Bonnie interacting with her before, during and after the procedure. I asked Lucky how he was able to convince Ade to get a pap smear on camera:

Well because during research I interviewed a lot of women. And almost all the women in Kalyana I interviewed, she was there, I was like come on come on let me just put you on camera and we'll talk about this. When she heard about my idea she was intrigued because her lesbian friend a few days before had talked to her and urged her to do a pap smear.[17]

Just what it means for a lesbian not married to a man choosing to have a pap smear for the sake of her health in Indonesia is nothing short of revolutionary, and Bonnie's jubilant mood is reflected in their drive home after the procedure. Bonnie crows, 'Kebangkitan nasionalis kerayaan satu abad.' (Feels like the nationalist awakening day). From the doctor with the big ears intoning the Lord's Prayer and Pancasila, the New Order political ideology, to Bonnie invoking revolution with her joke about the nationalist awakening day, this segment highlights how culture, politics, the state, medicine and religion conspire to deny women their right to decent health care.

The final segment *Raga'te Anak [For the Sake of the Kids]* is directed by Ucu Agustin, a journalist and now a documentary film-maker (she has gone on to make several other documentary feature films, including *Perempuan Kisah Dalam Guntingan [Women Behind the Cut]* (2008) about film censorship and *Konspiracy Hening [Conspiracy of Silence]* (2010) about the health-care system in Indonesia). This film is an extremely powerful portrait of two mothers, Nur and Mira, who work as stone-breakers by day and as prostitutes in a Chinese graveyard by night, in Gunung Bolo in the area of Tulungagung in East Java. Originally Ucu began her research with the question of why so many Indonesian women working abroad were HIV positive. She had assumed that they contracted the disease from their foreign employers. It turned out that researchers in East Java found that men married to TKWs had contracted HIV from prostitutes while their wives were abroad working, and the wives subsequently contracted it from their husbands.

So in fact *Pertaruhan [At Stake]* depicts three different economies of working women: the Chinese women in Hong Kong who need to work (like the employer of Ruwati in the first film), the Indonesian women who leave their husbands to go and work abroad (like Ryantini in the first film) and the Indonesian women who work as prostitutes and service the husbands of the workers sent abroad (like Mira and Nur in the fourth and final film).

The exotic sexual availability of the figure of the Indonesian woman, so typified in Paul Gauguin's figure of *Annah la Javanaise* in *Aita Tamari vahina Judith te parari* (1893), along with the nineteenth-century romanticism of Gustave Courbet's *The Stone Breakers* (1849–1850) – a work of social realism that scandalized the salon visitors of Paris – are collapsed, deconstructed and exploded in the person of Nur, a stout, hard-working woman who sits on the ground breaking stones with her bare hands while her toddler daughter plays nearby. Nur explains that she can make 40 dollars a month breaking stones into pebbles, and the rest of the money that she needs to feed her children and send them to school comes from her prostitution, by which she makes a dollar a client.

This representation of Nur is also a deconstruction of the model wife/mother of Kartini and the model of the over-sexualized prostitute of Gerwani that Silvia Tiwon has explicated are the two models for women during the Suharto era[18] : Nur is the mother who sacrifices herself for her children through her labour. The bright washed-out colours of the exterior day scenes of her breaking stones in a blazing red t-shirt in the hot sun provide a contrast to the black and white infrared filming of her work at night in the Chinese graveyard. Because this footage is infrared, the people's eyes become like shiny points, their expressions plainly visible to us viewers. The scene of illegal prostitution is a society of ghosts or walking dead. We recognize Nur and yet we don't recognize her, as she clucks at potential clients. Like an X-ray, these images are the inverse of the representation of the national ideology of what it means to be a 'perfect' mother.

The film also interviews the gangsters who extort the prostitutes for money. Another stone-breaker/prostitute, the slender, younger Mira, talks about the man with whom she lives – her companion or '*kiwir*'– who is not a pimp but does benefit from the money that she makes. Their work hazards are police raids, which force them to run away in the dark and sometimes hurt themselves; violent clients; and diseases, including HIV/AIDS. Near the end Mira has lost hope and Nur consoles her:

> Think of your parents and kid. It's sinful to think that way. Dying is human. We can't decide our lives. God does.

Raga'te Anak is the most gut-wrenching and riveting of these four very brave and challenging films because we are brought intimately into the lives of Mira and Nur, and see how their labour, for the sake of their children, takes a toll on their own health and well-being.

With the opening title of the film *Pertaruhan [At Stake],* one is already aware that something new is being shown:

> Bekerja sama dengan Kalyana Shira Foundation
> Mempersembahkan
> Pertaruhan
> Sebuah Karya Kokektif dari Workshop Project Change 2008
> [In conjunction with Kalyana Shira Foundation
> We offer you
> Pertaruhan
> A Collective Work from the Workshop Project Change 2008]

Although it is not uncommon for a documentary to be a collaboration of different voices, *Pertaruhan [At Stake]* was intended to be a commercial feature film, exhibited in major theatres all across Indonesia. In the US, commercial documentary films are marketed in theatres as the work of a (usually) male genius: one goes to be educated by Errol Morris or Davis Guggenheim, harangued by Michael Moore or Spike Lee, or watch Morgan Spurlock gorge. In the classic history of documentary, historian Erik Barnouw divided documentary directors into implicitly male character types, which included: explorer, reporter, advocate, bugler, prosecutor, chronicler, promoter, observer, catalyst, guerrilla and discoverer.[19] The antithesis of this would be a working collective; it is an omnibus film with four stories by five different film-makers whose names only appear at the end of the film.

As I have explained earlier, the film-makers and the collaborators often step in front of the camera, or are part of the community being filmed – unlike the traditional US documentary film-maker, who is a male outsider in a position of power owing to his technology or class status. Instead of one auteur we have five directors, all having participated in a learning workshop. Ani Ema Susanti, who directed the segment on overseas workers, was herself an overseas Indonesian worker in Hong Kong; the line producer Cinzia Rini Puspita smuggles in a hidden camera to get a pap smear; and another long-time Kalyana Shira associate, Ade Kusumaningrum – the 'anti-penetration lesbian' – also gets a pap smear and has her vagina penetrated for the first time. So the crew collaborated to an extent that is atypical for a documentary film, and themselves became the subjects of the film.

Finally, I would like to point out that the long tail of a Kalyana Shira film is much longer and more involved than a typical commercial US documentary because of how they transformed the 'roadshow'. The term 'roadshow' was originally used in 1960s Hollywood to signify the heavy marketing for an epic film, like *Camelot* (1967) or *The Sound of Music* (1965), as a prestigious cultural event. For the Kalyana Shira Foundation, 'roadshowing' *Pertaruhan [At Stake]* refers to the year that Dinata, co-producer Vivian Idris and several of the directors spent taking the film on the road to the people – to cities in Java, Sumatra, Bali, Kalimantan and Sulawesi, for special free screenings to women's groups, activists, students and government. Heated discussions were often provoked by these screenings. Director Lucky Kuswandi explained that sometimes the reactions were quite defensive, as in Lampung, Sumatra, where invited officials claimed that they had already done a lot for women.[20] Another director, Ani Ema Susanti, who wears a *krudung*, was asked by audience members in Bandung: 'Aren't you ashamed wearing a *krudung* and talking about lesbians?'[21] The point of the roadshow was to raise consciousness and promote social change.

In conclusion, *Pertaruhan [At Stake]* explores the different use of subjectivity in not just the content of the film, but in its actual production and exhibition. Although this is a Kalyana Shira production helmed by the producer Nia Dinata – who is head of a production house that has made more than ten feature films, including sex comedies and dramas, and many commercials, public-service announcements and music videos – *Pertaruhan [At Stake]* is marketed as an omnibus film intended to showcase the work of emerging documentary film-makers. The directors were trained in a workshop, and the five people whose film ideas were chosen were diverse: a former transnational worker who had worked as a caregiver and dog sitter in Hong Kong, a Western-educated Chinese Indonesian gay male, a young journalist beginning to study documentary, and two men who had worked in Indonesian TV. Moreover, Dinata and her foundation spent months bringing the film to special screenings all over Indonesia to raise consciousness and promote change towards women's health and sexuality. The collective voices of the film make a stand and call out the complexity and the joy of what it means to be Indonesian and a woman in the early part of the twenty-first century. The eye of the camera becomes the 'we' of Indonesian women and Indonesian cinema.

Notes

1. Stephan Klasen and Francesca Lamanna, 'The Impact of Gender Inequality in Education and Employment on Economic Growth: New Evidence for a Panel of Countries', *Feminist Economics*, 15, no. 3(2009): 116.
2. See Anu Rammohan, Meliyanni Johar, 'The Determinants of Married Women's Autonomy', *Feminist Economics*, 15, no. 4(2009): 51 and Mary Beth Mills, 'Gender and Inequality in the Global Labor Force', *Annual Review of Anthropology*, 32(2003): 48–49.
3. Krishna Sen, 'Indonesian Women at Work: Reframing the Subject', in Krishna Sen and Maila Stivens (eds), *Gender and Power in Affluent Asia* (London and New York: Routledge, 1998), 35. Sen writes specifically on the growing numbers of affluent working women targeted by the advertising industry.
4. Youna Kim, 'Female Individualization? Transnational Mobility and Media Consumption of Asian Women', *Media Culture and Society*, 32, no. 1 (2010): 27.
5. Dian Kuswandini, 'The Rise and Fall of Indonesia's Women's Movement', *The Jakarta Post* (21 April 2010), http:///www.thejakartapost.com/news/2010/04/21/the-rise-and-fall-indonesia's-women's-movement.html.
6. Mariani Dewi, 'Nia Dinata: All It Takes Is Courage', *The Jakarta Post* (29 March 2009), http://www.thejakartapost.com/news/2009/03/29/nia-dinata-all-it-takes-courage.html.
7. Interview with Nia Dinata, 22 December 2008, Jakarta.
8. Ibid.
9. Ibid.
10. Interview with Ani Ema Susanti, 20 December 2008, in Jakarta.
11. For more on the image of Kartini see Silvia Tiwon, 'Models and Maniacs', in Laurie Sears (ed.), *Fantasizing the Feminine in Indonesia* (Durham and London: Duke University Press, 1996), 47–70.
12. Interview, 20 December 2008 with Ani Ema Susanti, Jakarta, Indonesia.

13. Tom Boellsdorf, 'Dubbing Culture: Indonesian *Gay* and *Lesbi* Subjectivities and Ethnography in an Already Globalized World', *American Ethnologist* 30, no. 2(May 2003), 237.
14. Ibid., 236.
15. Ibid., 237.
16. Interview with Lucky Kuswandi, 5 August 2009, Jakarta.
17. Ibid.
18. Tiwon, *Fantasizing the Feminine in Indonesia*, 69.
19. Erik Barnouw, *Documentary: A History of the Non-Fiction Film* (New York and Oxford: Oxford University Press, 1993).
20. Interview with Lucky Kuswandi, 5 August 2009, in Jakarta.
21. Interview with Ani Ema Susanti, 20 December 2008, in Jakarta.

References

Barnouw, E. (1993) *Documentary: A History of the Non-Fiction Film*, New York: Oxford University Press.

Boellsdorf, T. (2003) 'Dubbing Culture: Indonesian *Gay* and *Lesbi* Subjectivities and Ethnography in an Already Globalized World', *American Ethnologist*, 30(2): 225–242.

Dewi, M. (2009) 'Nia Dinata: All It Takes Is Courage', *The Jakarta Post*, 29 March, http://www.thejakartapost.com/news/2009/03/29/nia-dinata-all-it-takes-courage.html.

Kim, Y. (2010) 'Female Individualization? Transnational Mobility and Media Consumption of Asian Women', *Media, Culture & Society*, 32(1): 26–43.

Klasen, S. and Lamanna, F. (2009) 'The Impact of Gender Inequality in Education and Employment on Economic Growth: New Evidence for a Panel of Countries', *Feminist Economics*, 15(3): 91–132.

Kuswandini, D. (2010) 'The Rise and Fall of Indonesia's Women's Movement', *The Jakarta Post*, http:///www.thejakartapost.com/news/2010/04/21/the-rise-and-fall-indonesia's-women's-movement.html.

Mills, M. (2003) 'Gender and Inequality in the Global Labor Force', *Annual Review of Anthropology*, 32: 41–62.

Rammohan, A. and Johar, M. (2009) 'The Determinants of Married Women's Autonomy', *Feminist Economics*, 15(4): 31–55.

Sen, K. (1998) 'Indonesian Women at Work: Reframing the Subject', in K. Sen and M. Stivens (eds), *Gender and Power in Affluent Asia*, pp. 35–62, London: Routledge.

The Jakarta Post (2010) '154 Bylaws Haunt Women, 15 More to Come', http://ww.thejakartapost.com/news/2010/01/30/154-bylaws-haunt-women-15-more-come.html.

Tiwon, S. (1996) 'Models and Maniacs', in L. Sears (ed.), *Fantasizing the Feminine in Indonesia*, pp. 47–70, Durham: Duke University Press.

Part III

New Consumption Practices of Female Individualization

9
Fandom, Consumption and Collectivity in the Philippine New Cinema: Nora and the Noranians

Bliss Cua Lim

National Artist Nick Joaquin called Nora Aunor the 'lowly *morenita* from Iriga', the dark-skinned, destitute provincial girl who rose to unparalleled prominence as the Philippines' first media-convergent superstar (de Manila, 1970: 6). The daughter of a train porter in Bicol province, Nora Aunor exploded into the nation's popular consciousness as an amateur singing contest champion on TV and radio at the end of the sixties. By 1970, at the age of 17, with 30 films and several music recordings to her credit, she crossed over from TV and music to a lucrative career as the nation's highest-paid film star (Zapanta, 1970: 42–44). Throughout the mid-seventies and eighties, Nora Aunor helmed her own film production company and took on critically acclaimed film roles in several canonical works of the Philippine New Cinema. Still professionally active today, Nora Aunor has been called 'the most accomplished transmedia star the Philippines has ever produced, spanning a career of four decades and counting' (Flores, 2000b: i), in music, TV, film and theatre.

The girl of meagre origins had been taunted with racist remarks in her childhood ('Nora *Negra*', other children called her), but she went on to forge a spectacular career that effectively 'broke the colour line in Philippine movies' (de Manila, 1970: 58). As I have argued elsewhere, Nora's superstardom in Philippine cinema's post-studio era is significant because she forced an unprecedented break with the Filipino film industry's reliance on mestizo/a stardom. Filipino film studios 'favored mestizas for principal roles because they approximated the Caucasian features of American icons' (Tiongson, 1992: 24). In the studio era, matinee idols were invariably mixed-race actors whose light skin and

European features allowed them to be packaged as local approxima-
tions of Hollywood stars. Mestizo/a stardom was a racialized politics
of casting that enshrined tall, fair-skinned mixed-race performers with
Euro-American features as the apex of physical beauty and cinematic
glamour. In the Philippine popular imagination, the social location of
the mestizo/a star is imagined as proximate to the white privilege of
Spanish and American colonizers, the postcolonial elite and the physical
appearance of Hollywood stars. More than a figure of race mixture, the
mestizo/a star in Filipino cinema is also imagined as situated between
the 'whiteness' of the Hollywood star or of the post/colonial elite, and
the 'brown-ness' of lower-income urban audiences who comprise the
bulk of the nation's filmgoers. The ascendancy of Nora, a 4 feet 11 inch
'Cinderella superstar' and a new 'brown beauty' [*kayumangging kali-
gatan*], issued a resounding challenge to the racial logic of mestizo/a
stardom. (Lim, 2009: 318–327).

One of Nora's culturally significant feats, then, is her star persona's
ability to refunction the previously abject ethnic figure of racialized and
impoverished provincial girlhood into a figure of triumph (Tolentino,
2006: iii). The oft-repeated trope of Nora's rise from water vendor to
transmedia superstar is a narrative condensation of how her superstardom managed to breach the expected limits of what could be
achieved by women disenfranchised by class, ethnicity, provincialism,
racialization and gender.

It has often been observed that Nora's mythology has not one but
two protagonists: the individual star, Nora herself, and the collectivity
of Noranian fans (De Guzman, 2005: viii; Flores, 2000b: 7). It is here
that we glimpse a key dynamic of Nora's transmedia stardom. On the
one hand, a rhetoric of exceptionalist individuation suffuses Nora's star
mythology across several vectors. An icon of what a uniquely gifted
and charismatic individual can accomplish in the face of poverty, discrimination and adversity, Nora is individuated – that is, singularized
and set apart – from other similarly disenfranchised Filipinas by the
heights and depths of her star biography. Her commercially profitable
and critically acclaimed career in music, film, TV and theatre is a narrative of exceptional achievement punctuated by a leitmotif of suffering,
as the star's struggles with financial insolvency, heartbreak, drug abuse
and alcoholism individualize Nora as both triumphant *and* tragic. On-
screen, Nora's racialized allure as the first dark-skinned superstar of
Philippine cinema likewise individualized her, marking her as atypical
amid the pantheon of fair-skinned mestizo/a movie idols who preceded
her. On the other hand, such elements of individualization in Nora's

star persona are counterbalanced by the collectivity of her devoted Noranian fans, who were widely perceived as lower-class, feminized and dark-skinned, much like their idol. In that sense, Nora's exceptionally individualized countenance as the first 'brown beauty' to challenge the neo-colonial hold of mestizo/a stardom in Philippine cinema has simultaneously been read as a collective embodiment of her steadfast following.

One movie reporter, for example, synecdochized Nora's 'coffee-brown skin' as 'the colour of the skin of the majority of movie fans, from the *utusan* [housemaid], to the *lavandera* [washerwoman], and from the fish vendor to the grade school *titser* [teacher]' (Zapanta, 1970: 43). With its emphasis on low-income domestic or feminized work – such as housemaid, laundrywoman or market seller – the remark exemplifies the continuing prominence of poor rural and urban women among Nora's famously devoted popular audience. As Neferti Tadiar notes:

> Nora Aunor's following might be seen as a form of 'class' and 'gender' inasmuch as a great many of her fans worked as domestic labour and, more importantly, inasmuch as Nora Aunor's identificatory trait was her personification of the *atsay* [maid], a figure embodying the combined racializing and sexualizing devaluations of menial labour and poor women. This is not to say that all of Nora Aunor's fans fit this dominant profile.
>
> (Tadiar, 2004: 332)

Collectively referred to as 'Noranians', Nora's enduring fan following has since traversed the barriers of class, gender and place to include middle-class professionals, gay and straight men and overseas Filipino workers engaged in the transnational labour economy.[1] To the popular mind, however, Noranians are iconically the impoverished urban and provincial women who can recall the raucous heyday of her popularity in the early 1970s. Thus, while not being composed exclusively of older women from underprivileged social origins, the resonance of the 'Noranian' audience as a historical configuration of reception in Philippine popular culture arguably retains its predominantly gendered and generational quality (Tolentino, 1999: 6–7).

In what follows, I trace the broad contours of individual aspiration and self-imagining as well as collective, star-focused media consumption among Nora's predominantly female fans. The first section explores the new dynamics of star–fan relationships inaugurated by Noranian fandom. Calling Nora 'the former water vendor who now peddles our hopes', one fan writes: 'Millions of Filipinos loved you because you embodied them [*kinatwan ninyo sila*]. Your triumph is the triumph of our impoverished fellow citizens.... If a water vendor could succeed, then so can every farmer, carpenter, manicurist, tailor, security guard, manual labourer, housemaid, overseas contract worker, prostitute, baker, janitor, fisherman, recycler, sidewalk vendor, midwife and laundrywoman.' (Bayron, 2005: 23). Such remarks exemplify the links between star embodiment and fan aspiration. Fandom has long been recognized as having both collective and individualizing aspects; fan letters, for example, express the 'fans' desire to emerge from anonymity, to create a concrete existence for themselves in relation to the star system' (Orgeron, 2003: 79). The individualizing aspects of aspirational self-imagining attempt to 'close the gap' between individual media performer and collective social audience through an array of cinematic and extra-cinematic identificatory practices (Stacey, 1991: 155) that hinge on a sense of mirroring and felt intimacies between Nora and Noranians. In particular, Nora's embodiment of undeserved suffering, both on- and off-screen, are paralleled by tropes of sacrificial consumption on the part of her most fervent fans.

The second section of this chapter closely considers *Bona* (directed by Lino Brocka, 1980) and *Himala* ([Miracle] (directed by Ishmael Bernal, 1982). In these two films, the Filipina superstar's collaboration with the premier directors of the New Cinema resulted in critical reflections on the limits of star worship. Cinematic allegories of Nora's relationship to her audiences, both films figure fans as self-abnegating female *alalay* [aides], and point off-screen to the dynamics of fan sacrifice, suffering, aspiration and political ambivalence in Nora's collective following.

The two 1980s Nora Aunor films explored in this chapter, *Bona* and *Himala*, are emblematic achievements of what has been called the New Cinema or the Second Golden Age of Philippine film – a period of artistic accomplishment beginning in 1975 (three years after Ferdinand Marcos' declaration of Martial Law) and ending in the February 1986 People Power Revolution that ousted Marcos from power. *Himala* models the accomplishments of two government institutions that crucially contributed to the emergence of New Cinema in the 1970s and 1980s: the Metro Manila Film Festival (MMFF) and the Experimental Cinema of the Philippines (ECP), the latter under the executive directorship of the dictator's eldest daughter, Imee Marcos (David, 1990: 1–17). Film historian Joel David suggests that part of the answer to the paradox of

Philippine New Cinema – why did cinematically accomplished, politically engaged films flourish during the repressive Marcos regime? – lies in the conditions of production and exhibition that these two institutions, the MMFF and the ECP, were able to provide (David, 1990: 1–17). This may explain why the works of the Philippine New Cinema often evinced a critical militancy and a defiance of state censorship in their content, yet relied on a certain degree of complicity with the Marcos administration in terms of their production and exhibition contexts. An early ECP production in which Nora both starred and served as creative consultant, *Himala* was seen as proof of the superstar's ties to the Marcos regime. Nora's involvement in the film was rumoured to have been influenced by the Marcos family's promise to 'overwrite' her outstanding tax debts (Flores, 2000b: 122).

The 1980s straddle two contentious political eras in the Philippines. First, the twilight of the Marcos regime (1965–1986), the 'strong man' administration that institutionalized what Neferti Tadiar calls the 'feminization of Philippine labour'; and second, the anti-Marcos movement that culminated in the 1986 EDSA Revolt or 'People Power' Revolution (EDSA is the acronym for Epifanio de los Santos Avenue in Metro Manila, where most of the demonstrations occurred). That popular uprising ushered in Corazon Aquino's presidential administration (1986–1992), which would preside over the 'nationalization of the domestic labour export industry'; the export of Filipinas engaged in domestic or sexual work comprise the overwhelming majority of Philippine migrant labour. Tadiar suggests that Nora's star persona – and most importantly, her massive Noranian following – energized certain aspects of Marcos' and Aquino's contending forces while remaining fundamentally 'tangential' to both. In other words, both before and after the 1980s, Nora and the Noranians were caught up in these political polarities but not reducible to them (Tadiar, 2004: 23–24). Accordingly, the final section of this study will explore the ambivalent politics of Noranian collectivity as it intersects with Nora's much-criticized endorsement of a series of corrupt political regimes in the Philippines, from the Marcos dictatorship to the Arroyo administration.

Closing the gap: Star–fan relationships and Noranian embodiment

Filipino film critics have long recognized that Nora forged a distinctively new relationship between stars and the national public (Landicho, 2005: 109). In retrospect, one strikingly new quality that emerged in the audience dynamics of the Noranians is the shortening of the distance between the individual exceptionalism of the star and the collective aspirations of her fans. Scholarship on classic Hollywood cinema consistently demarcates identification as a key facet of spectatorship in the American studio era (Mulvey, 1989; Stacey, 1991). In contrast, Filipino film commentators in the late studio and early post-studio period (the 1960s and 1970s) consistently recognized that the Philippine star system of the studio era, in relying on the 'impossible' glamour of stars living in unrealizable social worlds, actually impeded identification among low-income movie-goers who comprised most of the popular audience (de Manila, 1965: 6–7). Mestizo/a stars were beautiful idols whose lives were impossible to achieve; their instantly recognizable distance from fans elicited worship and adoration, but precluded identification. In contrast, Nora is evoked again and again in relation to her capacity to arouse identification and aspirational self-imagining among her predominantly female following. A movie reporter describes an encounter between Nora and her female fans, witnessed at the star's home: 'Women of all shapes and sizes rushed up to meet her, called out her name repeatedly, reached for her hands.... Watching her with her fans, we partly understood why they were tenaciously loyal to her ... Nora was their friend who just happens to be a star.' (de Guzman, 1970: 40).

In part, the ability of Nora's star persona to close the gap between star and fan, her intimation of an attainable proximity – or even kinship – with her own tribulations and successes, had to do with the capacity of Noranian embodiment to foster identification between actress and audience. The racial defiance of what I refer to as 'Noranian embodiment' inheres not only to Nora's own physical countenance but also pervades the sensational fascination with her a/typical star body on the part of her massive fan following among the urban and rural poor. Remarkably atypical of previous mestiza screen goddesses, but unexceptionally typical of the ordinary moviegoer, Noranian embodiment amounted to an oppositional form of valuation. In loving their star, Noranian devotees were also explicitly championing *their own* heretofore devalorized external appearance against the neo-colonial conflation of beauty and whiteness – a solidarity mapped on the axes of racial, classed and gendered alliances (Lim, 2009: 323). The Noranians upheld the achievements of the dark one, La Aunor, who accomplished both a real and symbolic triumph against the neo-colonial racial logic that equates beauty with whiteness ['*maganda ang maputi*'] (Tiongson, 1979: 12).

Alalay and sacrifical consumption: *Bona* and *Himala*

By the beginning of the 1980s, Nora had entered a period of considerable professional and personal difficulty. On the professional front, years
of heavy smoking and alcoholism had taken their toll on her legendary
singing voice, and she teetered on the verge of bankruptcy due to failed
investments and untrustworthy business partners (Peñaflor, 1979: 24,
31). Her production company NV Productions had been established in
1972 to fulfil Nora's dream of becoming a 'serious artist and producer'
(Almario, 1983: 142). By the mid-eighties, however, NV Productions,
along with several other companies she had established at the height of
her affluence, had folded, reportedly as a result of Nora's lack of over-
sight and the mismanagement of her businesses by trusted associates
who aggrandized themselves while the star's own finances collapsed.
Depressed by the failure of her marriage to actor Christopher De Leon,
the deaths of close family members, and charges of tax delinquency –
the Bureau of Internal Revenue ordered Nora to pay outstanding tax
obligations amounting to 2.4 million pesos – Nora publicly admitted to
having attempted suicide three times by the mid-eighties (Fernandez,
1980: 11; Villasana, 1985: 8, 35).

Confronted with a spate of personal and professional crises, Nora
dreamed of making a film that would tell her own story, 'chroni-
cle... her ascent from peddling drinking water in the railroad station
of Iriga to undisputed superstardom in Philippine movies', as well as
giving something back to the unwaveringly devoted 'public who ended
up forgiving and loving her' despite her many well documented fail-
ings (Constantino, 1979: 29). In 1982, Nora made a film that arguably
answers to that description, allegorizing Nora's life script with a surprisingly unblinking, unsentimental power. *Himala* was a virtuoso collaboration between Nora and two major talents in the Philippine New
Cinema, director Ishmael Bernal and screenwriter Ricky Lee.

Regarded as one of the country's finest cinematic achievements in the
1980s, *Himala* was made under time constraints so that it could compete
in the government-sponsored 1982 Metro Manila Film Festival, where it
swept the awards for Best Film, Director and Actress. *Himala's* canonical
position in Philippine film studies is partly due to Nora, who delivered
a performance of such quiet forcefulness that it has been hailed as the
finest performance of the period and of Philippine cinema itself (David,
1995: 58).

Himala is the story of Elsa (Nora Aunor), a 24-year-old domestic servant in a drought-stricken impoverished town, who claims to have seen

an apparition of the Virgin Mary during a solar eclipse. *Himala* follows Elsa's transformation from housemaid to faith healer, from wretched poverty to a brief, relatively lucrative and conspicuous sainthood. As a result of her growing fame as a faith healer, the little town commercializes, and Elsa herself is commodified (her blessed water is sold and her followers charge a fee for her healing). The film pivots around the demystification of her apparent miracles of faith healing, as a series of events undermine Elsa's claims to divinity: she and a female disciple are raped, and the sick begin to expire under her care. The narrative's central enigma – can Elsa truly perform miracles or is she a fraud? – is apparently answered by the film's final scene. In *Himala's* famous climax, Elsa, who has hardly spoken throughout the film, tells thousands upon thousands of her stunned devotees that there are no miracles (*'Walang Himala!'*), that all events, from success to misfortune, are not God's making but our own (Illustration 9.1). Following her stunning disclosure, Elsa is shot through the heart by an unknown assassin, and her closest disciples proclaim her sainthood. *Himala*, then, may be read as a story

Illustration 9.1 Elsa (Nora Aunor) addresses her followers in the closing scene of *Himala* ([Miracle], directed by Ishmael Bernal, 1982)

about a star belatedly attempting to disabuse her fans of their misperceptions; its bleak ending suggests that such attempts at demystification will inevitably be contained and re-inscribed through cult devotion. *Himala*'s story of how a young woman of marginal social status comes to be hailed as a divinity can be read as a reflexive allegory thematizing Nora's own fandom, tracing the movement of devotion across various registers, from the onscreen narrative to the star's off-screen cult following (Lim, 2004: 61–67).

For viewers familiar with what has been called 'the height of Noramania' ['*rurok ng Noramania*'] in the 1970s (de Guzman, 2005: 7), certain scenes in *Himala* elicit a shock of recognition, making the film a reflexive paradox – a highbrow New Cinema masterpiece that makes conscious allusion to the lowbrow, feminized mass audience of a phenomenally popular Filipina star. A growing multitude converges in and around the faith healer Elsa's tiny abode, hoping to experience a miracle. Such scenes recall one movie reporter's account of an 'excited sea of people', a group of about 500 fans who filled Nora's Valencia Street home to bursting; 'women and young girls who want to believe', longing to touch the superstar and kneeling at her feet. Watching Nora's effect on the Noranians, the journalist remarks, 'it is her smallness that overwhelms, her silence that drives the crowds wild' (Velarde, 1980: 8). This observation captures perfectly the tenor of several scenes in *Himala* in which the quiet faith healer exerts a magnetic effect on a riotous legion of devotees.

The film depicts the ardency and restlessness of the enormous crowds waiting for Elsa, and the attempts of a coterie of mostly female disciples to form a kind of 'cordon sanitaire' around her, echoing journalistic reports of how Nora's closest devotees or *alalay* [literally, aide or helper] strove to safeguard the superstar during public appearances (Kalaw, 1971: 28). In the fan anthology *Si Nora Aunor Sa Mga Noranian*, one woman – a former factory worker and member of the Federation of Nora Aunor Followers – describes herself as an overprotective *alalay* who, together with others in the star's staff, would form a circle around Nora, enabling the superstar to move through the teeming multitude of her fans relatively unscathed (dela Cruz, 2005: 61–62). Such accounts illuminate the off-screen referents of scenes in *Himala*, where *alalay* are prominent. In one subdued but memorable scene in *Himala*, Elsa is ministered to by a close-knit circle of her most ardent believers, all of whom are impoverished women: Chayong (Laura Centeno) a former schoolteacher; Sepa (Ama Quiambao), a housewife and mother of two; and Aling Saling (Vangie Labalan), Elsa's adoptive mother and a

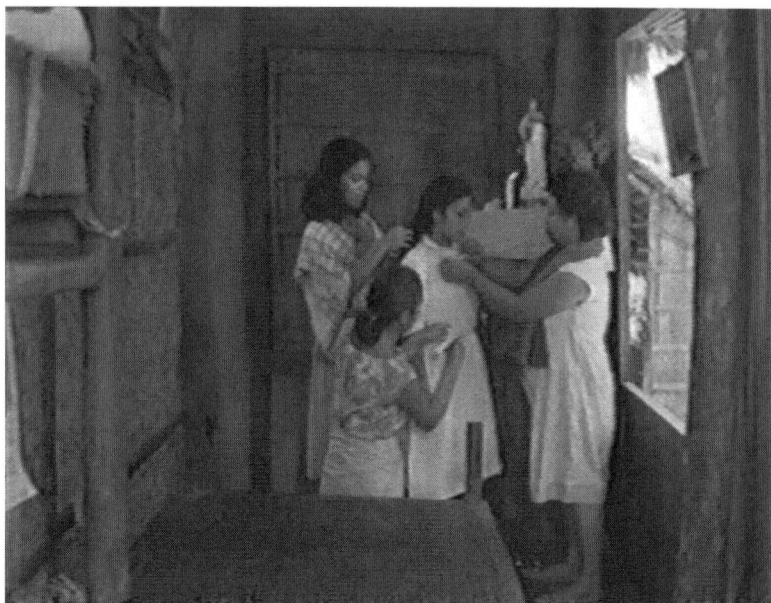

Illustration 9.2   Elsa (centre) is ministered to by a close-knit circle of her most ardent female devotees, or *alalay*, in *Himala*

housemaid like herself (Illustration 9.2). Unfolding in a long take and framed at a distance by a static camera, the women get Elsa dressed to meet her growing throng of devotees. The scene alludes to Nora's oft-remarked retinue of *alalay*, fans admitted into the actress' inner circle, forming part of her entourage and entering formal or informal service in the star's employ. In particular, the characters Chayong and Sepa in *Himala* are on-screen analogues to diehard Noranian *alalay* who, according to numerous accounts, eschewed ties to boyfriends, husbands and family members and neglected their jobs to serve their star (Caceres, 2005: 34; Dela Cruz, 2005: 61–63; de Guzman, 2005: x).

This filmic depiction of fan sacrifice extends beyond the film's inter-textual reference to Nora's off-screen retinue of *alalay*, enabling a consideration of the trope of 'sacrificial consumption' on the part of low-income Noranians. Nora's poorest fans frequently had to scrimp and save to afford the various media products that bore Nora's voice or visage – be it a film ticket, an audio recording, a movie magazine or a publicity photograph. Noranians skipped meals and walked to school or work to save up the requisite purchasing power for the star's various commodities (Diaz, 2005: 76; Reyes, 2005: 184; Roxas, 2005: 187). Similarly, a homemaker and female member of the fan organization Grand Alliance for Nora Aunor Philippines (GANAP) recalls rising at dawn to cook and pack provisions for an all-day trip to an urban movie theatre to watch Nora's newest film. Once admitted into the cinema for the cost of a single ticket (tickets ensured admission but did not restrict the number of screenings), Nora's frugal fans would stay the whole day, repeatedly watching her films while consuming packed dishes of rice and viands and eschewing the additional cost of concessions (Salazar, 2005: 187–188). The conspicuously sacrificial character of star-focused Noranian consumption prompted one journalist to ask:

> What does she possess that moves them to spend their hard-earned money on movie magazines and tabloids, on photos sold on sidewalks at 20 centavos each, on leis to offer her? What makes them abandon their studies and work, risk the ire of their parents and employers, brave the elements and travel great distances just to see her?
>
> (de Guzman, 1970: 37)

What is perhaps even more striking about a low-income audience's decision to forgo other needs or renounce their obligations to family and employers for their star is that Nora's media persona across the years increasingly shed its early character of escapist teenage froth in favour of an iconic embodiment of suffering – both in her melodramatic on-screen roles and the much-publicized travails of her off-screen biography. Why, then, did Noranians routinely make sacrifices in order to consume the spectacle of Nora in the grip of suffering?

Nicanor Tiongson mentions Nora in connection with a neo-colonial ideological value perpetuated by popular film and theatre. The idea that the oppressed are virtuous ['*mabuti ang inaapi*'] is a conceit that, in his view, enjoins audiences to adopt a passive acceptance of social injustice (Tiongson, 1979: 17). As several critics have noted, Nora incarnates the Filipino conception of suffering feminine virtue, the female martyr or *babaeng martir*. Scholars have drawn attention to the conception of sainthood exemplified by Nora even when she plays ostensibly secular, melodramatic film roles. She is repeatedly cast as a long-suffering woman who puts the needs and wishes of others before her own, the noble heroine of melodrama whose tribulation is all the more deeply felt by the audience because it is so unjust (Flores, 2000a: 94–95; Lim, 2004: 65–66; Tadiar, 2004: 227). Patrick Flores' discussion of the 'aesthetics of sufferance' in the affective-political horizon of Noranian reception illuminates the collective resonance of Nora's personification of oppression and forbearance:

> To suffer in film or to film sufferance is to reiterate the forces of popular, collective, and public sufferance in cinema as social space, and in doing so generates something new, disconfirms certain dominative modes, and makes the pain of sacrifice for redemption sufferable and necessary .... The term sufferance is favoured over suffering as it stresses the politics of overcoming a problematic site of pain in the same way that grievance reworks grief, or 'acting' processes the situation....

> Lexically, sufferance may mean 'the act or state of suffering', or the 'patience or endurance under suffering'.... The generative impulse of subjectivity emerges from subjection, rendering agents not solely compliant or complicity with power, but rather co-operators of its generation.
>
> (Flores, 2000b: 5–6)

For Flores, cinematic sufferance never inheres only to the figure of the anguished protagonist in a fictional narrative. Rather, sufferance resonates off-screen and extra-diegetically as 'public sufferance in cinema as social space'. Beyond advocating the need to endure hardship, the Noranian aesthetics of sufferance may also take on a resistive, politically agentive function by exposing and refusing to uphold structures of domination and by taking on the affective labour of overcoming pain or acting upon grief. Suffering, Flores compellingly suggests, can be generative, redemptive and collective. For the Noranians, then, suffering is not borne solely by an individual. The peaks and valleys of Nora's 40-year career – her unprecedented rise and critical acclaim, offset by a litany of failed romances, struggles with addiction, and legal and financial difficulties – are intersubjectively lived and collectively remembered by her audience of Noranians, the 'faith community' that not only consumes Nora's performances across media platforms but also remembers what their star has achieved and endured (Flores, 2000b: 11).

The collective, politically and affectively agentive character of suffering for Noranians is explored further in the last section of this chapter. At this juncture, however, it is useful to juxtapose the thematizing of fan sacrifice in *Himala* alongside another of Nora's New Cinema collaborations, a film that explored the centrality of sufferance to star worship: *Bona*. Directed by Lino Brocka, perhaps the best-known film-maker of the Philippine New Cinema, *Bona* was released in 1980 under the banner of Nora's own company NV Productions, with the star herself billed as executive producer, despite production delays due to the financial stresses caused by her unpaid tax obligations (Fernandez, 1980: 11, 14). The film was the Philippines' official entry to the Cannes Film Festival, and garnered Nora the prestigious Urian Award for Best Actress.

Whereas *Himala* exposes the religious devotion that underpins certain forms of fandom, *Bona* depicts fan desires carried to an extreme pitch of servility and exploitation. In *Himala*, the faith healer's aides or *alalay* – Chayong, Sepa and Aling Saling – play supporting roles; Elsa, the miracle worker-turned-superstar, is the film's central protagonist. In contrast, in *Bona*, the *alalay* takes central stage, with Nora playing the title character. *Himala* is about collective devotion to a charismatic female martyr; *Bona* is about a solitary female fan who renounces everything for undeserving male movie extra Gardo (Phillip Salvador), with disastrous results (Illustration 9.3). Conventional translations of the term *alalay* as assistant, helper or aide (or even the looser interpretation of the term as a member of a star's entourage) fail to capture the menial, servile and feminine connotations that the word often evokes. Yet untenable forms of female exploitation and servitude are precisely at the heart of *Bona*'s portrait of an *alalay*. Bona is the fan, who, in devoting herself to the unworthy bit-player Gardo is reduced to the status of an unpaid, emotionally abused and sexually available female domestic servant.

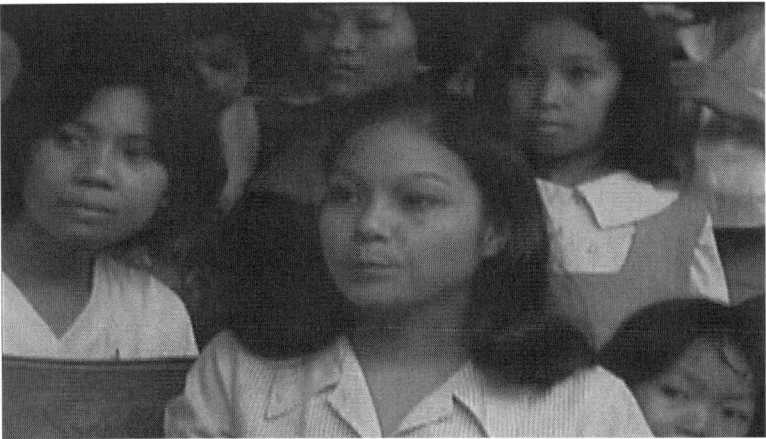

Illustration 9.3 Nora Aunor plays a movie fan in *Bona* (directed by Lino Brocka, 1980)

Referring to the presence of Nora's retinue of *alalay* on set while the actress was filming, a reporter wryly notes, 'research into Bona's character was needless on her part for she has known countless Bonas' (Parel, 1980: 32). In interviews, Nora has been critical of the demeaning connotation of the term *alalay*: 'Once my fans become close to me, I no longer treat them as fans. I treat them as friends.... In fact, I don't like calling them *alalay*.' (Stuart-Santiago, 1980: 32). *Bona* critiques the idea that becoming an obsessive *alalay* should be fandom's highest aspiration. Nora's 1980s New Cinema works suggest that there are more productive ways to channel fan aspirations, and warn against the co-optation of fan desires in the service of false promises (*Himala*) or self-destructive ends (*Bona*).

Abandoning her middle-class family to live with Gardo in the slums, Bona performs several uncompensated services for her movie idol, from cooking and keeping house to trailing along to the film set where she carries his bags, wipes his brow and stands ever at the ready to light his cigarette. Water forms a central motif in *Bona*: Bona's first significant encounter with Gardo involves his sharing her umbrella during a torrential downpour. Quickly adjusting to life with Gardo in the squatter colonies of Manila, Bona patiently waits in line with other slum residents at a communal tap and then carries heavy containers of water back to Gardo's shack, which lacks interior plumbing. Set in an era of pronounced water shortages in the urban capital of Manila, Bona's daily ritual of collecting and then heating water to prepare Gardo's bath becomes a conspicuous act of fan sacrifice, affording Gardo the everyday luxury of a hot bath under conditions where water is a scarce and precious resource (Illustration 9.4). An opportunistic womanizer, Gardo is oblivious to Bona's feelings and unappreciative of her labours. In the film's final scene, Bona boils water in preparation for Gardo's bath while he casually announces his plans to leave her to emigrate to the US in the company of a wealthy widow. Crushed by his cruel indifference and ostracized by her own family, Bona hurls scalding water at the selfish actor's body, refusing to suffer in silence any longer. With reference to this scene, one fan recalls:

> I came out of the movie theatre in a daze. Nora played the role of Bona. My own life as a fan. Blindly believing in, but finally abandoned by, her idol. That's when I saw it: even the patient endurance of suffering has its limits [*ang pagtitiis ay may hangganan*]. It will come to a boil in the fire of deception and abandonment.
>
> (Pascual, 2005: 159)

Illustration 9.4 In *Bona*, the eponymous heroine (Nora Aunor) bathes Gardo (Phillip Salvador)

As this response indicates, *Bona*'s memorable depiction of fan exploitation and vengeance overtly encouraged Nora's followers to critically reflect on the possibly self-abnegating effects of fan devotion to movie idols. Though at first seeming to encourage the patient endurance of suffering [*pagtitiis*], *Bona* ends with the *alalay* acting in her own interests at last, struggling to refuse her subjection and overcome her oppressive circumstances. In this sense, Bona is a cinematic sister to Elsa in *Himala*, another 'empowered servant' whose example 'inspires...women to act on their own claims' (Tadiar, 2004: 239).

The capacity of Nora's on-screen and off-screen star persona to galvanize women's aspirations resurfaces frequently in fan accounts. One Filipina – a provincial fan who went on to become a pre-school teacher in Japan – credits Nora with inspiring her to study to support her family financially and to attain upward social mobility for herself (Long, 2005: 114–115). Another fan reveals that Nora's film *'Merika* (dir. Gil Portes, 1984), about a Filipina nurse who migrates to the US to practise nursing, inspired her own dreams of becoming a nurse overseas (Mirandilla, 2005: 135). Such triumphalist accounts of women attaining their aspirations by swelling the ranks of diasporic Filipina workers – with women accounting for 75 per cent of the 10 million Filipino workers overseas by 2009 – have to be tempered, however, with the sobering reality that their search for a better life issues from a corrupt Philippine political and economic system that is unable to provide its citizens ample employment within the nation yet is overwhelmingly dependent on the dollar remittances generated by the export of primarily Filipina labour (San Juan, 2009: 99). As Roland Tolentino points out, 'For most Filipinas, to be an overseas contract worker is to be in a triple bind: first as a foreigner, second as a women in patriarchal societies, third as a woman working in professions regarded as menial and even socially undesirable.' (Tolentino, 1996: 58).

Political ambivalence and Noranian collectivity

While *Bona* and *Himala* are widely considered to be self-reflexive allusions to Nora's own persona and the devotion of Noranian audiences, most commentaries miss the significance of the fact that both films end with the star (Elsa) or actor (Gardo) destroyed at the hands of a fan. These films are less about star worship than the ambivalence of fan yearning, variously manifested as love, adulation, hope, disappointment and anger. Both films end by tempering exaggerated estimations of star power, instead recognizing the unruly power *in potentia* of Noranian collectivity, which may often contravene the declared wishes of the star herself.

Unmistakable parallels link the opening scene of *Bona* to the climactic conclusion of *Himala*. *Bona* opens with the January Catholic feast of the Black Nazarene, shot on location in Quiapo, the former commercial and cultural heart of Manila (Illustration 9.5). Brought to the Philippines in the seventeenth century via the Manila–Acapulco galleon trade, the

Illustration 9.5 *Bona* opens with a crowd scene at the Feast of the Black Nazarene in Quiapo, Manila

Black Nazarene is a life-sized image of a kneeling, dark-skinned Jesus that is reputed to be miraculous. By the 1920s, the image was attracting such large numbers of pilgrims that a commercial economy grew around its home, Quiapo Church. The January feast of the Black Christ has been called 'the day of the masses' and the 'greatest religious spectacle' in the Philippines, a dramatic admixture of commercial interest and religious fervour (de Manila, 1966: 67). Abandoned by the elite in the latter half of the twentieth century, the crowded Quiapo district then became identified with the majority of its tenants: low-income, working-class migrants from the provinces (Pamintuan, 2006: 2–7).

Bona's exposition introduces Nora's character as a devotee of the Black Nazarene, one of the many thousands who crowd around the Quiapo saint because its touch is said to heal the sick. The scene abruptly cuts to a shot of Bona's face on the sidelines of a movie set, clearly drawing an analogy between religious and cinematic devotion. Paralleling *Bona*'s opening scene, the closing sequence of *Himala* likewise highlights the religious resonances of star worship: Elsa's cruciform corpse is carried aloft by a grief-stricken multitude, establishing Nora's character as another dark-skinned Christ figure, albeit a feminine one (Illustration 9.6). Shot in Northern Ilocos with a cast of 3000

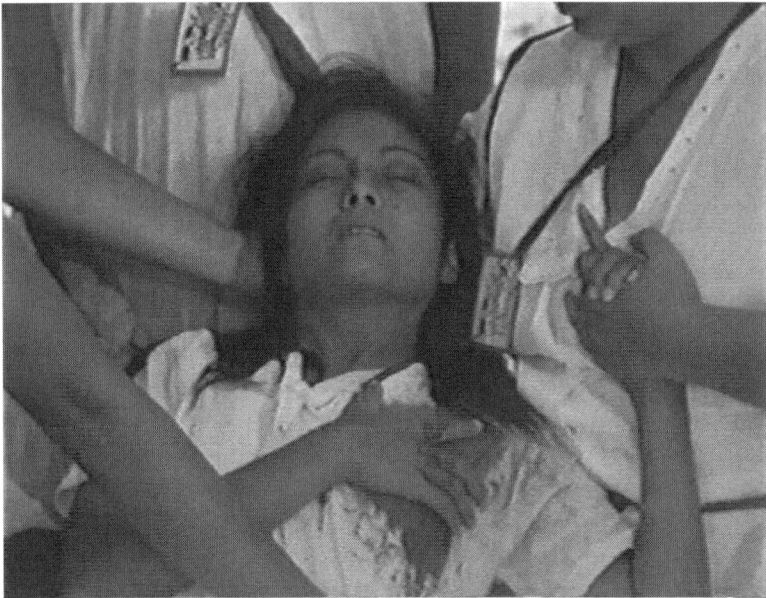

Illustration 9.6 *Himala* depicts Elsa as a kind of female Christ

extras, the scene in which the audience responds to Elsa's death with a frenzy of despair and violence has the pronounced character of a rural insurrection.

During Nora's heyday as a 1970s teen star, the throng of fans gathered around her prompted an observer to joke that the country was ripe for revolution, since a widespread uprising would doubtless take hold if Nora, the country's reigning superstar, were ever assassinated (de Guzman, 1970: 36). This is the very speculation that the end of *Himala* entertains in 1982, directly acknowledged by lines of dialogue in which a town official warns the mayor that the masses of Elsa's congregation were likely to spark a revolution.

Nora's meteoric rise in the early seventies coincided with an era of pronounced political unrest in the Philippines, as militant student leaders and other leftist groups led a series of demonstrations against the Marcos dictatorship. These were the very protests that provoked the declaration of Martial Law in 1972. The disenfranchised legion of Noranians that gathered whenever the superstar was scheduled to make an appearance was often compared to a nascent protest movement in size and scale. A writer for the *Weekly Graphic* complained, however, of the apolitical character of Noranian collectivity in the early 1970s:

> Nora Aunor... today commands the biggest and most formidable unarmed force in the Philippines. Her fans remain silent over the fascism of the state, but have epileptic fits of fury whenever an unfavourable remark is uttered about their idol.
>
> (Guerrero, 1971: 10)

As the journalist's impatient remark reveals, the young transmedia superstar and her following seemed indifferent to the radical political climate of the times. I would argue, however, that the conspicuously classed, gendered and racialized valences of Noranian embodiment had unmistakable nationalist and populist resonances. Noranians were well known, for example, to fiercely refute racist, elitist or misogynistic slurs hurled against Nora by her detractors; such fan behaviour discloses an espousal of anti-hegemonic values (Demafeliz, 2005: 66). Aware that Nora embodied the popular youth as much as the student leaders of the First Quarter Storm represented the radicalism of that era, the Marcos regime sought to cultivate Nora's support as early as 1971. During a resurgence of student protests, first lady Imelda Marcos summoned Nora to Malacañang Palace. Flattered but wary, Nora declined the Marcos' invitation to live in the palace and continue her studies alongside the

Marcos children, saying only that accepting such offers might be tricky ['*mahirap nang tanggapin*'] (Kalaw, 1971: 29).

Scholars have posited that the resistive or oppositional tendencies of Noranian collectivity were realized in the 1980s and 1990s. Having produced and starred in one of the first mainstream Filipino films to be critical of the presence of US military bases in the Philippines (*Minsa'y isang gamu-gamo* [Once a Moth], directed by Lupita Aquino-Kashiwahara, 1976), Nora is credited with her ability to 'coordinate collective sentiment' in a growing anti-imperialist, anti-base movement that culminated in the protests of 1990–1991 (Flores, 2000b: 237). It has also been suggested that Noranian collectivity 'prefigured the event of People Power' – a wave of non-violent demonstrations that deposed the authoritarian Marcos regime in February 1986 (Tadiar, 2004: 226). In 1995, Nora played the title role of an oppressed overseas Filipina worker in *The Flor Contemplacion Story* (directed Joel Lamangan), a film that broke domestic box-office records in recounting the Singaporean government's execution of Flor Contemplacion for murders that the Filipino public believed her innocent of. Provoking widespread protests against the Philippine government's failure to provide Contemplacion with requisite legal and social support, Contemplacion's story exposed the Philippine government's unwitting collusion with wealthier nations where overseas Filipina workers often experience abuse and death (San Juan, 2009: 123–124). For Flores, Nora's performance is a cinematic coordination of 'mourning, or *pagluluksa*, for Flor Contemplacion... enacting the cultural process of transforming *awa* [pity] into *damay* [commiseration] or *pakikidalamhati* [sharing of grief], and finally into *pakikiisa* [solidarity]'. Nora's film, Flores argues, 'refunctions the commodification of grief into a virtue of collective action' (Flores, 2000a: 85).

Such politically progressive expressions of Noranian collectivity notwithstanding, Nora herself has been repeatedly supportive of a series of corrupt and repressive presidential regimes. Nora cast her lot with the Marcos government in the 1986 snap presidential elections, angering and profoundly alienating her previously devoted Noranian following (Flores, 2000a: 88; Tadiar, 2004: 233). Two weeks before Marcos was ousted from power, the Tagalog weekly *Liwayway* reported with shocked disapproval that Nora was campaigning for Marcos. It was rumoured that Nora had been paid seven million pesos for her support of the dictatorship (Villasana, 1986: 34). Though Nora drew harsh criticism for her pro-Marcos stance, she also sheltered and inspired fans who had been brutalized by the regime for supporting Corazon

Aquino and the anti-Marcos opposition (Guy, 2005: 104; Pascual, 2005: 153–159). A decade later, Nora threw her support behind the successful campaign of then-vice-president Joseph Estrada, who would be elected to the presidency in 1998 but ousted over allegations of corruption in 2001. A co-founder of the Noranian fan organization GANAP recalls serving as Nora's emissary to Estrada during his vice-presidency, planning the involvement of Noranians in a 1997 charter-change rally. (Charter-change movements to revise the 1986 Philippine Constitution have been criticized for cynically attempting to extend term limits, thus allowing current officials to remain in power.) The fan recounts what is most likely an inappropriate act on the part of a public official. Vice-president Estrada is described as gifting the leaders of Nora's fan club with wristwatches in appreciation (or inducement) of Noranian support (Polistico, 2005: 169), recalling the corrupt practice of *paghahakot* [inducing the poor to show up at political rallies by offering money, food and transportation, or intimidating them into attending via threats of violence]. Most recently, Nora supported the presidential candidacy of Gloria Macapagal-Arroyo, who emphasized her physical resemblance to Nora during her successful but controversial 2004 electoral campaign. Rumours circulated that Nora had been paid six million pesos in return for her endorsement of Arroyo (Flores, 2008: 125). An unsuccessful impeachment case was subsequently filed against President Arroyo in 2005 over allegations of electoral fraud in the sensational 'Hello Garci' case. In 2011, over a year after the end of her presidency, Arroyo was arrested for alleged electoral sabotage.

As this brief encapsulation of Nora's ambivalent political involvements reveals, Nora has both channelled anti-hegemonic collective sentiment and aided traditional politicians' cynical attempts to capture the support of her enormous populist fan base. Whether true or false, persistent rumours that the habitually cash-strapped star accepted lavish payments in return for her endorsement of corrupt regimes underscores the degree to which she was widely perceived to be manipulating her famously self-sacrificing Noranian base for selfish personal gain.

Nestor De Guzman notes that the Noranian response to the star's various political missteps has been measured. In general most fans regret Nora's questionable political partisanship, but some forgive it and even admire her ability to take a politically unpopular stand. Nonetheless, Noranians have voiced a wish that Nora stop endorsing or campaigning for politicians so as not to be tainted by them. For the fans, 'Nora's reign will last longer than that of politicians, who come and go' (de Guzman, 2005: xiii). Implicit in this championing of Nora's lasting cultural – rather than political – legacy is also a canny disarticulation of Nora's unquestionable significance as a media star from her tainted track record in Philippine politics. Noranian star worship, however, stops short of compliance with the star's political endorsements, the cynicism of which has been recognized. Like the devotees and *alalay* who contravene the star's wishes in *Himala* and *Bona*, instead electing to act on their own behalf, Noranian fans have historically not always voted in compliance with Nora's directives. Crucially, Nora vis-à-vis the Noranians must be recognized as linked but autonomous social agents.

Although political administrations that wooed Nora to curry favour with the Noranians attempted to interpellate the latter as a potential electoral voting bloc, the Noranians appear to have self-identified as an organized consumer bloc, not as a political force doing their star's bidding. In the early 1970s, Nora's product endorsements sparked supply shortages, with Nora's famous advertising campaign for Dial soap credited with stimulating product demands that far outpaced marketing predictions (Quirino, 1971: 45). Despite their meagre financial resources as individuals, the Noranians were well aware of the immense consumer power that they wielded as a collective, and were willing to bring this power to bear on campaigns that by turns affirmed or defended Nora's career. In the late 1980s, learning that the channel RPN-9 planned to cancel Nora's TV show *Superstar*, the Noranians mounted a national campaign and collected more than a million signatures in support of the show, which first aired in 1975 (Arce, 2005: 21). *Superstar* moved to another broadcast station in 1990 and went on to become the longest-running variety show in Philippine TV history, spanning a period of 22 years. Noranian consumption patterns, however, did not translate into electoral obeisance to Nora's reactionary political endorsements. Flores writes that Nora was 'almost lynched during the EDSA Revolution' for supporting the Marcos dictatorship during the 1986 snap presidential election (Flores, 2000a: 88–89).

Across the highs and lows of Nora's career, the Noranians reversed the conventional star–fan dynamic by functioning as Nora's would-be redeemer, with the fans frequently offering to rescue the star from her own legendary fiscal imprudence. Recalling their success in raising funds for the National Mental Hospital in 1978 during the '*Mamera Para Kay Nora* [A Penny for Nora]' campaign, the Noranians repeatedly offered to salvage their star from professional or financial crisis by mounting fundraising campaigns in the 1980s, either by raising enough to produce her TV show themselves, or by collecting the millions of pesos needed to settle Nora's crippling tax debts. To her credit, Nora declined these generous Noranian initiatives on her behalf, doubtless aware that most of her fans were poor rural and urban folk whose participation in such large-scale fundraising campaigns would amount to a nationwide act of collective sacrifice (Arce, 2005: 20–21; Fernandez, 1980: 11; Lo, 1984: 14).

What is perhaps surprising, then, is that Nora selflessly refused to take advantage of Noranian offers for fiscal rescue while reportedly trying to manipulate their political sympathies in exchange for personal financial gain at other junctures of her career. Such vacillation recalls the political ambivalence of both the Philippine New Cinema itself – a movement that often articulated opposition to the Marcos regime while remaining reliant on the filmic institutions it had established – and the heterogeneous political charge of Noranian consumption and collectivity.

Note

1. See in particular, *Si Nora Aunor Sa Mga Noranian* (2005), a groundbreaking anthology of fan writing edited by Nestor De Guzman. Consisting primarily of contributions from Noranians active in three fan clubs, the anthology showcases the multi-generational range of the Noranian following, with authors ranging in age from 22 to 71 years old at the time of publication. Recollections by women and gay men are prominent in the collection. The Federation of Nora Aunor Followers was established in 1980 and gathered under a single umbrella institution various fan groups active in the 1970s, including many veteran Noranians who were already grandmothers by the time the anthology was published; the eldest Federation member at the time was a 94-year-old female fan. The other two fan groups that contributed to the anthology were the Grand Alliance for Nora Aunor Philippines (GANAP), established in 1990 and known for its charitable and philanthropic projects; and the US-based International Circle of Online Noranians (ICON), founded in 2000, with a network of more than 600 members by 2005.

References

Almario, V. (1983) 'Cinderella Superstar: The Life and Legend of Nora Aunor', in R. Guerrero (ed.), *Readings in Philippine Cinema*, pp. 135–143, Manila: Experimental Cinema of the Philippines.

Arce, O. (2005) 'My Prayer', in N. de Guzman (ed.), *Si Nora Aunor Sa Mga Noranian: Mga Paggunita at Pagtatapat*, pp. 18–22, Quezon City: Milflores Publishing.

Bayron, R. (2005) 'Nora Ng Pag-Asa', in N. de Guzman (ed.), *Si Nora Aunor Sa Mga Noranian: Mga Paggunita at Pagtatapat*, pp. 23–25, Quezon City: Milflores Publishing.

Caceres, G. (2005) 'Together Again', in N. de Guzman (ed.), *Si Nora Aunor Sa Mga Noranian: Mga Paggunita at Pagtatapat*, pp. 32–35, Quezon City: Milflores Publishing.

Constantino, R. (1979) 'Is Nora Aunor Fed Up with Showbiz and Vice Versa?' *Expressweek*, 22 March, pp. 28–29.

David, J. (1990) 'A Second Golden Age (An Informal History)', in Pasig (ed.), *The National Pastime: Contemporary Philippine Cinema*, pp. 1–17, Metro Manila: Anvil Publishing.

David, J. (1995) *Fields of Vision: Critical Applications in Recent Philippine Cinema*, Quezon City: Ateneo de Manila University Press.

de Guzman, N. (ed.) (2005) *Si Nora Aunor Sa Mga Noranian: Mga Paggunita at Pagtatapat*, Quezon City: Milflores Publishing.

de Guzman, Z. (1970) 'Nora, Nora, Nora', *Now*, 3(1): 36–38, 40–41.

de Manila, Q. (1965) 'Don't Rock the Star System!', *Philippines Free Press*, 58(31): 6–7, 30–32, 34, 36.

de Manila, Q. (1966) 'The Day of Downtown', *Philippines Free Press*, 59(2): 6, 67–68.

de Manila, Q. (1970) 'Golden Girl', *Philippines Free Press*, 63(28): 6–7, 57–59.

Dela Cruz, N. (2005) 'A Promise of Love', in N. de Guzman (ed.), *Si Nora Aunor Sa Mga Noranian: Mga Paggunita at Pagtatapat*, pp. 61–63, Quezon City: Milflores Publishing.

Demafeliz, J. (2005) 'Pearly Shells', in N. De Guzman (ed.), *Si Nora Aunor Sa Mga Noranian: Mga Paggunita at Pagtatapat*, p. 66, Quezon City: Milflores Publishing.

Diaz, A. Jr. (2005) 'Himala', in N. De Guzman (ed.), *Si Nora Aunor Sa Mga Noranian: Mga Paggunita at Pagtatapat*, pp. 47–49, Quezon City: Milflores Publishing.

Fernandez, M. (1980) 'Nora Aunor: Still the Queen of Woes', *Parade*, 2(10): 11, 14.

Flores, P. (2000a) 'The Dissemination of Nora Aunor', in R. Tolentino (ed.), *Geopolitics of the Visible: Essays on Philippine Film Cultures*, pp. 77–95, Quezon City: Ateneo de Manila University Press.

Flores, P. (2000b) 'Makulay Na Daigdig: Nora Aunor and the Aesthetics of Sufferance', PhD dissertation, University of the Philippines, Diliman, Quezon City.

Flores, P. (2008) 'Hanapbuhay Sa Mga Pelikula Ni Nora Aunor', in C. Paz (ed.), *Ginhawa, Kapalaran, Dalamhati: Essays on Well-Being, Opportunity, Destiny, and Anguish*, pp. 117–125, Diliman, Quezon City: University of the Philippines Press.

Guerrero, A. (1971) 'A Study in Speculation: Nora and the Golden Budhha', *Weekly Graphic*, 37(52): 10–11.

Guy, L. (2005) 'Ang Lalaking Nangarap Maging Nora Aunor', in N. de Guzman (ed.), *Si Nora Aunor Sa Mga Noranian: Mga Paggunita at Pagtatapat*, pp. 98–106, Quezon City: Milflores Publishing.

Kalaw, L. (1971) 'Getting to Know Nora – and Liking Her', *Asia-Philippines Leader*, 1(3): 27–29, 34.

Landicho, D. (2005) 'Bakit Nila Mahal Si Nora Aunor?', in N. de Guzman (ed.), *Si Nora Aunor Sa Mga Noranian: Mga Paggunita at Pagtatapat*, pp. 107–109, Quezon City: Milflores Publishing.

Lim, B. (2004) 'Cult Fiction: Himala and Bakya Temporality', *Spectator*, 24(2): 61–72.

Lim, B. (2009) 'Sharon's Noranian Turn: Stardom, Embodiment, and Language in Philippine Cinema', *Discourse*, 31(3): 319–358.

Lo, R. (1984) 'Nora Aunor: Up from the Doldrums', *Celebrity*, September: 7, 9–10, 12, 14–15.

Long, M. (2005) 'Inspirasyon', in N. de Guzman (ed.), *Si Nora Aunor Sa Mga Noranian: Mga Paggunita at Pagtatapat*, pp. 114–117, Quezon City: Milflores Publishing.

Mirandilla, V. (2005) 'Merika', in N. de Guzman (ed.), *Si Nora Aunor Sa Mga Noranian: Mga Paggunita at Pagtatapat*, pp. 132–139, Quezon City: Milflores Publishing.

Mulvey, L. (1989) 'Visual Pleasure and Narrative Cinema', in *Visual and Other Pleasures*, pp. 14–26, Bloomington: Indiana University Press.

Orgeron, M. (2003) 'Making It in Hollywood: Clara Bow, Fandom, and Consumer Culture', *Cinema Journal*, 42(4): 76–97.

Pamintuan, J. (2006) 'Pagmamapa Ng Pagbabagong Heograpikal Historikal at Kultural Ng Quiapo', *Plaridel*, 3(3): 1–7.

Parel, T. (1980) 'Behind the Scenes with Bona', *The Review*, 3(6): 27–34.

Pascual, W. Jr. (2005) 'Patotoo Sa Pelikula Ng Batang Nagpakasakit', in N. de Guzman (ed.), *Si Nora Aunor Sa Mga Noranian: Mga Paggunita at Pagtatapat*, pp. 153–159, Quezon City: Milflores Publishing.

Peñaflor, E. (1979) 'The Girl on a Pedestal', *Focus Philippines*, 24 June (31).

Polistico, G. (2005) 'Bilangin Ang Bituin Sa Langit', in N. de Guzman (ed.), *Si Nora Aunor Sa Mga Noranian: Mga Paggunita at Pagtatapat*, pp. 166–170, Quezon City: Milflores Publishing.

Quirino, J. (1971) 'The Legend Grows: Nora Revisited and Updated', *Asia-Philippines Leader*, 1(22): 20–21, 45–46.

Reyes, Y. (2005) 'Superstar Ng Buhay Ko', in N. de Guzman (ed.), *Si Nora Aunor Sa Mga Noranian: Mga Paggunita at Pagtatapat*, pp. 183–185, Quezon City: Milflores Publishing.

Roxas, M. (2005) 'Tadtarin Man Ako Ng Pinong-Pino', in N. de Guzman (ed.), *Si Nora Aunor Sa Mga Noranian: Mga Paggunita at Pagtatapat*, pp. 186–190, Quezon City: Milflores Publishing.

San Juan E. Jr. (2009) 'Overseas Filipino Workers: The Making of an Asian-Pacific Diaspora', *The Global South*, 3(2): 99–129.

Salazar, R. (2005) 'Guy and Pip', in N. de Guzman (ed.), *Si Nora Aunor Sa Mga Noranian: Mga Paggunita at Pagtatapat*, pp. 197–200, Quezon City: Milflores Publishing.

Stacey, J. (1991) 'Feminine Fascinations: Forms of Identification in Star-Audience Relations', in C. Gledhill (ed.), *Stardom: Industry of Desire*, pp. 141–163, London: Routledge.

Stuart-Santiago, A. (1980) 'Superstar Blues', *Parade*, 2(31): 31–32.

Tadiar, N. (2004) *Fantasy-Production: Sexual Economies and Other Philippine Consequences for the New World Order*, Quezon City: Ateneo de Manila University Press.

Tiongson, N. (1979) 'Si Kristo, Ronnie Poe, at Iba Pang "Idolo": Apat Na Pagpapahalaga Sa Dula at Pelikulang Pilipino', *Sagisag*, 4(9): 11–39.

Tiongson, N. (1992) 'The Filipino Film Industry', *East-West Film Journal* 6(2): 23–61.

Tolentino, R. (1996) 'Bodies, Letters, Catalogs: Filipinas in Transnational Space', *Social Text*, 48: 49–76.

Tolentino, R. (1999) 'Icons, Genres, and Values', *Pelikula*, 1(1): 6–7.

Tolentino, R. (2006) 'Media and Ethnicity', *Plaridel*, 3(3): iii–viii.

Velarde, E. (1980) 'The Constant Star', *Celebrity*, October: 8–10, 12–14, 16–17.

Villasana, G. (1985) 'Si Nora Aunor Ngayon', *Liwayway*, September: 8, 26, 35, 39.

Villasana, G. (1986) 'Nora Aunor Nagkampanya Para Kay Marcos!', *Liwayway*, February: 7, 22, 34.

Zapanta, P. (1970) 'The Girl Who Made Good', *Sunday Times Magazine*, September: 42–45.

10

'To Do Whatever She Wants': Miss India, Bollywood and the Gendered Self

Susan Dewey

'Miss India is a platform for a girl to do whatever she wants,' explained Avantika, an 18-year-old contestant at the annual Miss India beauty pageant. Although the 'anything' she mentions usually means Bollywood stardom, many Indian girls believe that the pageant grants its participants life-transforming opportunities to enter social arenas to which they would otherwise never have access. Amidst India's rapid economic deregulation and subsequent influx of international media, many Indians refer to their Miss India pageant winners, seven of whom have gone on to win the Miss Universe and Miss World titles, as their country's 'global ambassadors'.

Yet the potential for young women to access such rapid upward mobility in media-related fields is tied to their abilities to impress others through their beauty, grace and, above all, their underlying adherence to gendered social norms. Miss India thus presents an apparent paradox by reinforcing gendered stereotypes while simultaneously espousing a discourse of individual female achievement that calls upon contestants to become what the pageant terms 'women of substance'. By situating this cultural phenomenon within the broader context of female individualization and mass media in India, this chapter will explore the complex means by which many relatively privileged, young urban Indian women engage in the construction of gendered self-identity, whether they participate in Miss India or not.

At the time that Avantika affirmed her belief in the potentially limitless possibilities presented by the Miss India contest, she was one of hundreds of young urban women in India who hoped to attain Bollywood stardom through their participation in the pageant. Many such young women, almost all of whom self-identify as 'middle class', envision the pageant as a pathway into lucrative media careers that India's highly stratified class system otherwise forbids them. To understand the reasoning behind the level of investment that Avantika places in the Miss India pageant, we must examine two interrelated questions: (1) Why have socio-economic changes sparked the interest of so many young urban Indian women in pursuing media-related careers, and (2) what role has the expanding media played in female individualization in urban India?

Situated within the framework of pervasive ongoing socio-economic change in India, this chapter pays close attention to how young urban Indian women working in media-related professions formulate and act upon their desires for social mobility and individual autonomy. It is true that such women are extraordinarily privileged because of their advanced education, ability to travel abroad and their work in (or aspirations to work in) high-income professions that require socializing at night, but their views are nonetheless important due to their prevalence in contemporary urban Indian popular culture. Young women like Avantika negotiate a complex psychological and cultural terrain informed by their social class, ethno-religious community, professional aspirations and, of course, the everyday realities of life in urban India.

Situating Miss India in 'India Incorporated'

The term 'India Incorporated' first entered popular argot in the mid-1990s, and quickly gained currency as an apt description of the enthusiasm many Mumbai business and film-industry professionals felt about the reforms that accompanied structural adjustment. These reforms specifically amounted to a new pro-foreign investment industrial policy, the introduction of private banks, a liberalized import/export regime, cuts in social spending to reduce fiscal deficits, and amendments to laws in support of all of these reforms (Chopra et al., 1995). These policies vastly altered the commodity and consumption choices available to those with disposable incomes, as part of a pattern that further marginalizes already disadvantaged groups throughout the world following the implementation of structural adjustment programmes (Qadeer et al., 2001).

Structural adjustment facilitated the expansion of an already prolific media industry in India, as the changes brought about by the introduction of international media and thousands of Indian-run cable networks were vast and over-arching. The idea of 'India Incorporated' rather unsubtly positioned India as a thriving economic machine prepared to enter the world economy on equal terms with other, wealthier nations. Numerous discussions in both popular culture and company boardrooms actively debated how the country should be what diverse figures, including senior government officials and Hindi film producers, termed 'marketed' to the rest of the world (Bandyopadhyay and Morais, 2005).

Anthropologists working throughout Asia have observed a pervasive association between the implementation of neo-liberal economic policies and individuals' use of the terms 'modern' and 'fashion' as synonyms for individual choice (Gerke, 2000; Jones, 2003; Liechty, 2003). As anthropologist Shoma Munshi notes, 'the discourse about the "modern woman", particularly in Asian contexts, is underpinned by ideas of social progress, improvement and "acceptable modernity"' (Munshi, 2001: 6). Young women's widespread aspiration to social mobility through consumer consumption takes place in just such a context, and yet is also relatively confined to individuals who came of age during the economic reforms that preceded structural adjustment in the early 1990s.

The culture of consumption that arose following the implementation of structural adjustment policies sharply contrasts with the austere post-independence economic policies that focused upon reducing poverty and supporting national industries (Nayar, 2001). Neo-liberal economic policies also welcomed major international media corporations to India, thus allowing for the expansion and further elaboration upon the already prolific Mumbai-based film industry known as Bollywood. Numerous scholars have discussed Bollywood's extensive influence and popularity throughout South Asia and its diaspora, and many have noted that the cult of personality surrounding popular actresses is unlike anywhere else in the world (Dwyer, 2000; Kasbekar, 2003). While this phenomenon long predates structural adjustment, the removal of most restrictions on international media and the concomitant increase in the amount of competition faced by Bollywood film producers led to a restructuring of the industry. These shifts in Bollywood film production mirrored many of the broader neo-liberal goals of efficiency, productivity and 'international standards' based upon a western European and North American template.

Some of the most salient changes to Bollywood and other forms of Indian popular culture resulted from the 1994 introduction of the international satellite network STAR TV – a broadcasting conglomerate that beams predominantly North American TV programmes throughout

Asia from its head offices in Hong Kong (Page and Crawley, 2001). The implementation of the Prasar Bharati (Broadcasting Corporation of India) Act in 1997 removed government controls from the formerly state-administered TV network, resulting in the deregulation of national media and the proliferation of Indian-run cable TV networks. (Munshi, 2001). Individuals throughout urban India began routinely to use the media-centric English-language phrase 'MTV culture' to describe a philosophy of life that privileges individuality, the right to self-expression and celebrates conspicuous consumption in a new market economy. Those possessed of what anthropologist Gordon Mathews calls the 'receiving equipment' to take advantage of this brave new world of MTV culture did so with abandon in the newly opened nightclubs and other entertainment venues. When asked to define what 'MTV culture' meant, a young manager of a fitness spa explained:

> MTV culture has come about ever since satellite channels have come into our homes. Now we want to be like that, we want to dress like that. Fitness has become very important because everyone wants to wear tight jeans and short skirts and look good. Basically, people in Mumbai work out and make their money so they can go out at night and party, and go out in style, in the best labels. That's MTV culture.

These socio-economic changes were also strikingly gendered, and prompted a veritable revolution in urban Indian beauty culture. Prior to liberalization, Indian women had two brands of lipstick and cold cream to choose from, a number which skyrocketed to 250 new beauty products released by the multipurpose corporation Hindustan Lever in 1994 alone. French cosmetics giant L'Oreal spent more than 30 million dollars on the local manufacturing of beauty products in India in the same year (Dewey, 2008). As a senior executive at the Mumbai offices of Hindustan Lever told me during an interview, 'The Indian woman no longer compares herself to other Indians. She uses international concepts of beauty.' When I interviewed Satya Saran, the then-editor of *Femina* magazine, she was quick to note that images of female beauty had 'changed amazingly in the last five or six years because of the multinationals coming in. They brought images of beauty with them which were very different from what we had, and there we internationalized our images of beauty, and today we see that reflected in the way that young women look.'

During the course of a number of interviews I carried out at Mumbai's burgeoning gyms and spas, almost everyone mentioned the media as a powerful factor in influencing what they saw as a beautiful body. Individuals I spoke with often mentioned a deeply rooted connection between individual physical self-cultivation and often-used terms like 'awakening' to describe such cultural shifts. One personal trainer explained that urban India had experienced 'a certain awakening, actually, due to the international exposure on TV, where we're seeing beautiful people most of the time'. Indeed, many young women in Indian cities with economies that are at least superficially bolstered by economic liberalization seek to capitalize on the allure of new media, new commodities and an independent lifestyle that would have been unthinkable for their parents. Many such young women, particularly in Mumbai, have aspirations to work as models or actresses – jobs that hold magical qualities for them because of the ability to generate large sums of money for relatively little work.

The allure of fame and wealth in a media-related profession is made especially attractive to youth by the almost total lack of social mobility in India, and for good reason: a one-day modelling or film shoot can earn twice the monthly salary of the average college graduate. Modelling or acting are two of the only means by which a young person who self-identifies as part of the Indian middle class can become wealthy, famous and, above all, a youthful symbol of a new 'India Incorporated'. During the course of an interview I conducted with a popular Hindi film actress, who self-identified as middle class, she noted that such work 'was my only chance to make something of my life. Before, when I worked in an advertising agency, the people who now beg me to come to their parties wouldn't even look at me'.

Such aspirations and tales of success have inspired an equal number of small businesses eager to capitalize on young urban people's desires for social mobility. During an interview I conducted with a former Hindi film actress who started a Mumbai modelling school with hundreds of students, the actress was adamant that this potential for social mobility was a direct result of the new forms of media brought about by structural adjustment's economic reforms. She claimed that her school offered 'endless opportunity' to her students, and noted that, 'so much has happened all of a sudden that there's room for almost anyone to make something of her life'. For 15,000 rupees (about US $300), her students receive eight weeks of daily training by media industry specialists, including stylists, models, actresses and photographers. This is an exorbitantly high fee for most families, but the allure of social mobility is such that many young people rationalize the expense as an investment in their future, which they hope will extend beyond the low pay and long hours that most college graduates find in their first job. 'It's definitely about upward mobility for the young' the actress explained, 'with so much glamour and money attached to it, how could it not be?'

Situating Miss India within India

In holding such aspirations, young women ascribe to a media culture with a strongly subversive potential that is by no means confined to urban India. *Gurlz*, a Mumbai-based fashion magazine that entered circulation in the late 1990s, hosted a contest for readers called 'Design Your Dreams' in which readers were invited to send their clothing designs to the magazine with the promise of featuring the winners in a future issue. The magazine received nearly 500 entries, and all but two featured tight-fitting and skin-baring ensembles rather than the loose-fitting, modest garments typically worn by Indian women in public. A sketched entry from Jaipur in North India, for example, consisted of a cleavage-baring black spandex bikini top and faux chain-mail miniskirt. Another entry from Ludhiana, a conservative city in the northern state of Punjab, featured a sheer mesh gown with a bathing suit worn underneath.

What made young women in Jaipur and Ludhiana – mid-sized north Indian cities where modest dress for females of all ages is both the expectation and the norm – design garments that they could never wear in public in their home cities? The consistency with which such young women associated being scantily clad with modernity points to a way of being 'in fashion' that has everything to do with perceptions of female autonomy, at least in terms of being able to choose what to wear. A group of Mumbai adolescent girls with whom I carried out a focus group on the subject of dress and individual identity were divided in their opinions on the subject. Some dismissed their classmates' desires to wear provocative clothing as a form of what they termed 'aping the West', while others insisted that, were it not for what they called 'India's backwardness', girls and women would not need to think so carefully about their choice of garments. One particularly reflective young woman, who had spent several years living with her parents in the US, took the middle ground by noting:

> Wearing skimpy clothes in the West makes people think you are a bimbo-type, but here in India it means you are interested in fashion. It's because in our families we aren't so free to make decisions

about the big things, so we choose the small-small issues, like wearing skimpy clothes. You see, the word 'fashion' is misunderstood by our old Indian thinking. According to some girls, fashion is wearing short clothes, and a little bit of exposure here and there is also fashion.

As the speaker hints above, young women's choices about what to wear occur on tense fault lines that span generational differences. Hence the post-liberalization social changes surrounding individual rights to choose that centred upon beauty, consumption and sexuality were, of course, embedded in gendered social values that police women's sexuality. These tensions are evident in multiple spheres of popular culture as well. For instance, Hindi film actresses often appear on the covers of magazines in revealing clothing that, prior to liberalization's influx of US and western European media, would have been (and to some degree still is) taboo. However, these revealing forms of dress belie the deeper and enduring reality that, despite their fame and popularity, such women hold a deeply ambivalent social status in a moral economy that places a high value on premarital female chastity and absolute post-marital fidelity.

Most marriages in India are arranged with careful regard to social class as well as educational and ethno-religious background. Nonetheless, a number of professional urban women are increasingly opting for greater individual control over life-partner selection processes, as evidenced by the later age at which many such women choose to marry in Mumbai. Women working in media-related professions evince somewhat divergent views regarding relationships that stem in part from their individual experiences and marital status, and yet three striking commonalities emerged in the course of my interviews with women. The first is a high degree of overlap between the companionate ideal of finding an equal (Wardlow and Hirsch, 2006) and the cross-generational preference, when arranging a marriage, for matching individuals from similar backgrounds. Second is the common belief that women working in the media possess a unique set of bargaining skills, particularly beauty, education and earning power, that helps to mitigate what some view as restrictive community norms. Finally, women also consistently mentioned that they felt an uncomfortably high degree of pressure regarding their futures, particularly with respect to marriage.

Many social scientists have argued that marriage itself is a historically recent idea that is often rather deceptively labelled 'traditional' – a term that implies that a social practice has always been stable and runs the risk of branding all variations on it as something contrary to convention. Sociologist Noel Gist observed as early as 1954 that the advent of mass media, specifically in the form of Bollywood films, coincided with the consolidation of national legislation on marriage in a newly independent India. Writing on the growing popularity of matrimonial advertisements in nationally syndicated Indian newspapers, Gist predicted a decline in arranged marriages because 'the procedure itself is not satisfactory for those persons for whom "freedom" has meant freedom to select a husband or wife' (Gist, 1954: 481).

Gist's mid-century predictions regarding the demise of extended family involvement in the arrangement marriages were, of course, premature. One of independent India's most challenging tasks lay in the codification of marriage laws, as gendered norms regarding heterosexual unions are powerful indices of social change and ways of thinking about the family. Efforts in the early and mid-1950s to systematize these divergent norms resulted in an enduringly controversial set of laws known as the Hindu Code Bill, which included the Hindu Marriage Act of 1955, which, among other things, prohibits polygyny and mandates the ages of 18 and 21 for brides and bridegrooms, respectively. Scholar-activist Madhu Kishwar (1994) notes that the level of attention paid by colonial officials and post-independence leaders alike to defining marriage in limited, state-regulated terms clearly indicates that such rules were never set in stone and remain, rather unsurprisingly, in flux today.

Yet such debates about what constitutes an appropriate marriage are ongoing and regularly acted out on Bollywood screens, in newspaper accounts of 'sham marriages' carried out by unscrupulous men who consummate and flee, and, most importantly, among family members and friends. Bollywood films and other forms of Indian popular culture are replete with tales of romantic love and companionate marriages, particularly in the famous cinematic plot formula of two lovers who are torn apart by class or religion, only to be reunited with family approval through some happy twist of fate.

Hence while family norms are certainly being reconfigured in multiple ways for women who work in media-related professions in Mumbai, such reconfiguration takes place within in a set of pre-existing norms. Very few of the female media professionals that I interviewed lived in extended family arrangements, but almost none of them lived alone. Those who still lived with their parents experienced a close guarding of their sexuality despite their sometimes significant economic contributions to the household. One woman I interviewed protested such structures in her characterization of the limited scope women had for relationships with their male peers, lamenting that, 'those of us who choose to stay single because we have careers that we are passionate about get stuck with all the [male] weirdoes who are not married, or we are with married men'. An unmarried executive at a multinational corporation expressed her discontent with such norms by discussing the deep generational divides between her own world view and that of her parents, with whom she lived:

> See, what I would really love is to move to Europe and work and spend my weekends travelling, but my parents could never accept that. My father wouldn't even be able to accept me living on my own in Mumbai, let alone in another country. That is a problem for me, but I can't do anything about it. And my mother- I mean, when my mother got married, before her wedding someone told her to use cold cream and she didn't know what that was. How can I possibly relate to her?

The issue here is not cold cream, but rather notions of appropriate female behaviour. In this vignette, cold cream serves as a signifier for urban knowledge and the world view that accompanies it. The generation gap that exists between this woman and her mother is thus both chronological and cultural, and tellingly employs the metaphor of beauty culture (and lack of knowledge about it) as a symbol of different ways of thinking about womanhood and independence. Most of my interlocutors noted that the ability of young women to make such choices lies partly in one's geographical location in India, about which quite a few young women observed something to the effect of 'Mumbai is the only place in India where women can be whatever they want'. One unmarried film director in her late twenties noted:

> In Mumbai, women get to be freer than in Delhi because there are so many actresses here, so many creative people. With so many such people, it isn't as likely that people will want to keep their daughters locked up at home, like they do in Delhi. Mumbai is where all the advanced, more international and media savvy people live, and so naturally women are going to be more advanced and international as well.

A female assistant director I interviewed about her work on a popular TV show explained her belief that the media had been instrumental in encouraging women to take on new roles as soldiers and police officers. 'It's all because of us, because of TV,' she explained, 'we in media make women realize that they have greater opportunities than they thought they did, and that they can do more than just get married.' This sentiment was echoed by a junior editor at *Femina* magazine, who opined that women in Mumbai, where the magazine is published, serve as role models for the rest of India:

Mumbai women have a much more liberal mindset. They are freer because of the opportunities that Mumbai gives, and its cosmopolitan nature. All women in India yearn for that Mumbai kind of freedom. We see that in the letters we get [from readers]. We are a national magazine, so we can see that sometimes women living in smaller towns have quite radical ideas, but they cannot live them.

Many young women who work in the media share similar views of Mumbai women as uniquely able to make choices that allow them to chart their own life course. Such attitudes were particularly explicit when women discussed their views on workplace relations between men and women. A staff member at a prestigious spa catering to many Bollywood professionals acknowledged how employers specifically hire women workers in customer relations to capitalize upon what she (and many others) viewed as an inherently sexual dynamic between men and women. She felt that this was a particularly clever business strategy on the part of the almost exclusively male management, as 'men will agree to more things if they are proposed by a pretty woman. This is wrong, but we have to live this way if we want to work'.

Almost all of the women I interviewed cited the strong cultural association that women's individual decision-making has with female sexual promiscuity. Throughout India, cultural norms regarding that normalize male desire have been historically balanced by systems that make sexual access to women to whom they are not married difficult for men. For actresses and other women working in the media, aggressive male sexuality continues to be the norm without the safeguards that exist for women in the rest of India, such as the supervision of interactions between unrelated men and women.

Considering the rhetoric of independence so commonly voiced by Mumbai women, it is a curious paradox that while rural people may have the same ideas about male sexuality as their urban counterparts, rural women are potentially more protected from unwanted sexual attention via a system in which their male family members regulate sexual access to them. Many Hindu textual traditions understand female sexuality as double-edged in nature, with women in constant danger of falling victim to predatory male lust and yet able to 'digest' more sexually than men (Wadley, 1994). Anjali, an aspiring actress, succinctly summed up what she viewed as the state of affairs among her Mumbai peer group by noting that men remained sexually aggressive while a number of women increasingly emulated what she characterized as 'male behaviour':

> This women being honorary men business absolutely has to go. This promiscuous behavior, 'oh, I slept with him, no big deal'. It's ridiculous, really. Why should women lower themselves nine steps instead of men taking one step forward? I don't see the difference between this and the past, honestly. It's a different set of behaviors, that's all, with women accepting and even endorsing a system that favors men.

Women are consequently left alone to negotiate sexual norms tilted heavily in the favour of men, which exist simultaneously with increased cultural messages that encourage women to engage in intimate relationships before (and sometimes outside of) marriage. Such relationships must necessarily be kept hidden from family members and, sometimes, from friends, because they are so taboo. Such secrecy not only encourages unsafe sexual behaviour and reduces women's abilities to make informed decisions but also creates a system in which any negative repercussions that women encounter are constructed as their own fault.

Hence young women working in media-related professions in Mumbai operate under multiple levels of restrictions. Their gender, professional ambitions, independence and cultivation of their beauty renders them both objects of desire and at risk of sexual harassment from employers and others in positions of power. Tania clearly mentioned this in her description of why she wanted to enter Miss India, noting that she felt the pageant

> ... was my only chance to make something of my life, because this is the one place that if you want to get into media you know the men are not going to be funny with you, because it is such a prestigious event that they restrain themselves.

It is in this cultural context that young women enter the Miss India pageant, full of their own notions of what achieving their fullest potential might mean and, at least in some ways, free from the threat of the sexual harassment that they might face in other media venues.

Miss India and the limits of female agency

The process of choosing a Miss India begins every year in August or September, when *Femina* magazine publishes entry forms on its website, in issues of the magazine, and in its parent publication *The Times of India*. Several thousand young women, most of whom live in the main urban centres of Delhi, Mumbai and Bangalore, submit photographs of themselves along with completed entry forms affirming that they are more than 5'7" tall, less than 25 years of age, unmarried and biologically female. Pageant officials select approximately 25 young women from this pool of applicants to participate in a pre-pageant 30-day residential training seminar in Mumbai, where the contestants attend fitness classes twice a day and have all of their meals catered by a well known dietician. This opportunity to meet with the individuals who train them, all of whom are extremely renowned media professionals, gives the young women an opportunity to create social networks that will benefit them long after the pageant has finished (Dewey, 2008). As 2003 pageant contestant Mareesha explained, 'Even if you don't win, you gain something, so it's not a wasted effort. You make so many contacts, by the end you have 15 different options – serials, ramp, whatever.'

The ability to participate in such networks, however, is contingent upon the ability of individual young women to fit a predetermined mould. Young women at the Miss India pageant aspire to literally embody and to evince, through their culturally sanctioned expressions of individual self-confidence and ambition, what is discursively constructed in South Asia as 'international standards'. Such standards are inculcated at the training programme by a group known as 'the experts', comprising a host of Bollywood celebrities and other media professionals well known in Mumbai and elsewhere in India. Those with whom the contestants have daily contact include, at a minimum, a choreographer, fashion designer, dietician, personal trainer, hair stylist, self-styled 'grooming expert', make-up artist and a spiritual guide who relies upon syncretic Hindu-Buddhist philosophy in imparting advice. At scheduled intervals in their tightly packed days, the young women also meet Bollywood film producers, directors and others closely connected to the otherwise very tightly knit world of the media.

Young women enter the training programme fully aware that participation requires extensive physical and cultural transformations that involve, in some cases, a complete personal transformation. Radha, a contestant from Delhi, told me that 'the training programme means that you kill whatever you are in terms of lifestyle in order to handle celebrity'. Shonali, from Calcutta, echoed this sentiment in noting that the experts at the training programme 'turn you into a complete lady, but when people watch you more and more, your concept of individuality just goes'. Such statements are somewhat at odds with the rhetoric of confidence and ambition espoused at the pageant. As contestants use their knowledge gained at the training programme to form new relationships with themselves and the world around them, they are clearly aware that they must also ascribe to cultural norms surrounding appropriate roles for young women.

One of the most dramatic physical transformations during the training programme involves skin colour, as every single one of the young women undergoes some kind of skin-lightening treatment. The resident dermatologist Dr Jamuna Pai emphasized the need for all the contestants to chemically lighten their skin through the use of the peeling agents Retin-A and glycolic acid and, in the case of isolated darker patches of skin, laser treatments. When I asked Dr Pai why light skin was such a concern, she explained:

> Fair skin is an obsession with us, it's a fixation. Even with the fairest of the fair, they feel they want to be fairer. It isn't important anymore, because the international winners are getting darker and darker [in skin color]...but we still lighten their skin here because it gives the girls extra confidence when they go abroad.

Miss India participants must maintain a rather precarious balance between simultaneously cultivating their own individual ambitions and creating the appearance of embodying all the desirable qualities of Miss India. This tension is evident in recurring training programme discussions about 'confidence', which signifies everything from extraordinary beauty to eloquent public speaking. Training programme participant Anita explained that, 'Miss India has everything to do with inner confidence, because in India girls are not that independent at this age.' In the name of cultivating such confidence, then, young women undergo dramatic physical transformations involving their body shape and skin colour.

Indeed, pageant organizers and experts often laud a young woman's willingness to enthusiastically undertake such transformations as a predictor of her future success. The pageant's resident personal trainer

Mickey Mehta insisted that the young women who worked the hardest at modifying their bodies and inner selves were those who often went on to win. Drawing upon nearly a decade of experience helping contestants to lose weight and sculpt their bodies into the lean shape desired at the pageant, he noted that:

> The ones who keep working hard despite everything are the ones who win. I've seen many such girls. I worked the hardest with [eventual Miss World winner] Diana Hayden, who lost almost 15 kilos, and then there was [eventual Miss World winner] Yukta Mookhey, who was so huge [overweight] that people just wrote her off completely, but during the training she worked so hard that she lost 12 kilos and then on her way to Miss World she lost more.

Mehta's association between losing weight, hard work, and eventual success underscores the unique world of the pageant, where young women work hard to become underweight and use their 'confidence' to largely answer questions in a pleasing, apolitical manner.

All the same, more than one contestant whispered conspiratorially to me, 'I don't give a damn about world peace. I just want to be famous.' This desire, however elaborately veiled under discourses of idealized femininity, inspires young women to consciously mould themselves under the watchful gaze of the experts throughout the course of the training programme. As Hemant Trevedi, an eminent Indian fashion designer and the Miss India pageant choreographer rhetorically asked all of the contestants on the first day of the training programme, 'To those who criticize beauty pageants as frivolous, I ask: tell me where else in India or the world can 20-year-old girls stand up to speak and actually have people listen to them?' Trevedi's statement speaks volumes about the terms upon which young women are, indeed, able to speak and be heard in a professional field that simultaneously requires their participation while devaluing their role as actors and agents.

Conclusion

In *No Shame for the Sun: Lives of Professional Pakistani Women*, feminist scholar Shahla Haeri (2002) seeks to privilege 'the women's discourse, and to underscore the women's uniqueness by making them visible...like the sun that shines brilliantly and publically'. The women whose lives and views on relationships and work are described in this chapter already live extremely public lives by virtue of their work in or around media-related fields in India's largest, most culturally diverse city. Their views on marriage and their professional lives reveal that much of what such women aspire to rests upon the premise of their equality with men. Ironically enough, we see that the ways in which they seek to gain that equality often end up replicating the processes that enable male privilege in the first place. Young women like Avantika, whose belief in the power of the Miss India pageant to transform female lives opened this chapter, clearly do obtain opportunities for social mobility through their participation in such events. However, the terms upon which they are able to do so are cross-cut by enduring gender norms that carry a heavy, conflicted cultural weight.

References

Bandyopadhyay, R. and Morais, D. (2005) 'Representative Dissonance: India's Self and Western Image', *Annals of Tourism Research*, 32(4): 1006–1021.

Chopra, A., Collins, C., Hemmings, R., Parker, K., Chu, W. and Fratzscher, O. (1995) 'India: Economic Reforms and Growth', International Monetary Fund Occasional Paper, 134. Washington: International Monetary Fund.

Dewey, S. (2008) *Making Miss India Miss World: Constructing Gender, Power, and the Nation in Postliberalization India*, Syracuse: Syracuse University Press.

Dwyer, R. (2000) *All You Want Is Money, All You Need Is Love: Sex and Romance in Modern India*, pp. 135–158, London: Cassell.

Gerke, S. (2000) 'Global Lifestyles under Local Conditions: The New Indonesian Middle Class', in C. Beng-Huat (ed.), *Consumption in Asia: Lifestyles and Identities*, London: Routledge.

Gist, N. (1954) 'Mate Selection and Mass Communication in India', *The Public Opinion Quarterly*, 17(4): 481–495.

Haeri, S. (2002) *No Shame for the Sun: Lives of Professional Pakistani Women*, Syracuse: Syracuse University Press.

Jones, C. (2003) 'Dress for *Sukses*: Fashioning Femininity and Nationality in Urban Indonesia', in S. Niessen, A. Leshkowich and C. Jones (eds), *Re-Orienting Fashion: The Globalization of Asian Dress*, pp. 185–213, New York: Berg.

Kasbekar, A. (2003) 'Hidden Pleasures: Negotiating the Myth of the Feminine Ideal in Popular Hindi Cinema', in R. Dwyer and C. Pinney (eds), *Pleasure and the Nation: The History, Politics and Consumption of Public Culture in India*, pp. 286–308, London: SOAS.

Kishwar, M. (1994) 'Codified Hindu Law: Myth and Reality', *Economic and Political Weekly*, 29(33): 2145–2161.

Liechty, M. (2003) *Suitably Modern: Making Middle Class Culture in a New Consumer Society*, Princeton: Princeton University Press.

Munshi, S. (2001) 'Introduction', in S. Munshi (ed.), *Images of the 'Modern Woman' in Asia: Global Media, Local Meanings*, pp. 1–16, London: Curzon.

Nayar, B. (2001) *Globalization and Nationalism: The Changing Balance in India's Economic Policy, 1950–2000*, Delhi: Sage.

Page, D. and Crawley, W. (2001) *Satellites over South Asia: Broadcasting Culture and the Public Interest*, London: Sage.

Qadeer, I., Sen, K. and Nayar, K. (2001) *Public Health and the Poverty of Reforms: The South Asian Predicament*, Delhi: Sage.

Susan, Wadley (1994) *Struggling with Destiny in Karimpur*, 1925–1984, Berkeley: University of California Press.

Wardlow, H. and Hirsch, J. (2006) 'Introduction', in J. Hirsch and H. Wardlow (eds), *Modern Loves: The Anthropology of Romantic Love and Companionate Marriages*, pp. 1–22, Ann Arbor: University of Michigan Press.

11
Post-Socialist Articulation of Gender Positions: Contested Public Sphere of Reality Dating Shows

Jing Wu

Popular culture and public consciousness in mainland China can be described as post-socialist in the twenty-first century, though many argue that socialist memories, desires and legacies still linger in the field of culture and ideology and exert power in multiple forms and under unexpected circumstances (Rofel, 1999; Hanser, 2006; Ho and Ng, 2008; Erwin et al., 2009). A post-socialist culture places emphasis on individualism, materialism and a de-politicized view of the mundaneness of everyday life as antidotes to the collectivism, self-sacrificial puritanism and class struggle that characterize the nucleus of socialist ideology. In place of the increasingly emptied-out socialist cultural values, tradition and the market are two central forces that provide social identity and cultural meaning in the vicissitude of the 'free' and globalized economic and social sphere. Whatever their differences and contradictions, the revitalized traditional culture and newly introduced market converge on the theme of family value and domesticity. It is within this theme that popular sentiment about gender and gender roles figure prominently, and the socialist legacy of women's independence and equality with men is questioned, resignified and toppled most heavily.

Female individualization is one significant idea that is caught in the complex interaction and crossfiring of various cultural traditions of gender discourse. Socialism promoted gender equality but condemned individualism. In the post-socialist era, it is generally considered backward and conservative to subsume individual interests under collective goals. The sense that a modern culture should encourage individuals to pursue their own happiness and that the success of society is mostly based on individual efforts and market competition has greatly reduced the legitimacy of socialism as a modern ideology. However, the idea of individualization is also intermingled with a pre-socialist understanding of social roles as naturally given, especially gender roles. Socialist corrections of the gender relationship through education, legislation and policies of equal opportunity in the public sphere are thus ironically considered to be behind the times, blind to sexual differences and antithetical to modern trends. Women in contemporary China are therefore facing paradoxical expectations to achieve more as an individual and at the same time perform more naturally female roles as supporters of the family, community and men. Socialist tradition has laid the ground for women to gain happiness and success independently of men, yet a capitalist economy creates new barriers for women to have comparable achievement with men and undermines the ideal of individualization as an achievable goal for women. The infiltration of commercialism in the mass media has also seen representations of women as the sex objects of men and as bodily creatures become more prominent and widespread in mainstream culture, while unconventional imaginations about women's lifestyle are mostly confined to the realm of high culture. The imagination and self-imagination of gender positions and gender roles are unavoidably implicated in social aspirations to modernity and varying understandings of what it means to be modern and progressive.

This chapter aims to explicate the intricacies of post-socialist gender discourses that permeate the Chinese mass media today, using the specific example of a popular reality dating show, *Take Me Out (Fei Cheng Wu Rao)*. The show came out in early 2010, and quickly became the most watched and talked about reality genre in China because of its unusual format and controversial commentaries of female and male participants on each other, which are symptomatic of the contested gender stereotypes and gender ideologies that already circulate prominently in the wider society. The programme is significant to explore, as it ties together several lose ends of social and discursive development in contemporary China, especially concerning female individualization and the social discourses that both encourage and condemn this new image of female lifestyle. One issue is the rising concern over the difficulty of finding the right person to marry among the urban, middle-class generations that were born after the 1970s. The one-child policy; changing lifestyles of the urban white-collar workers; precarious interpersonal relationships in modern life; and better-educated career women who find it hard to locate equally, if not more prominent, men to marry are all recognized by social critics as the reasons behind this phenomenon (Zhang, 2007; Zuo and Xia, 2008; Chen, 2009; Zhou, 2010). The topic has become a major stalk of mass-media discourse, as well as in popular debates on interactive new media. The mainstream discussion is heavily slanted towards seeing women (rather than men) who stay single beyond the average marriage age as socially and psychologically problematic – to the extent that the term 'leftover women' (sheng nv) has been coined to label the heterogeneous group of female adults who stay single for various reasons. The reality dating programme *Take Me Out* is centred on the process of choice and evaluation between men and women, so issues such as different self-understandings of the two gender positions and their varying expectations of each other frequently surface. This provides a rich intertextual resource to explore the precarious, ambiguous and contested ways of gender interpellation and gender relationship in contemporary China, especially how female individualization is represented and dealt with.

The second discursive field has to do with a rising commercial culture that increasingly targets the young and the dreamful in order to boost sales based on manufactured desires, fantasies and fears that can lead to new consumption practices. Entertainment programming, like reality TV, is closely tied in with the promotional apparatus. Not only are product placements and commercial announcements within programmes taken for granted and rationalized within the TV industry, but also the content as a whole is constructed around the notion that lifestyles presented in it are amiable with and conducive to the normalization of the commodity defined environment of the urban middle class. The naturalization of commodity as an integral part of a happy life is frequently manifested in *Take Me Out*, as participants examine their potential dates' career, income and material conditions. The blatant materialism expressed by some female participants has been the source of huge controversy among the audience and general public, and has even incurred heavy handed censorship by the regulatory body of the state. One of the new restrictions enforced on reality dating shows is that the organizer should be very scrupulous in their selection of participants, from the tens of thousands of applicants, to ensure that they are really serious about finding a date rather than using the chance to get the 15 minutes of fame by speaking outrageously on TV. In practice, this is hard to manage, and producers try to reduce risk by editing sections and utterances that are deemed inappropriate or insensitive. Not surprisingly, censorship creates its own backlash. By accusing the show of expressing and glorifying moral degradation and materialism, it reminds people of the already obsolete value system of socialism, and encourages them to notice and reflect upon the death of socialist culture under the current regime. At the same time, censorship belies the government's claim that individual gain can amount to collective good in a market economy. There is also the irony and hypocrisy of accusing women of putting individual comfort and material gain above family value and true love by an ideological institution whose cultural legitimacy partly comes from the promise to liberate women from the oppressive tradition of family, obedience and self-sacrifice. It is therefore interesting to explore how socialist, traditional and consumerist ideas of gender relationship, women's position in society and the institution of the family confront, intermingle and negotiate with each other within the larger discursive field generated by the reality TV show.

Finally, it is necessary to consider the genre of reality TV and its unique development in China. Reality programming began its encroachment into prime-time TV in Western countries during the 1980s. With low production costs, the convenience of product placement and targeted merchandising, chances of audience participation and the appearance of realism, the reality TV genre combines the economic, social and aesthetic aspirations of the era of neo-liberal globalization so well that it has become one of the major genres of networks and cable TV, as well as new forms of interactive TV (Raphael, 2009). Through format trading and localized content, reality TV is welcomed by most TV channels in China. This reality dating show is a successful case. By letting real people exhibit their lives, thoughts and behaviours on stage, reality TV has the paradoxical effect of revealing some hidden realities of society while exerting a disciplinary force on those individuals who expose themselves to public scrutiny (Andrejevic, 2002). Dating shows form such a platform on which gender performance, self-identity and hegemonic gender discourses confront, contend and negotiate. *Take Me Out* is especially interesting because its women participants, and sometimes the men too, are notorious for their eagerness to express and argue on stage, even if it damages their chances of making a good impression on their potential dates.

New gender discourses of post-socialist China

One of the most cited achievements of Chinese socialism is the degree of gender equality realized in an East Asian society, a region that is known for the cultural value of emphasizing women's obedience to men and to authority. Socialism has emphasized the equal ability of women to participate in the public sphere of education and production, towards the collective cause of socialist modernity. By the 1980s, Chinese women, especially among the urban population, were enjoying much more power and equality in many social fields.

However, because socialist gender discourse mostly focuses on the public sphere, concerning the private sphere of sexuality and sexual relationships within the family, socialist teachings have only superficial moral dictums of mutual respect, tolerance and sharing to offer. The most significant reason for this is that sexuality and family life are not considered very important in socialist culture, even for their role as a stabilizing force in society. China's public authorities used to be active in offering a matchmaking service to young citizens in place of the tradition of arranged marriage, but through this they cultivated a sense of love and binding between two persons as the basis for a more energetic life devoted to socialism. Sexual desires, bodily attraction and economic status are downplayed in a cultural environment that is against materialism and individualism. In this sense, socialist gender politics are top-down and unbalanced, with cultural norms of obedience and self-sacrifice in the domestic sphere rarely addressed and questioned as long as they fit well with the agenda of state-building. The concept of family and the gender relationships involved are not adequately problematized from a feminist standpoint, and they are simply borrowed from the traditional culture to serve the cause of a new social order.

With the introduction of a market economy and the promotion of a more individualist and materialist cultural consciousness based on material gains, self-love and happiness, gender discourses and realities in China have changed drastically since the 1990s. On the one hand, a capitalist economy created new disadvantages for women in the job market while much of their social welfare was withering away. Thus, women started to experience great contradictions between what they were brought up to believe about women's rights and independence and what they had to face in everyday life and the workplace. On the other hand, with the socialist ideology losing its credibility, traditional culture and the newly emerging commercial culture soon came in to fill the vacuum. The ideas of sexuality, women's virtue, gender roles in society and their relationship to modern ways of life became prominent in post-socialist gender discourses.

It is the post-socialist discursive field that starts to highlight the issues of individuality and its ramifications in the domestic sphere, both to make cultural inroads towards global capitalism and to cast criticism on socialist culture. In her article *Postfeminist Media Culture:*

Elements of a Sensibility, Gill argues that a post-femininity cultural sensibility includes: 'The notion that femininity is a bodily property; the shift from objectification to subjectification; an emphasis upon self-surveillance, monitoring and self-discipline; a focus on individualism, choice and empowerment; the dominance of a makeover paradigm; and a resurgence of ideas about natural sexual difference.' She also explores the connection between the new cultural sensibility in America and neo-liberalism (Gill, 2007). Even though China did not have a proper feminist movement *per se*, socialism is generally seen as an overarching category that institutionalizes not only class, but also gender and ethnic equality. Therefore, the post-socialist structure of feeling does have structural and thematic resemblance to post-feminist and neo-liberal theories of individual freedom and responsibility against the idea that it is social, cultural and gender power structures that shape and influence an individual's chances for development. Moreover, post-socialism not only promotes individualism as liberation from the oppressive collectivism of the past but also prepares a cultural tolerance for the reduction of public services – education, medical care and housing – that is euphorically referred to as 'economic reform' in contemporary China. The latter has a greater impact on women because domestic labour – childcare, education and the daily job of taking care of the family – are usually considered to be a woman's responsibility. While the state has shirked its duty in compensating or helping out with domestic labour, it is women who cushion most of the impact on families that are left alone to their own means.

What is significant about post-socialist gender discourses is that they are not simply antithetical to socialist ideas. Just like what Gill argues about post-feminism, post-socialism is the converging platform for the play of various traditions of gender ideology, including socialist, traditional and commercialized subjectivity influenced by global capitalism and neo-liberal ideas (Gill, 2007). Ideas of gender position and gender identity coordinate and confront each other at the same time. For example, the explosive growth of the fashion industry, cosmetic merchandising and makeover programmes aimed at improving the female body in various ways point to the pervasive idea of femininity as bodily features and that women should constantly monitor and discipline their bodies to maintain gender security and social status. On the other hand, all these activities are promoted by the media as ways to enhance individuality and a sense of self-pride for women. Women are supposedly doing these things for no one but themselves, and they are acting out of their own choice and following their heart to become more naturally women, rather than under any pressure from external forces to achieve an illusionary equality with men. Thus, objective social and cultural forces that shape women's lives and limit women's choices are materialized in the language of female subjectivity, individuality, personal freedom and self-determination. Likewise, traditional values about women's virtue intermingle with the socialist legacy of sharing, self-sacrifice and taking care of others, in the ideological project to reconstitute the idea of family as a safe site of love and caring against the vicious and threatening social field of the market or human competition. Socialism used to denigrate the institution of family as being the tool of patriarchal domination and oppressive to women and children, so the socialist state was reinvented to be the new big family of equals. Now, with the collapse of the 'big family', the small family regains favour in contemporary culture.

The post-socialist gender discourse can be described as multi-vocal and contradictory. Liberating narratives of women's independence and self-respect co-exist with the neo-liberal sensitivity of the self needing constant upgrading in order to catch up – the idea that femininity is natural and that women should follow authoritative teachings on how to reshape their bodies and manage their appearances to be more feminine and attract the same audience and satisfy the same marketing initiatives. Family values and individualism are promoted to the same goal of achieving stability and happiness in an era of drastic social change.

Take Me Out and the carnival of gender performance

Reality dating shows started to hit Chinese screens in early 2010. *Take Me Out* is not the first one, but it became the most successful and influential soon after its first airing on 15 January 2010. The rules of the game are relatively simple. Twenty-four women participants are on stage to evaluate and choose one man at a time. There are three rounds for the participants to make up their minds: love at first sight, re-evaluation and the final decision. They can turn off the light in front of them at any time during the three rounds to say no to the man. Videos of the man's self-introduction are shown, in which the participant describes his personality, profession, temperament, visions of love and marriage, and other related issues. His friends are also invited to say a few words about him. Throughout the process, the host, two discussants sitting by the stage and any one of the 24 women participants can ask questions or converse with the man at centre stage. After the final decision, women cannot change their minds, and it is the man's turn to choose. If no woman has her light on, the man fails and goes off. If one woman has her light on, the man has to decide if he agrees to date her. If more than one has their light on, then the man gets to pick two of them and ask a few more questions to make up his mind. At the end of each section, the failed male participant or the successfully matched couple get a few seconds to say something off-stage in front of the camera.

Unlike its Western counterparts, *Take Me Out* does not have eye-popping surveillance camera shots of couples actually dating. Without juicy visuals fixed on bodies and sex, the localized reality dating show focuses mostly on the verbal exchanges between participants on-stage. With the setting of one man against 24 women, and with the host and the discussants intervening constantly to comment on either side of the interchange, dialogues easily amount to more generalized and abstract issues of gender identity, value conflicts, lifestyle choices and personality tests. The sensationalism that gets the show both a high rating and a bad reputation does not come from the commonly expected reason of sexual indecency or deviance, but for the outspoken politically incorrect ideas about love, marriage and family. The audience is shocked and perhaps awed each time someone says something outrageous, and it eagerly expects a dramatic reaction from the participants – usually the men. A newly issued regulation to tame reality dating shows, and their wild ideologies specifically, stipulates that participants should be true to their intention of looking for a date, in the belief that it is those who are not sincere that create verbal excess on purpose to catch eyeballs instead of true love.

The term 'reality' here refers to the format of letting real people rather than actors perform under dramatic circumstances, which has the dual effects of representing more 'authentic' life to those who have a sociological interest in knowing about people and their ways of living, and being more sensational and entertaining to voyeuristic consumers (Raphael, 2009). Most contemporary reality shows have extremely contrived and impossible situations under which the participants should act. Performativity is embedded in the very rules of the genre and this is well understood by most participants and by more and more savvy audiences (Andrejevic, 2009). What is worth watching on a reality TV is how well amateurs play the roles assigned to them, which is usually considered to be their innermost nature concealed by everyday life. Reality dating shows in this sense are platforms of gender performance and collective script writing. *Take Me Out* excels among all of them, because it has the sharpest self-awareness of its inevitable performativity and consciously makes use of it to secure a unique style of a show that is supposedly raw and artless. Gender performance is integral to the social processes of gender subjectification as well as objectification (Butler, 2004). Given scripts of gender roles are explored, tested and recreated every time they are played out in *Take Me Out*. The real fun of the show comes not from its utility but from the excess of pretension, staging and contradictions of the individual performances of gender. Thus, the censors are editing their own tales, trying to bite out the key elements of the show while hoping to maintain its success on the cultural market.

Compared with previous reality shows, the mise-en-scène of *Take Me Out* is quite extravagantly designed. The 24 women participants walk onto the stage when the programme begins, and they stand in a semi-circle waiting for a male participant to be carried onto the stage by an elevator accompanied by loud music and flashing lights. Close-ups, panning shots and a quick editing of the participants' reactions are a common feature of the show to enhance suspension and drama. Both on stage and in front of the TV, an atmosphere of high drama and eventful encountering is created, rather than a cosy everyday environment where people can interact more calmly. The women participants are trained on dressing and make-up, while the men are left to their own accord. Women's appearances are highly standardized, with super-feminine, 'princess' styles of dressing and make-up dominating the screen. Skirts, silky fabric, ribbons, long curly hair, bowknots and smoky eyes are common, out of which the one or two with trousers, suits, a T-shirt or short hair stand out as unusual.

For many of the women participants, the programme has become a chance to dress up extravagantly and put on the façade of a movie star just for fun. When they start talking, the words do anything but conform to the Cinderella or Snow White cloak that they put on their bodies. One man after another finds out that instead of having the supreme opportunity to lay claim to a beautiful woman, by coming to the programme they are actually going through a series of agonizing tests. Their appearance and their words are constantly under scrutiny and harshly criticized by these women. Everything about the men participants – their bodies, fashion tastes, hobbies, personalities and social values – is in danger of being questioned, interrogated and sometimes ridiculed. The men also realize that they are in a difficult situation; fight back or retreat? If they choose to retreat, they may get some symbolic support from the host, but risk losing face and becoming a laughing stock for the audience. But if they decide to fight back, they may bring out a sense of sisterhood among all the women participants and become the target of a collective attack by a group of intelligent women. Neither is fun for the participants, but both are extremely entertaining for the audience – although Internet discussions have shown that the audience has extreme feelings towards those daring, defiant and outspoken women. Mostly the audiences express dislike, discomfort or even hatred of the women who show too much self-confidence and a condescending attitude towards men.

This kind of carnivalesque playfulness to disturb and disrupt the unreflective patriarchal consciousness is a contentious feature of the post-socialist gender discourses of China, especially with the coming of new media and more channels for women to articulate unconventional ideas of gender relations. Mu Zimei, a female magazine editor who almost single-handedly popularized blogging in China in 2003, did so by detailing her sexual relationships with numerous men, including public figures, in her blogs (Yang, 2009: 114). In her (in)famous sex diaries, she not only bragged about her sexuality and described sex as a way towards true freedom, but also ridiculed men's sexual power with an air of cosmopolitanism that began to emerge with China's new class of women with a good education and promising careers. In both traditional and socialist cultures, women's sexuality is considered dangerous and corrupting. There is no other sin more evil than a woman being sexually desiring and promiscuous. While both men and women's sexual desires are discouraged for the higher causes of nation and socialism, women's sexuality is especially guarded against as it has a precarious relationship with these collective agendas that are masculine in content. Some argue that in the post-socialist era, men's sexual power is re-articulated and revitalized to be symbiotic, or better, to incarnate rather than undermine the revolutionary and nationalist spirit in mass culture texts such as TV dramas and popular novels (Wu, 2006; Song, 2010). Women's sexuality, however, remains antithetical and undermining to meta-narratives of history, and thus needs to be disciplined and contained.

Take Me Out is an unusual case in that it is on national TV during prime time and is in a genre that is connected with mass entertainment and shameless commercialism. Cultural performances with some feminist repercussions can be played out, though not necessarily with clear feminist agendas or informed with feminist politics. The acknowledgement and exertion of female sexual desires is a regular occurrence in the conversations among participants. Comments like, 'I want to see the muscles under your shirt', 'I don't like slim guys', 'I appreciate your body' or 'he is the kind of dish I like' are expressed constantly by women participants. This unusual degree of self-expression and assertiveness is achieved because the women on stage, selected out of tens of thousands of applicants, are mostly artists, professionals, freelancers, managers or business owners. The women participants are highly articulate, self-confident and able to create an interesting show that depends on verbal exchanges.

The display of femininity as bodily features and the blatant exhibition of female sexual desires destabilize the show's theme of love towards marriage. The women, usually in their mid- or late twenties, show more interest in flirting with the idea of having a date than in seriously picking up a man on stage. For example, one woman participant claims that she will not choose a man who does not fall in love with her at first sight. Another woman says that she is a queen and she can accept someone no less than a king. Another poses hard questions and ridicules men all the time, to the extent that everyone expects her to launch an attack when there comes some 'Mr Feeling Good'. It is obvious that, for many participants, to stay on stage and get notorious is more satisfying than finding a date. They play excessively with the public stereotype of well-educated and professional women being anxious to get men's attention, but explode the idea by separating female sexual fantasy from its socially sanctioned place in the family. The show's implicit alliance with cosmopolitan culture and global capitalism makes it tolerant and even celebratory of the idea of female sexual independence, at the demise of male supremacy and the dominant ideology of family values that fill the post-socialist cultural vacuum. However, as liberating as it may be to demonstrate women's self-reliance and self-determination concerning issues of body, gender relationship and family, the discourse of female sexual independence does not stand alone as an absolute value. It is inevitably entangled with the emerging disciplining regime of the body and sexuality at the onslaught of a globalizing commercial culture, which is no less standardizing and restraining than any previous restrictions on the human body and sex.

The moral panic of modernity and women as scapegoats

Giddens (1991) has discussed the destabilizing effect of modernity on an individual's relationship with established institutions of identity and morality. He makes the point that projects to reshape and rebuild the individual constantly are central to the reflexive mechanism of modern life. These institutionally sustained projects have both liberating and repressive possibilities, and they are intricately connected to global transformations of social structure (Giddens, 1991). In an era of the saturation of mass communication technologies, mediated experience has become a major instrument for articulating, negotiating and shaping personal identities and a sense of the world (Riesman, 1950). The explosive development of reality-based or so-called user-generated programming on contemporary Chinese TV is symptomatic of the economic, social and cultural responses to structural transformations in post-socialist China.

One of the most characteristic genre that plays the role of remoulding individual consciousness under new social conditions is talk shows based on ordinary people's problems. Family fights, financial disputes among relatives, parent–children conflicts, and various other topics that are concerned with morality, tradition, self-identity and similar issues of the 'private sphere' find their way onto national TV. This kind of programming fulfils the dual tasks of creating low-cost and relatively high-rating shows, and also offering moral and practical guidance to ordinary people in service of social stability.

Take Me Out can be seen as a variation of such a genre of reality talk shows. The two discussants are presented as experts in relationships and personality. They work together with the host to cast authoritative comments on the participants. Their comments are often direct, harsh and sarcastic, but the participants are unlike the guests in those therapeutic talk shows where they come to seek suggestions and education from the elite. The strong women of *Take Me Out* just come to occupy centre stage, and they do not care less about being agreeable to the host, experts, male suitors or the audience.

The most frequently cited case of the programme's celebration of immorality is the famous answer given by a woman to her suitor's invitation to join him on a date on his bicycle. She replied coldly, 'I'd rather cry on the back seat of a BMW than have a good laugh on your bike'. A boy taking a girl on a bicycle ride is the classical image of pure, authentic and heart-wrenching romantic love in socialist literature and mass culture. It symbolizes the simplicity and carefreeness of the good old days, when a 'pure relationship' could really be achieved without the intervening factors of social status, family background and material conditions. Ma Nuo, a model and part-time actress who spoke the unspeakable on national TV, soon became public enemy no. 1. Mass Internet searching of her profiles and personal background goes on wildly, while thousands have posted messages on Bulletin Board System (BBS) venting their indignation.

Ma Nuo is just one example of the 'bandwagon' strategies that plague today's commercial media – if it can catch eyeballs, anything goes.

She causes additional panic because she is on TV – the most ideologically restricted media in contemporary China. What places the show in the ranks of the formerly mentioned talk shows is its notoriety in the public exhibition of destructive individualism in issues related to love, relationship and family.

Unlike these shows, however, the focus of *Take Me Out* is not to provide a reassuring resolution of the unsettling spiritual crisis of modernity, but to display its features and consequences, with women being the primary carrier, and the three supposedly objective and intelligent (two men and one woman) expert characters being its witnesses and playing out the public outcry on TV. It is this feature that alarms the censors, not the degree of sensationalism *per se*, but the lack of textual closure to contain and correct the horrendous acts that sabotage public morality. The reality TV genre helps to bring a certain degree of textual instability and openness into the beacon of ideological state apparatus.

However, moral panic is also a form of ideological control, albeit this is collectively imposed and serves not as cure but catharsis. With more power to cast a comment, cut short other's speech and have the final say in case of a debate, and with the opportunity of editing the conversations, the host and discussants have the rhetorical advantage of representing common sense and public opinion against the irrationality of the participants. The programme as a whole frames the carnivalesque performance of many female participants as pathological, as a symptom of the social disease that is shameless materialism and a loss of belief. Women are seen to be impossible and destructive to social order, because they want too much for themselves and their desire runs so wild that they have lost any understanding of true love and happiness.

The show's way of educating these women is not through moral denunciation but through upholding opposite examples of female virtue. Xia Yan is repeatedly mentioned as an example by the programme host Meng Fei whenever he tries to preach to the audience about the secret of true love. Xia Yan is a college student who has a cute face and a quiet disposition. She seldom speaks on stage, and when she does she makes meaningless comments. Meng Fei affectionately calls her the 'sleepwalking girl'. In one episode, a graduate student studying computer music composition named Li Quan came to the programme claiming that he was fascinated by Xia Yan's angelic voice and only came to sing a song for her. After his song, Xia Yan happily walked away with him and this episode has become legendary ever since.

Xia Yan stands as a clear contrast to those sharp-tongued women who fault men on almost every aspect and who are never satisfied. She is muddy minded, does not know what she wants and has no specific judgement on men. She is weak and easily swayed and pushed around by others, as the programme's discussant Le Jia concludes. Le Jia dutifully reminds her to make up her own mind, but that is obviously wasted when the studio audience claps their hands and chants 'go with him' enthusiastically. In their script, and in the script of the programme, there is no way that Xia Yan could reject the man. Furthermore, since the programme does not offer follow-ups on how well relationships that started on the show developed afterwards, the audience has to take the on-screen ending as the real end of the story and imagine that 'they live happily together ever after'. Equally metaphoric is Ma Nuo's ending on the show. She keeps her light on for a man until it is his turn to make a choice. He chooses Ma Nuo as his date, but sings a song to thank another woman for her strong support of him before he turns to her. Ma Nuo tries to back up, claiming that it is infuriating to see her suitor flirt with another woman in front of her. The host Meng Fei cuts her short, saying that she could choose to break up with him immediately after the show, but a rule is a rule and she has to go with him on the programme. The audience is relieved to see that the insatiable Ma Nuo does not get a happy ending, just like they are satisfied with the romantic settlement of Xia Yan.

Modernity may bring freedom of choice and self-determination, but also uncertainty, alienation and rootlessness. Experiencing the fastest economic development and drastic social restructuring in all of human history, the sense of disorientation and disconnection is felt sharply in all strata of Chinese society, with different forms and to various degrees. Mediated collective matchmaking is both symptomatic of and responsive to the modern consequence of loneliness that infects the urban middle class. Through televised communication and self-disclosure, the cultural logic of reality dating shows is a collective effort of soul searching and consolation; trying to bring together isolated individuals and bind them with the basic human emotion of love. With the TV programme, however, it can be disheartening to sense that the degree of miscommunication between genders and the pathetic success rate have made it more of an enlargement than a cure of the wound. The format of 24 assertive women against one passive man makes women the real spectacle of the social problem. They repeatedly demonstrate the startling disregard of moral order and a rejection of the given temperament of femininity. Given rare cases of success like Xia Yan, or vehement public condemnation of assertive characters like Ma Nuo on the Internet, the intertextual environment of the show dismisses women's liberation and independence as destructive and disruptive. When trying to showcase the new self-determination of womanhood, the daring women of *Take Me Out* also reveal a seemingly terrifying idea that having a man's care and protection may not be a necessary condition for happiness, or that a man could only be treated as a medium towards something else – ostensibly money and power. Thus, what starts out as a subversive and refreshing TV format may end up churning out a conservative message that the downside of modernity manifests itself in woman's liberation, which in turn sabotages the sacred institutions of family/marriage and disturbs the happiness of everyday life.

Contested public sphere, or sites of gender formation surveillance?

Reality dating shows like *Take Me Out* can be read as a new form of public sphere. The genre combines claims of reality and features of theatricality, excess and playfulness. Real people are coming onto the stage to expose their lives, values and dispositions, bypassing the literary, moral and ideological authorship that dominates much of Chinese TV. Non-traditional ideas of gender roles and the manifestation of gender subjectivity are proliferating in China. This show brings diversity and counter-images to the conservative gender discourses of post-socialist China. Women participants are eager to show that they are in charge, that they are choosing men based on their bodies, and that they are smarter than men.

One of the early participants of *Take Me Out*, Xie Jia, represents such a case of transgression. She is a college student studying art management, and is rumoured to be a lesbian. She is one of the few women who dresses in a style that crosses gender lines, with short hair, jackets and trousers. She admits publicly that she comes to the programme as someone who is interested in observing programme development and management. Her style on the show is of a philosophical commentator, providing a rational analysis of everyday attitudes towards life – encouraging people to be his or her self, to insist on the things that they are truly interested in and to defy traditional stereotypes. She shows an alternative style of femininity that has great intellectual agency and cannot be essentialized into certain bodily features.

Counter-balancing this kind of resistance, however, is the show's overall faithfulness to conventional representations of male and female bodies. The show's women participants all receive some instruction on their appearance and they mostly look gorgeous – much in tone with the show's commercial outlook. Fatness is almost a taboo for the programme, and the participants are quite sensitive to the issue of body weight whenever the topic of food is brought up. In one episode, a male participant who is a chef says that he is good at making both Eastern and Western cuisines and does not mind cooking for his girlfriend at home. Although this is a good opportunity for women to encourage men to be caring and helpful with domestic chores, one slightly chubby woman asks what his recipe would be for 'balloon babies' like herself, turning the topic back to the disciplining of women's bodies for the sake of sexual attractiveness to men. If the heavy body is considered unacceptable for women, slimness is the stigma for men, as women participants often claim that they do not like men to be too slim, which signifies a lack of power and manliness.

Despite the unusual demonstration of extremely assertive female agency, *Take Me Out* and its participants share some common sense about gender relations between a heterosexual couple: the man should be older than the woman, and a woman can have her own career but a good man must be successful in socially recognized professions. Questions of the influence of class on intimate relationships almost never come up, for the whole organization and intention of the programme is limited to the urban middle class. These conventional ideas are self-imposed and self-scripted by the participants, as much as shaped by the production team and media apparatus, which testifies to the limitations of a public sphere built around the parameters of capital, individuality, consumption and the market. Mediated experiences are important sites where identities are being formed, negotiated and contested in contemporary consumer society. Popular media culture like *Take Me Out* is a site of entanglement, articulation and confrontation of the newly emerging gender discourses of post-socialist China, becoming a vital subject for critical exploration.

References

Andrejevic, M. (2002) 'The Work of Being Watched: Interactive Media and the Exploitation of Self-Disclosure', *Critical Studies in Media Communication*, 19(2): 230–248.

Andrejevic, M. (2009) 'Visceral Literacy: Reality TV, Savvy Viewers, and Auto-Spies', in S. Murray and L. Ouellette (eds), *Reality TV: Remaking Television Culture*, New York: New York University Press.

Butler, J. (2004) *Undoing Gender*, New York: Routledge.

Chen, Q. (2009) 'The Changes in Women's Ideas on Marriage: From the Perspective of Daily Language', *Journal of Yichun College*, 31(5): 116–118.

Erwin, K., Adams, V. and Le, P. (2009) 'Glorious Deeds: Work Unit Blood Donation and Postsocialist Desires in Urban China', *Body & Society*, 15(2): 51–70.

Hanser, A. (2006) 'Sales Floor Trajectories: Distinction and Service in Postsocialist China', *Ethnography*, 7(4): 461–491.

Ho, W. and Ng, E. (2008) 'Public Amnesia and Multiple Modernities in Shanghai: Narrating the Postsocialist Future in a Former Socialist Model Community', *Journal of Contemporary Ethnography*, 37(4): 383–416.

Giddens, A. (1991) *Modernity and Self-Identity: Self and Society in the Late Modern Age*, Stanford: Stanford University Press.

Gill, R. (2007) 'Postfeminist Media Culture: Elements of a Sensibility', *European Journal of Cultural Studies*, 10(2): 147–166.

Raphael, R. (2009) 'The Political Economic Origins of Reality-TV', in S. Murray and L. Ouellette (eds), *Reality TV: Remaking Television Culture*, New York: New York University Press.

Riesman, D. (1950) *The Lonely Crowd*, New Haven: Yale University Press.

Rofel, L. (1999) *Other Modernities: Gendered Yearnings in China after Socialism*, Berkeley: University of California Press.

Song, G. (2010) 'Chinese Masculinities Revisited: Male Images in Contemporary Television Drama Serials', *Modern China*, 36(4): 404–434.

Wu, J. (2006) 'Nostalgia as Content Creativity: Cultural Industries and the Popular Sentiment', *International Journal of Cultural Studies*, 9(3): 359–368.

Yang, G. (2009) *The Power of the Internet in China: Citizen Activism Online*, New York: Columbia University Press.

Zhang, L. (2007) 'A Sociological Study of the "Leftover Women" Phenomenon', *Journal of Shanxi College for Youth Administrators*, 20(4): 8–10.

Zhou, S. (2010) 'Leftover Women and Gender Domination', *Youth Study*, 5: 14–18.

Zuo, X. and Xia, D. (2008) 'Construction of Women and Women Constructing: Sociological Perspectives on the Leftover Women's Crisis', *Collection of Women's Studies*, 88(5): 11–16.

12
Female Individualization and Illiberal Pragmatism: Blogging and New Life Politics in Singapore

Audrey Yue

The last few decades of accelerated postcolonial modernization in Singapore have created a highly educated polity. Recent developments in the country's transition to the new knowledge and creative economy have also witnessed the rise of a media-savvy and entrepreneurial population. As new cultural economic policies have appropriated the technologies of sex, sexuality and gender to envision the contemporary nation state, women in Singapore have been at the forefront and been the beneficiaries of these changes.

This chapter uses three case studies of female blogging to show how women, as producers and consumers of social media, have seized upon new media technologies to fashion new female self-narratives. While these self-narratives construct a new life politics based on reflexive lifestyling, I argue that they are enshrined in the ideology of illiberal pragmatism. Illiberal pragmatism refers to the ambivalence between rationality and irrationality, liberalism and non-liberalism that regulates the pragmatic interventions of government. From the iconic image of the famed 'Singapore Girl' in the 1970s, to the gendered policies on female reproduction and marriage in the 1980s, the interventions of illiberal pragmatism have regulated women, and in turn constituted their subjectivity.

The first section will review critically how gendered state policies have shaped women's identities through the ideology and practice of illiberal pragmatism. It will show how illiberal pragmatism neutralizes gender norms and creates compliant female subjects, but also provides the conditions to fashion new female life politics. The second section will demonstrate these new modes of female life politics in the social media of blogging. I will examine award-winning blogs by teenagers, adult women and transgenders to consider the performances of hetero-normative, hegemonic and trans-femininities. New consumption practices of female individualization, this chapter will argue, are constituted by illiberal pragmatism as a logic that not only governs identities and produces new subjectivities but also enables new practices that are complicit with and resistant to its ideology.

The illiberal pragmatics of gendered state policies: Social control and life politics

When Singapore gained independence in 1965, it was a 'third-world' country that relied on colonial entrepôt trade. Women were mostly uneducated, did not work and lived in extended patriarchal households as mothers, wives and daughters. With the transition to a manufacturing society, education was encouraged and women began participating in the labour force. Singapore's subsequent transformation from a regional finance hub into its current status as a global city saw female literacy rise to 96.3 per cent in 2009 (Statistics Singapore, 2010), with 54 per cent of the female population in the workforce (MCDYS, 2009: 12).

Family values underpin the cornerstone of Singapore society and affect women's sexuality through marriage and reproduction. In the early developmental years of postcolonial independence, families were discouraged from having more than two children. As women became more independent through work and education, they began to marry later and have fewer children. The country now has one of the lowest birth rates in the world (MCDYS, 2009: 10). Only 38 per cent of women are married (NPS, 2010: 2), and singlehood is highest among those with university qualifications (NPS, 2010: 5). Despite Singapore's pro-family trend, there are now more single women, and those married are delaying parenthood. Divorce has also increased, from 7.1 per 1000 resident population in 2002 to 8.1 in 2007 (MCDYS, 2009: 10). Women's changing socio-economic status in education, work, marriage, family and sexuality show how gender is associated with the nation's modernity.

Nirmala Purushotam discusses the envisioning of the modern Singapore nation through the figure of 'the middle-class woman'. Such a woman is portrayed in the mass media as upwardly mobile, liberated and sometimes even feminist. Purushotam argues that the nation constructs itself as modern by providing the material conditions for women to achieve socio-economic progress, but also ensuring that they are bounded by the traditions of the family. First, women's access to work and education masked cheap labour as social progress (Purushotam, 2002: 338). Second, women's social progress is contained by promoting family values as socially responsible communitarian values (Purushotam, 2002: 344). Engendering women through the discourses of woman-as-labour and woman-as-family, modernity is constituted in and through gendered state policies.

In the mid-1980s, new reproductive policies were introduced to encourage well-educated women to bear more children and accept a mothering role (Heng and Devan, 1992; Oehlers, 1998). Central to the working of this policy is illiberal pragmatism. On the one hand, female liberalization – where women appeared to be liberated through their visible presence as wage-earners and participants in the public sphere – suited the growing materialistic economy, with rising family incomes and an increased ability to consume. On the other hand, women's emancipation was at the same time constrained by the state's control of their bodies and reproductive capacities. These twin processes of liberalism and non-liberalism – illiberalism – are undergirded by a pragmatism that forms the common-sense ideology of the state's performance principle – what Chua defines as 'being practical in the sense of earning a living' (Chua, 1997: 131), and Tan refers to as 'pragmatic patriarchy' (Tan, 2008: 78). These associations between biological reproduction and a racialized discourse of nationalism reveal how gender has become a biopolitical project of state modernity.

Nation-building strategies of gendered state policies reinforce state power. They establish regular and predictable relations between state and society so that people structure life-decisions around these policies (Teo, 2007: 423). They encourage Singaporeans to identify themselves as members of families, rather than by gender or ethnically based identities, which diminishes the possibility of gender-based resistance to state policies. Such policies 'solidify the state's claim to being the only agent able to balance the twin tensions that are at the core of the nation's survival' (Teo, 2007: 423). While gendered state policies should provoke negative reactions among women, they were regarded as natural and inevitable by Singaporeans: 'The political discourse around the family [sic] recasts the state not as a selective or hypocritical defender of traditions but as a sincere agent doing the best it can under difficult conditions not of its own making' (Teo, 2009: 534). Examining policies aimed at boosting marriage and fertility, Teo argues that they generate 'self-consciously Singaporean meanings and normative practices' and legitimate the state's conservative position towards the family (Teo, 2010: 337). Teo's remarks show how Singaporean women, by subsuming gender inequality under the greater good of the state, are interpellated by the ideology of illiberal pragmatism that neutralizes patriarchal gender norms as common sense and pragmatic not only for the state and society, but also for the individual. Singapore's gendered state policies have clearly enabled women to be visible and active participants in the public sphere. The social engineering of gendered state policies has also created a milieu of illiberal pragmatism that shapes female identities and subjectivities. Two practices of subject-formation are evident: first, through techniques of interpellation that create compliant gendered subjects; second, through techniques of critical reflexivity that transform gender relations. These techniques are encapsulated in the critical debates on life politics.

Different to emancipatory politics concerned with unshackling the underprivileged from hierarchies of unequal power and exploitation (Giddens, 1991: 211), life politics is more concerned with choice rather than life chances:

> Life politics does not primarily concern the conditions which liberate us in order to make choices: it is a politics *of* choice. While emancipatory politics is a politics of life chances, life politics is a politics of lifestyle.
>
> (Giddens, 1991: 214)

Tied to the practices of self-actualization, life politics narrates how self-identities are shaped, transformed and reflexively sustained in the rapidly evolving configurations of the local and global, and has the capacity to reduce inequality through new strategies of 'lifestyle bargaining' (Giddens, 1996: 374). This concept has become a popular tool to discuss contemporary identities and everyday life, especially with the proliferation of a consumer lifestyle and the growth of a user-generated convergent media culture. Criticisms of the celebratory overtures of life politics point to how the thesis does not simply herald new modes of self-actualization, but also new forms of social control. Elchardus suggests a tension between individualization and self-actualization, and argues that processes of tastes and choices are shaped by social patterns: 'Social control is exercised by molding the factors that determine choices and that influence the feeling, thinking and acting of individuals, such as knowledge, competence, taste, convictions, cultural frames and forms, routines, and meanings' (Elchardus, 2009: 153). Examining the practices of social media, Hearn argues that the 'reflexive project of the self' is a form of 'self-branding' that 'illustrate[s] the erosion of any meaningful distinction between notions of the self and capitalist processes of production and consumption' (Hearn, 2008: 197). Lamenting the loss of a self outside of capitalism, she argues that '[t]he function of the branded self is purely rhetorical; its goal is to produce cultural value and, potentially, material profit' (Hearn, 2008: 198).

Rather than highlighting the polemics of life politics, the two fields of debates are equally relevant to the logic of illiberal pragmatics that underpins women's life politics in Singapore. On one level, life politics speaks to women's abilities to make liberal lifestyle choices that determine how they actualize their identities; on the other hand, it suggests that these choices are imbued in non-liberal modes of social control that are determined by structural forces such as the interventions of government and capitalism. These two practices are evident in feminist reworkings of life politics.

Mulinari and Sandell examine how changes in family and gender relations impact on the public as much as private spheres, and suggest that rather than locating gender relations in the private domain, 'gender and gender relations permeate all areas of society' (Mulinari and Sandell, 2009: 495). Brooks and Wee (2008) show how Singaporean women transform gender relations by using critical reflexivity to rework state-gendered values in their everyday practices. These continuums across emancipatory/life politics, self/collective and private/public are highlighted in Bakardjieva's use of the term, 'subactivism', to refer to the intersection between citizenship and everyday life (Bakardjieva, 2009: 92). A form of politics outside of formal institutions, subactivism is 'a kind of politics that unfolds at the level of subjective experience and is submerged in the flow of everyday life. It is constituted by small-scale, often individual, decisions and actions that have either a political or ethical frame of reference (or both) and are difficult to capture using the traditional tools with which political participation is measured' (Bakardjieva, 2009: 92).

For women in Singapore, the subactivism of life politics is a useful framework to consider how social media bring private interests into the public sphere and redraw the boundary between the public and private. As Bakarjieva states, '[T]he Internet transforms the process of identification by exploding the number of discourses and subject positions to which the individual becomes exposed, as well as multiplying the participation forms available at that individual's fingertips' (Bakarjieva, 2009: 94). By '[facilitating] the loosely structured networks and affinity ties of this brand of late modern politics', social media offer the potential to mobilize social networks around the subactivism of life politics (Bennett,

2009: 13). This is demonstrated in the following three case studies on female and transgender blogging.

Blogging and the performance of femininities: From hegemony to subactivism

Singaporean uses of new media are shaped by the subactivism of life politics. The Internet, for example, is used more for 'goal-directed behaviour (using email, information seeking)... than experiential behaviour (such as playing games and instant messaging)' (Choi, 2008: 155). Similarly, social media sites enhance the quality of 'social interaction' (Phua, 2010; Skoric et al., 2009a) rather than increased political participation (Skoric et al., 2009b). These practices do not structurally redistribute unequal power but demonstrate the subactivist acquisition of everyday citizenship necessary for the cultivation of the self.

Blogging, one of the earliest forms of social media, has and continues to be highly popular in Singapore. There is even a government-sponsored 'Singapore Blog Awards', introduced in 2009, which recognizes the innovative genres of the medium (omg, 2011). Following the trend in Asia, Singaporean female bloggers have also risen to prominence in the country – those such as Esther Chia (2001), Fay Hokulani (2008), Arissa Ha (2010), Jessica Loh (2006), Nadia Suadi (2010), Priscilla Lee (2006) and Wendy Cheng (2003) (see Anon, 2010).

The women's blogs share a few common features. They are usually from young women in their late teens and early twenties – students, models, personal trainers or school-leavers looking for work – who have been authoring their blogs for more than three years. Chia (2001), for example, has been publishing for eleven years; Suadi (2010), eight years; and Lee (2006), five years. The medium's diary-structure of progressive entries lends itself well to the performance of identity as a literal form of serialized life narration. Stories about school examinations, friendships, families and relationships fill the posts, together with photos and videos of food, travel, clothes and fashion. As the young adult years are also transitional years, the archives show changing subjectivities through identity accumulation and management. The motif of student-to-worker is most common; with it, evolving social networks and self-representation. Combining text, images, animation and sound, a personal discourse is broadened with embedded multimedia and links to create new ties and social networks. Hjorth (2009) discusses these as practices of new media customization that create 'micro-narratives formed through visual, textual and aural modes of communication' (Hjorth, 2009: 118). Rather than macro-narratives, micro-narratives – what Hjorth calls 'imaging' rather than 'imagined' communities (ala Anderson) (2009: 117) – instantiate techniques of individualization rather than collectivization. For young Singaporean women, this identity follows an East Asian pop culture modernity that celebrates the 'kawaii' and 'kogal' cultures of J-pop and K-pop. This is especially evident in Cheng's performance of young adult femininity.

Cheng (2003) has been authoring her blog *Xiaxue* since 2003, when she was a media communications student. Asia's most awarded female blogger, she has won prizes, including the 'most popular blog' in the Asia Pacific region and the 'best Asian blog' online. Now married to an American, and living in and writing from Dallas, her site receives between 50,000 and 200,000 visits a day. In the beginning when she was a student, she shared updates of her everyday life, including examination results and part-time jobs. As she grows in popularity with her wit and humour, her blogs begin to contain photos and commentaries on food, restaurants and nightclubs. Her family and expanding circle of friends feature prominently in these posts that combine private networks with the public culture of food and nightlife. When her reviews begin to take on a more 'professional' outlook – usually through close-up photos of food menus and speciality dishes – they start to generate more public comments, with each post attracting a few hundred responses; thus calibrating individual taste to collective cultural capital.

A significant feature of Cheng's blog is her diary of physical transformation. She began writing as a young woman with long black hair who favours t-shirts and miniskirts. These photos are usually framed in long shot, showing her partying with friends or working. Her surgical transformation began around 2006 with a nose job, cut eyes, whitened teeth, tattooed freckles, fake eyelashes and long blond hair. With these, her photos began to be framed in close-ups, showing the results of the medical interventions. The entries also detail her experiences of these surgeries, and the processes of bodily recovery and ongoing physical maintenance. This image, complete with platform shoes and colourful false nails, replicates the J-pop fashion of 'gyaru'. Cheng's new image peaked in popularity in 2010, when she was invited to the US by Michelle Phan to make a *YouTube* video, *Disney Princess*. Phan, of Vietnamese-American descent, is *YouTube's* most subscribed female channel video star, whose videos are famed for their online tutorials on make-up. *Disney Princess* shows the visit of these two similarly styled young women to Disneyland, and their encounters with the characters and stars of the theme park. As simultaneously spectators and characters, Cheng and Phan disrupt the monoculture of Disneyland through their apparent anime-style cosplay that imbues these young women with a distinct East Asian pop-cultural femininity.

Cheng's online self-narrative supports her offline physical makeover. Documenting and performing the transitional staging of this identity as a form of life biography, her blog shows how the ideal young adult East Asian femininity can be acquired through self-improvement and validated through a micro-narrative of images, texts and videos. Her life biography can be considered a form of subactivism as it involves a Foucauldian ethics of care that inscribes the subject through practices of careful self-cultivation and management (Foucault, 1985). Her narrative of female individualization differs from Kim's account of how transnational mobility has enabled Asian women to move away from social norms and create a new life biography. Kim uses the concept of female individualization to show how the media promote a 'plurality of individual lifestyles' that encourage new ways of conceiving the self 'in more individualist terms, marked by an outward-looking reflexivity' (Kim, 2010: 40). Kim suggests that for women in patriarchal and traditional Asian societies, these mediated experiences have enabled them to be mobile and transnational, thereby 'disembedding' them from these hierarchies. For her, these practices of transnational mobility constitute 'a form of defection from an expected normative biography' (Kim, 2010: 41). While Cheng is undoubtedly transnational and mobile, both in terms of geographical mobility and in transcultural practices of consumption, her femininity, rooted in East Asian pop-culture modernity, is performed to meet the expectations of social and cultural norms. For most of the Singaporean Chinese population, these norms find resonance in the representations of East Asian popular culture. East Asian pop has a hegemonic hold in Singapore through its status as the dominant form of local popular culture that expresses the shared values of Confucian femininity and identity (Chua, 2008). Narrating her transition from a student-daughter to a single working girl and now a wife, Cheng's performance of an East Asian pop-cultural femininity reinforces rather than transgresses these values.

As authors mature and become more skilled in their identity presentation, and as their blogs begin to take on a unique 'voice' (such as a focus on health, cosmetic surgery, make-up, haute couture or sports fashion), these blogs begin to contain advertorials, powered by blogging advertising companies such as Nuffnang (2007) – the first and now most prominent company in the Asia-Pacific region with more than 80,000 bloggers in their community network and high-profile clients such as Nike, Sony, Nokia and Citibank. These advertorials are also accompanied by a do-it-yourself category that shows how simple makeover exercises can help young women instantly update their style and potentially improve their femininity. These personal empowerment practices relate directly to the material consumption of shopping, eating and exercise, and are especially encouraged if they are undertaken through the featured shops, brands and restaurants.

The popularity of these blogs has elevated these women to the status of celebrity bloggers, creating a do-it-yourself young female lifestyle culture where gurus are ordinary peers who have become role models as a result of a simple makeover achieved through, usually, easy and cheap fast fashion, and/or a health regime of body improvement. Combining the commercial and personal, advertorial female blogging readily engages a form of commodified hetero-femininity that prepares them for incorporation into the dominant ideology of romance capitalism (Hudson, 2004), which is a creative economic policy of cool capital leveraged through the consumption of sex, femininity and marriage. Significantly, these practices perform a hetero-normative femininity that not only constitutes and transforms female adolescents into well-groomed young women; they also, as the earlier section has pointed out, create compliant female subjects, whose ideologies are resonant with gendered state policies. This is especially evident in the site of the 2010 Singapore Blog Awards winner, Violet Lim.

Lim's (2011) blog, *Diary of a Matchmaker*, began in 2006 and currently contains 271 posts in 19 categories with 1066 comments. Although it is not a high-visited site, Lim's status as self-help author, co-founder of Lunch Actually – a successful offline dating company – and director of online dating site *Eteract*, has lent credibility to the authority of the blog, where she writes with a mix of personal experiences and professional advice. Such a constructed self-reflexivity has, not surprisingly, won her the prize in the 'Most Insightful Blog' category in the Singapore Blog Awards. According to the Awards website, this category is 'for serious blogs with interesting and revealing insights, analytical reports, dealing with various social issues' (omg, 2011). Key tagged topics include 'relationships insight', 'perhaps love', 'life lessons' and 'dating reality'. These posts approach the discourses of courtship and marriage from the point of view of single and married women; for the former, how to prepare for dates and recognize the right man; for the latter, how to keep a marriage healthy and what to expect from child-rearing. These discourses reflect the ideology of gendered state policies to raise marriage rates, fertility and procreation. The blog's performance of such an adult hege-monic femininity shows the interpellation of these discourses in the everyday life of women. Through experience and advice, she presents state values as post-feminist personal values, encouraging women to be proactive, and empowering them with a veneer of choice and agency, including how to dress, eat and talk during a date. Like Cheng's self-fashioning hetero-femininity, Lim's makeover practices recall the TV genre of makeover reality shows. Through neo-liberal techniques of self-improvement, this popular genre has the propensity to construct the good citizen (Ouellette and Hay, 2008).

On her blog, Lim introduces herself through her role model, Ally McBeal, the lawyer from the successful US TV series. Lim's life biog-raphy mirrors McBeal's; before becoming a successful businesswoman, she too was also trained as a lawyer. Her business acumen reflects the motif of self-entrepreneurship demonstrated in the blog. She repre-sents the exemplary successful woman as one able to balance career, marriage and children, and whose success results from the ethical cultivation of such an identity. When these identities are performed through the blog and naturalized as life politics via the perspective of her experiences, they assume a self-actualized normative biogra-phy. These practices 're-embed' an ideal patriarchal and Confucian femininity for a nation that finds it necessary to defend and secure traditional values against its own inexorable logic of cosmopolitan globalization. Through such performativity, blogs like Lim's reinforce illiberal pragmatism by promoting state femininity as ideal adult femininity.

The blogs discussed above evince two forms of subactivist life pol-itics. First, female teenagers and young woman perform an idealized East Asian femininity that reinforces Confucian norms and partici-pates in the commodification of hetero-femininity. These claims take place at the level of everyday life rather than political participation where citizenship is constituted through capital accumulation and ethi-cal self-cultivation. Rather than challenge the status quo, these practices are complicit with illiberal pragmatism and resonate with the state ideologies of romance capitalism and materialist consumerism. Sec-ond, ideal adult femininity is performed to respond directly to state femininity, showing how state-gendered policies have interpellated women through practices of self-fashioning that also support illiberal pragmatism. Like the female individualization of young women, these practices of adult women are also subactivist through the ethical care of self-cultivation and self-actualization. The following will discuss how transgender blogging and the formation of trans-femininity replicate these norms but are also subculturally political.

Ms Chor Lor's (hereafter MCL) *Blog of a Singaporean Transgender* (2009) also assumes the narrative of life politics discussed above. However, rather than the performance of idealized teenage and adult femininities, this blog shows how a transgender sexuality and trans-femininity are acquired. The blog started in January 2009, and currently has about 260,000 hits. It is a highly regular blog, with about one to five postings a week. Categories include everyday topics such as 'All About Dogs', 'comics', 'cool', 'fiction', 'food' and 'funny', as well as more specific types relating to the broader discourses of homosexuality, such as 'a gay story', 'gays', 'GLBT' (gay, lesbian, bisexual, transsexual), 'lesbians', 'health', 'Singapore Gay Scene' and 'transgender'. Of significance here is the category of 'A Transgender Story' (hereafter ATS), which is serialized into 49 posts. ATS, which began on 3 March 2009, is an account of the author's life story, from a male childhood, her awareness of her same-sex-attracted sexuality and her transition to a female adulthood.

ATS begins with an account of a working-class childhood in a one-room flat on a public housing estate. With a father in jail and a mother working long hours as a hawker assistant, MCL recounts her filial duty (sibling care, cooking and washing) and juxtaposing this with friendships that developed into homosocial bonding and homosexual encounters. These encounters are introduced through a rite-of-passage discourse such as 'crush', 'first love', 'first kiss', 'first boyfriend', and so forth, as well as through a school–work transition, from primary to secondary school, first job and so on. Replicating the life cycle, this serialized narrative, written in the first person, follows the structural motif of an autobiographical coming-out transgender story.

Trans-femininity, defined as a hybrid of male femininity (Halberstam, 1998), is acquired through denaturalizing normative masculinity and performing a femininity that can also be medically enhanced through surgical gender reassignment. This is evident in ATS through practices of dress, deportment and breast augmentation. In the beginning, as the author comes to realize her same-sex attraction, she begins to reveal her desire for a less masculinized and more feminine body. Using words like 'man enough' to describe the ideal masculinity of her boyfriend, she attributes a normative maleness to straight-acting homosexuality, which in turn calibrates her femininity. As she befriends a group of transsexuals and transgender prostitutes in the northern seaside township of Changi Village, she begins to learn the codes of cross-dressing. When her borrowed dress from her mother is deemed too 'aunty' by the group, she learns the finer details of generational femininity. She keeps her hair long, learns to put on make-up and starts to assume the public identity of a woman in everyday life. Made easier by her job as a retail assistant in the fashion industry, these modes of embodiment attest to femininity as a performance that is socially constructed, quickly mimicked and promptly internalized. As she begins to transition medically using hormones, she also recounts how her breast implant surgery is funded by a man she met on the Internet, who wants nothing more than to go with her to Thailand and foot the medical bill. These practices of femininity, from the length of hair to the types of bra, suggest a normative deportment that is also transgressive.

Transgressive femininity is evident in her screen name, Ms Chor Lor. 'Chor Lor' is Hokkien for 'rough' and 'unrefined'. This pseudonym connotes a femininity that is uncouth and crude. Indeed, she describes this hybrid sexuality as 'She's a man. He's a woman.' She also rides a bike, burps, talks loudly, eats with her mouth open, does not wear a skirt and puts on little make-up. Unlike the idealized demure and porcelain Asian femininity of most Singaporean Chinese women, MCL transgresses these stereotypes by heightening the accepted and embodied frames of this femininity. Life politics has indeed allowed MCL to disembed from these traditions of hegemonic adult femininity and re-embed a new hybrid femininity that gives agency to a pre-op transgender living in an oppressive regime. Authenticity is authored into the blog with voice recordings of her drag song performance, and long-framed photos of her in various stages of transition. MCL's new female life politics is explicitly subactivist and subcultural.

Subactivism is not only evident in the embodied practices of trans-femininity described above. It is also inscribed in the appropriation of exemplary everyday spaces that localize a Singaporean transgender subjectivity. In ATS, local spaces such as public housing estates, department stores, shopping malls and military training camps are recoded to fit the tactical cultivation of working-class trans-femininity. The void decks and common staircases of public housing allowed MCL to avoid her family when she was growing up. During her time as a sex worker, they double as changing rooms so she can secretly dress up in fetish wear without alerting her family to her 'abject' profession. Writing of her job experiences at Sogo and Takashimaya department stores, and recounting her introduction to make-up and long hair as a cosmetic retail assistant, and especially how she performs as a drag act for the opening of one of the stores, she twists these exemplary spaces of Singaporean modernity with self-styled expressions of trans-femininity. As an army clerk during the two-year compulsory military service, she imbues national masculinity with her hyperfemininity and recodes herself as a 'queen' of the camps. Class, sexuality and modernity are embodied in these trans practices that permeate the spaces of everyday life. While subjective and personal, these subactivist practices appropriate the institutional and carve out a claim to citizenship based on spatial, cultural and gender rights that facilitate access to trans participation and representation.

Armstrong (2004) uses the concept of a 'subaltern counter public' to show how young feminists use the Web 'to build networks and create space to articulate their interests and experiences', and argues such tactics constitute a 'vernacular feminism' (Armstrong, 2004: 92, 94). Harcourt (2004) also points to how these platforms are used, especially in contexts where women are denied other forms of political participation. Although MCL's blog demonstrates the oppositional discourse of a subaltern counter public, as well as expresses a vernacular transfemininity, her subactivist practices do not challenge the status quo but are more related to the narrations of personal life experiences that underpin the individualization of life politics. In other words, rather than emancipatory politics that reflects the same modernizing tendencies as the Western post-Stonewall liberationist discourse, MCL's blog shows transgender sexuality as a form of life politics that is also part of the commodified discourse of lifestyle.

Powered by Nuffnang and Google, her blog page is surrounded by rows of advertising. Instead of the mainstream fashion advertorials of the celebrity female bloggers identified earlier, advertising is bannerstyle and confined to the side menu, and more geared towards the lifestyling of gender transition. Products available include online purchases for male-to-female hormones, voice coaching for a more feminized voice and even online psychologist clinics for the treatment of gender dysphoria. Dating links also proliferate the site. These are ambiguously polysexual, from Asian singles looking for marriage, to heterosexual and gay personals. Accompanying these are also travel, hotel, car and dining advertisements that are location-specific to the reader. Two modes of commodification are evident: first, the identity instruments that enable gender transitioning as a lifestyle, from body and voice to sex and relationships; second, the broader niche market of pink tourism that is targeted towards to the general readership and identified through the sidebar link to *ClustrMap*, which allows users to track visitor locations. Outside Singapore, which forms the majority of the readership, it is interesting to note that most readers come from the US and Europe rather than the Asia-Pacific region. These advertising banners demonstrate the logic of illiberal pragmatism that surrounds Singapore's sexual politics. Elsewhere I have discussed how sexuality is used as a tool for the nation's cultural policy developments that promote cultural and societal liberalism on the one hand but continue to criminalize homosexuality on the other (Yue, 2006, 2007a, 2007b, 2011). MCL's blog attests to this logic: while gender reassignment and pink tourism are encouraged because they normalize gender identities and add to the income of the economy, transgender rights are invisible and homosexuality is illegal. For MCL, new transgender life politics do not challenge the status quo but are enabled by its queer complicity to the illiberal pragmatism of cultural liberalism that underpins the romance capitalism of the new creative economy.

According to Beck and Beck-Gernsheim (2002), individualization is not the same as the process of individualism. Their use of the term 'disembedding' points to the breakdown of traditional norms experienced in the social transformation of contemporary modernity. Individualization is a concept used to explain how people deal with these changes in their identity and everyday life. In such a milieu – what has been seminally termed 'reflexive modernity' – new social arrangements emerge that are indeterminate and immediate, 'characterized by choice' (Beck and Beck-Gernsheim, 2002: ix). 'Choice' does not simply mean the liberation from traditional roles; it refers more to how individuals are now compelled to organize and manage their own lives by coordinating them within the new constraints and controls that are imposed. This process of coordination is what is referred to as 're-embedding', highlighting the new forms of reintegration (Beck and Beck-Gernsheim, 2002: 203). Key to re-embedding is the self-fashioning of a new biography: '[T]he normal biography thus becomes the elective biography, the reflexive biography, the do-it-yourself biography' (Beck and Beck-Gernsheim, 2002: 3).

In the three case studies examined, young, adult and transgender women transform their identity by performing hegemonic and trans-femininities that conform to the new institutional norms of East Asian pop capitalism, state engineering and transsexual biomedicine. Young women use the consumer choices of shopping, food and health to create their own self-cultures that are also calibrated and validated by newly formed and chosen reflexive social networks. These ties are in turn nurtured, maintained and renewed by the continued transformation of their self-biographies. Similarly, adult women use the pro-family choice of heterosexual courtship to stage an aesthetic post-feminist lifestyle that is, on the one hand, self-determined by their practice of freedom, but on the other hand, overdetermined by the expected norms of marriage and parenthood. Likewise, trans-women perform the tasks required of gender normativity and acquire the standards demanded of straight-acting femininity. Tastes, choices and identities are self-organized and individually managed to ameliorate deviations and conform to changing preferences and life stages that are constantly adapting to the changing institutional conditions of capital, state and resource. In this sense, female individualization is a process of dialogues, negotiations and compromise that opens up 'precarious freedoms' (Beck and Beck-Gernsheim, 2002: 16); subactivism, as such, is experienced at the subpolitical level of the local, where 'an ethics of everyday life' is materialized (Beck and Beck-Gernsheim, 2002: 213). As a social media, blogging exemplifies these new conditions of life politics and individualization that engage the logic of flows rather than structure. For Singapore's global reordering, it creates new female subjects who comply with and are resistant to the governance of illiberal pragmatics.

Conclusion

This chapter began by showing how the illiberal pragmatism of Singapore's state-gendered policies has neutralized gender norms, produced compliant female subjects and created the conditions for possible new female life politics. Rather than celebrating life politics as individualistic, this chapter has suggested that female narratives of self-actualization were also structured by the forces of Confucian tradition, developmental modernity and global capitalism. Using the concept of subactivism to refer to everyday practices and actions that traverse the private/public and self/collective, this chapter has shown how the subactivism of female blogging has enabled gender and sexual minorities to fashion self-biographies and make claims to citizenship in their everyday life.

Blogging allows young women to perform a commodified East Asian pop-cultural hetero-femininity that prepares them for incorporation into idealized state femininity. Blogging allows adult women to perform a hegemonic femininity that fits the social-engineering ethos of gendered state policies. Through the ethical governance of self-cultivation and self-regulation, both performatives are subactivist and demonstrate how female subjects are interpellated into good citizens.

The self-fashioning tactics of transgender blogging follow these ethical frames, where the new sexual identities produced are complicit and transgressive. Trans-femininity is complicit through its embodied consumption of self-transformation, and transgressive through its excess of hybrid sexuality that challenges gender normativity. Subactivism is both individualized and collectively subcultural, anchoring the local and subterranean informality of transgenders and their claims to sexual citizenship and everyday survival.

These results demonstrate two characteristics of gendered social-media consumption: while media use creates alternative public spheres, these are micro and subcultural; while transforming identity, identities performed are more individual and less collective. These characteristics support emerging studies that suggest that while men spend more time online and claim more developed skills than women (Hargittai, 2007), women tend to embrace the identity formation potentials of new and social media better (Pujazon-Zazik and Park, 2010). In Singapore, these practices have governed new female subjectivities that are hegemonic, complicit and transgressive.

References

Anon (2010) 'Singapore's Top Female Bloggers Came Together To Learn More about Cervical Cancer', 21 May, http://www.pocc.sg/blog/2010/05/singapores-top-female-bloggers-come-together-to-learn-more-about-cervical-cancer/, accessed on 2 February 2011.

Armstrong, J. (2004) 'Web Grrrls, Guerilla Tactics: Young Feminisms on the Web', in D. Gauntlett and R. Horsley (eds), *Web Studies*, pp. 92–102, New York: Oxford University Press.

Bakardjieva, M. (2009) 'Subactivism: Lifeworld and Politics in the Age of the Internet', *The Information Society*, 25: 91–104.

Bennett, W. (2009 [2004]) 'Branded Political Communication: Lifestyle Politics, Logo Campaigns, and the Rise of Global Citizenship', in M. Micheletti, A. Follesdal and D. Stolle (eds), *The Politics Behind Products*, pp. 101–126, New Brunswick: Transaction Books.

Beck, U. and Beck-Gernsheim, E. (2002) *Individualization: Institutionalized Individualism and Its Social and Political Consequences*, London: Sage.

Brooks, A. and Wee, L. (2008) 'Reflexivity and the Transformation of Gender Identity: Reviewing the Potential for Change in a Cosmopolitan City', *Sociology*, 42(3): 503–521.

Cheng, W. (2003) *Xiaxue*, http://xiaxue.blogspot.com/, accessed on 2 January 2011.

Chia, E. (2001) *The Miracle Season*, http://the-miracle-season.blogspot.com/, accessed on 2 January 2011.

Chua, B. (1997) *Political Legitimacy and Housing: Stakeholding in Singapore*, New York: Routledge.

Chua, B. (2008) 'Structure of Identification and Distancing in Watching East Asian Television Drama', in B. Chua and K. Iwabuchi (eds), *East Asian Pop Culture: Analysing the Korean Wave*, pp. 73–90, Hong Kong: Hong Kong University Press.

Choi, A. (2008) 'Internet Use in Singapore: Findings from a National Survey', *Observatorio Journal*, 6: 151–168.

Elchardus, M. (2009) 'Self-control as Social Control: The Emergence of Symbolic Society', *Poetics*, 37: 146–161.

Foucault, M. (1985) *The History of Sexuality, Volume 2: The Use of Pleasure*, New York: Vintage Books.

Giddens, A. (1991) *Modernity and Self-identity: Self and Society in the Late Modern Age*, Cambridge: Polity.

Giddens, A. (1996) 'Affluence, Poverty and the Idea of a Post-Scarcity Society', *Development and Change*, 27, 365–377.

Ha, A. (2010) *Monoxious*, http://www.monoxious.com/, accessed on 2 January 2011.

Halberstam, J. (1998) *Female Masculinity*, Durham: Duke University Press.

Harcourt, W. (2004) 'World Wide Women and the Web', in D. Gauntlett and R. Horsley (eds), *Web Studies*, pp. 243–253, New York: Oxford University Press.

Hargittai, E. (2007) 'Whose Space? Differences Among Users and Non-Users of Social Network Sites', *Journal of Computer-Mediated Communication*, http://jcmc.indiana.edu/vol13/issue1/hargittai.html, accessed on 16 January 2011.

Hearn, A. (2008) 'Meat, Mask, Burden: Probing the Contours of the Branded Self', *Journal of Consumer Culture*, 8(2): 197–217.

Heng, G. and Devan, J. (1992) 'State Fatherhood: The Politics of Nationalism, Sexuality and Race in Singapore', in A. Parker, M. Russo, D. Sommer and P. Yaeger (eds), *Nationalisms and Sexualities*, pp. 343–364, New York: Routledge.

Hokulani, F. (2008) *With Love Fay*, http://www.withlovefay.com/, accessed on 2 January 2011.

Hjorth, L. (2009) 'Web U2: Emerging Online Communities and Gendered Intimacy in the Asia-Pacific region', *Knowledge, Technology and Policy*, 22: 117–124.

Hudson, C. (2004) 'Romancing Singapore: Economies of Love in a Shrinking Population', in R. Cribb (ed.), *Asia Examined: Proceedings of the 15th Biennial Conference of the ASAA, 2004, Canberra, Australia*, Canberra: The Australian National University.

Kim, Y. (2010) 'Female Individualization? Transnational Mobility and Media Consumption of Asian Women', *Media, Culture & Society*, 32(1): 25–43.

Lee, P. (2006) *Deadpris*, http://www.deadpris.com/, accessed on 2 January 2011.

Lim, V. (2011) *Diary of a Matchmaker*, http://www.violetlim.com/, accessed on 30 January 2011.

Loh, J. (2006) *Underage Girl*, http://www.underage-girl.blogspot.com/, accessed on 2 January 2011.

Ministry of Community Development, Youth and Sports (MCDYS) (2009) *Singapore's Fourth Periodic Report to the UN Committee for the Convention of the Elimination of all Forms of Discrimination against Women*, Singapore: Strategic Planning, Research and Development Division.

Mulinari, D. and Sandell, K. (2009) 'A Feminist Re-Reading of Theories of Late Modernity: Beck, Giddens and the Location of Gender', *Critical Sociology*, 35(4): 493–507.

Ms Chor Lor (2009) *Blog of a Singaporean Transgender*, http://mschorlor.com/, accessed on 5 February 2011.

National Population Secretariat (NPS) (2010) *Population in Brief 2010*, Singapore: Prime Minister's Office.

Nuffnang (2007) *Nuffnang: Asia's First Blog Advertising Community*, http://www.nuffnang.com/, accessed on 7 February 2011.

Oehlers, A. (1998) 'A Woman's Economic Role: A Historical Survey of Singapore', *Asian Women*, 7: 55–66.

omg (2011) *Singapore Blog Awards Website*, http://sgblogawards.omy.sg/, accessed on 2 January 2011.

Ouellette, L. and Hay, J. (2008) 'Makeover Television, Governmentality and the Good Citizen', *Continuum*, 22(4): 471–484.

Phua, S. (2010) 'Singapore's Social Media Scene', http://www.clicktrue.biz/blog/social-media-marketing/singapores-social-media-scene/#, accessed on 19 December 2010.

Purushotam, N. (2002) 'Woman' as Boundary: Raising the Communitarian Against Critical Imaginings', *Inter-Asia Cultural Studies*, 3(3): 337–350.

Pujazon-Zazik, M. and Park, J. (2010) 'To Tweet, or Not to Tweet: Gender Differences and Potential Positive and Negative Health Outcomes of Adolescents' Social Internet Use', *American Journal of Men's Health*, 4(1): 77–85.

Skoric, M., Ying, D. and Ng, Y. (2009a) 'Bowling Online, Not Alone: Online Social Capital and Political Participation in Singapore', *Journal of Computer-Mediated Communication*, 14: 414–433.

Skoric, M., Sim, C., Juan, H. and Fang, P. (2009b) 'Podcasting and Politics in Singapore: An Experimental Study of Medium Effects', *Journal of Contemporary Eastern Asia*, 8(2): 27–43.

Statistics Singapore (2010) *Key Indicators on Gender*, Singapore: Singapore Department of Statistics.

Suadi, N. (2010) *Nadnut*, http://www.nadnut.com/, accessed on 2 January 2011.

Tan, E. (2008) 'A Union of Gender Equality and Pragmatic Patriarchy: International Marriages and Citizenship Laws in Singapore', *Citizenship Studies*, 12(1): 73–89.

Teo, Y. (2007) 'Inequality for the Greater Good: Gendered State Rule in Singapore', *Critical Asian Studies*, 39(3): 423–445.

Teo, Y. (2009) 'Gender Disarmed: How Gendered Policies Produce Gender-Neutral Politics in Singapore', *Signs*, 34(3): 533–558.

Teo, Y. (2010) 'Shaping the Singapore Family, Producing the State and Society', *Economy and Society*, 39(3): 337–359.

Yue, A. (2006) 'The Regional Culture of New Asia: Cultural Governance and Creative Industries in Singapore', *International Journal of Cultural Policy*, 12(1): 17–33.

Yue, A. (2007a) 'Creative Queer Singapore: The Illiberal Pragmatics of Cultural Production', *Gay and Lesbian Issues and Psychology Review*, 3(3): 149–105.

Yue, A. (2007b) 'Hawking in the Creative City: *Rice Rhapsody*, Sexuality and the Cultural Politics of New Asia in Singapore', *Feminist Media Studies*, 7(4): 365–380.

Yue, A. (2011), 'Doing Cultural Citizenship in the Global Media Hub: Illiberal Pragmatics and Lesbian Consumption Practices in Singapore', in R. Hegde (ed.), *Circuits of Visibility: Gender and Transnational Media Cultures*, pp. 250–267, New York: New York University Press.

Index